Sanja Tepavcevic

Global Crises, Resilience, and Future Challenges
Experiences of Post-Yugoslav and Post-Soviet Migrants

T0285581

Balkan Politics and Society

Edited by Jelena Dzankic and Soeren Keil

Sanja Tepavcevic

GLOBAL CRISES, RESILIENCE, AND FUTURE CHALLENGES

Experiences of Post-Yugoslav and Post-Soviet Migrants

Bibliografische Information der Deutschen Nationalbibliothek

Die Deutsche Nationalbibliothek verzeichnet diese Publikation in der Deutschen Nationalbibliografie; detaillierte bibliografische Daten sind im Internet über http://dnb.d-nb.de abrufbar.

Bibliographic information published by the Deutsche Nationalbibliothek

Die Deutsche Nationalbibliothek lists this publication in the Deutsche Nationalbibliografie; detailed bibliographic data are available in the Internet at http://dnb.d-nb.de.

ISBN-13: 978-3-8382-1800-7

© *ibidem*-Verlag, Hannover-Stuttgart 2024

Alle Rechte vorbehalten

Table of Contents

Chapter 8
Conclusions: (Imagined) Global Crises and (Imagined)
Migrant Communities—Lessons from the Shortest Century... 245

List of Figures and Tables

Abstract

The idea to write this book was born during my teaching fellowship at the International Relations Department of the Faculty of Social Sciences at Eotvos Lorand University, Budapest in the Spring of 2017. I created and taught an MA course titled "Interests in Clash, the Clash of Interests: the Balkans and Great Powers". The major aim of this course was to explain the causes and consequences of the 1990s wars in the Balkans. During one of the seminar exercises, which was based on real persons who experienced the siege of Sarajevo in varying personal contexts, the students were asked what they would do if they were in the place of these individuals. Most of the students responded that they would try to leave the city and the country, taking someone close with them.

Unlike many books to which I refer, this book is neither a chronicle nor an analysis of the siege of Sarajevo, the war in Bosnia, the former Yugoslavia and genocides. Nor is it solely an analysis of the collapses of Yugoslavia and USSR. Additionally, it is not solely a book about the current war in Ukraine, though these topics are present throughout the book.

Taking a comparative approach, and inevitably crossing the disciplinary boundaries, "Global Crises, Resilience, and Future Challenges" examines the impact of the collapses of the former Soviet Union and former Yugoslavia on migration trajectories of their population and on their resilience in consecutive global crises. These consecutive global crises, include the collapse of the Socialist bloc, the global financial crisis, the COVID-19 pandemic, and the war in Ukraine. Because of these crises, the lives of post-Yugoslav and post-Soviet individuals and communities are frequently on the move. How do the most affected individuals within these populations manage to survive global crises? How do their experiences from previous crises influence their behavior when a new global crisis emerges? By situating their narratives and participant observations into Albert Hirschman's framework of 'Exit, Voice, and Loyalty' and combining them with concepts of resilience borrowed from social, behavioral, and natural sciences, this book presents stories of survival and lessons in resilience.

Devotion

To the loving memory of my family members Dragan, Ana, Boro Tepavcevic, and Ratko Tomic who survived the siege of Sarajevo; and in remembrance of my school mates Elvir Karacic, Sejo Klempic, Nedzad Subasic and Lejla Kolar, who tragically did not survive the siege. To the memory of Petko Tepavcevic, Dragan Kadijevic, Rajko Lozo, who did not survive the siege. I honor those who endured the siege and chose to stay, as well as those who escaped the war and sought a new beginning elsewhere. To the memory of all, who do not survive current conflicts; and to all, who do it and strive for a future free from exclusion and conflict.

Acknowledgements

Writing this book has been a painful process of analyzing and understanding the emergence and evaporation of human communities. I am grateful for the support provided by the Institute of Advanced Studies Koszeg (IASK) research fellowship grant in 2022 to turn this research into a monograph. Minor part of research was supported by the RFBR, Grant No. 19-511-23001 (2019-2022). I would like to express my sincere appreciation to the Director of iASK's Polanyi Center, Jody Jensen, as well as the most dedicated librarians of iASK Library, Eszter Takacs and Henrietta Doka. I am also grateful to my colleagues from iASK, Ferenc Miszlivetz, Izabella Agardi, Attila Pok, Ivana Stepanovic, and Aniko Magashazi, for their valuable suggestions and comments on my early presentation of this book in March 2022. I would like to extend my gratitude to Laszlo Karvalics and James Skelly for engaging in numerous informal conversations on the topics of narratives in micro-memory, traumas, and identity. I would also like to take this opportunity to thank my colleague from Budapest-based International Association Dialogue, Irina Molodikova for her insights into post-Soviet migrants' identities.

Additionally, I would also like to express my appreciation to the students of the MA International Studies Program of the Department of Modern Philology and Social Sciences at the University of Pannonia, Koszeg Campus, Hungary for their engaging discussions.

Special thanks are also due to all the anonymous respondents who participated in formal and informal conversations, focus groups, and online surveys. Their narratives have served as vital data for this book. My deep appreciation goes to an anonymous reviewer for valuable comments and suggestions on how to make a better use of secondary literature to support arguments made throughout the monograph. I also thank my truly British member of my family, Masha Milovanovich for her help in making this monograph clear and readable.

I would like to express my deep gratitude to my family members, Emma, Biljana, Minja, and Pasha for their unwavering love, attention, patience, and immense support throughout the research and writing process. I am also grateful to Maja, Rajka, Vanja, and Dragana and for their enduring love and moral support.

Last but equally important, I would like to extend my heartfelt thanks to my old and new friends who have been a constant source of inspiration throughout the writing of this book. Among them I want to acknowledge Lidiya Anantolevna, Vesna, Ira, Inela, Milica, Jasmina, Nina, Sanja, Tanja, Vanja, Nika, Darja, Deni, Jesenko, Isidora, Milos, Fredza, Dzo, Milana, Maja, Vid, Kata, Jure, Ana, Nikolina, Zlata, Katya, Yura, Natalia, Oleg, Senaida, Kolin, Ilya, Natasha, Anna, Vadym, Dima, Zhenya, Lyosha, Zoran, Bojan, Tija, Boris, Misho and many others whose support and friendship played a significant role in this journey.

PART I

PART I

Chapter 1
Shortest 21st Century —
Series of Global Crises from the
'End of History' to the New Threat of the
Nuclear War

"Speaking of crisis of whatever nature, we convey firstly the feeling of uncertainty, of our ignorance of the direction in which the affairs are about to turn—and secondly the urge to intervene" (Bauman & Bordoni, 2014, p. 7).

Introduction

This book delves into the exploration and comparison of the challenges faced by the citizens of former Yugoslavia and the former Soviet Union during the global crises of the late 20th century and the first two decades of the 21st century. It specifically examines their resilience through migration and migrant experience, shaped by the political, economic, and security orders. Building upon Eric Hobsbawm (1994) analogies of the 'long 19th century'— which he referred to as the period between the French Revolution and the beginning of World War I—and 'short 20th century'—characterizing the period between 1914—1989—I propose that the 21st century has been the 'shortest' in the history of human kind. This briefest 'century' commenced with the dissolution of the socialist bloc in 1989-1991 and concluded with Russia's invasion of Ukraine on February 24, 2022.

The collapse of the post-World War II bipolar world system in 1989 was prompted by the pro-democratic revolutions in the socialist countries of Central and Eastern Europe. Its result was the collapse of the world's second superpower, the Soviet Union, in 1991, along with simultaneous dominance of the world's first superpower, the USA. In 1991, the political scientist Francis Fukuyama famously characterized the outcomes of these transformations as "The End of History." This term signified the triumph of liberalism over other ideologies and the belief that, from that point onward, the world would progressively evolve towards democracy and a market-based economy.

Led by the US economically, this period has been marked by initial attempts to implement the liberal policies of the International Monetary Fund (IMF) and World Bank (WB). These international economic organizations proposed a standardized reform approach for post-socialist and previously decolonized developing countries, consisting of four sequential steps—stabilization, liberalization, institutionalization, and privatization. This approach is commonly referred to as the SLIP agenda or the Washington Consensus. In general, the reform assumed market deregulation as the one-size-fits-all 'golden straight jacket' or various forms of a liberal market economy (Friedman, 2000) as the solution to address the issues faces by former socialist states and former European colonies in Africa and Asia (Jackson, 2009). Over the past thirty years, rapid globalization has resulted in unprecedented economic, political and social interconnectedness and interdependence. However, this was only the first visible and predominantly positive effect of the process. During the implementation of these reforms, many post-socialist countries in Central Eastern Europe and across the former Soviet Union encountered a blend of nationalism and liberal market ideology, with attempts to promote democratization dominating the political scene.

Therefore, just as Hobsbawm (1994) predicted, it is unsurprising that this period has generated a full spectrum of both sequential and simultaneous global crises. Firstly, in the 1990s, a series of local wars of dissolution plagued mostly post-Yugoslav territories, but also some post-Soviet regions. These conflicts, including Bosnia and Herzegovina (Sokolovic, 2006) and Kosovo (Judah, 2000) in the Balkans; Transnistria in Moldova (Chamberlain-Creanga, 2006), Nagorno-Karabakh in Azerbaijan, and Abkhazia and South Ossetia in Georgia (King, 2001), remained unresolved, frozen, and had the potential to escalate. The issues of collective identities such as national, religious, and ethnic, significantly influenced the trajectories of these conflicts. The most recent conflict in Ukraine originated from Russia's annexation of Crimea. It escalated into a violent conflict in Donbas and eventually turned into a full-fledged invasion by Russia, beginning on February 24, 2022. In many respects, this conflict also symbolizes the ongoing repercussions of the collapse of the USSR, particularly regarding issues surrounding collective identity, with national identity being the most contentious aspect.

Secondly, as part of a parallel process, there was a series of color revolutions in post-socialist Europe and Eurasia between 2000 and 2005 (Kobrinskaya, 2005). These revolutions can be seen as a continuation of the 20th century's democratic uprisings, which originally occurred in Hungary, Czechoslovakia, and Poland during the Cold War and later extended to the post-Soviet and post-Yugoslav regions. Starting with Serbia's 'tractor' revolution in 2000, similar movements emerged in the post-Soviet Caucasus, Eastern Europe, and Central Asia. Examples include Georgia's 'Revolution of Roses' in 2003, Ukraine's Orange Revolution in 2004 (Aslund & McFaul, 2006; Nygren, 2007), and even the 'Snow' Revolution in Russia in 2011 (Holmes & Krastev, 2012). These revolutions revolved around the question of collective identity and aimed to establish economically successful democratic regimes.

Thirdly, the global war on terrorism commenced with the unprecedented terrorist attacks on the USA on September 11, 2001. Subsequently, there was a brief yet remarkable US-Russian anti-terrorist coalition formed to support the US military operation in Afghanistan. This coalition itself emerged from the Russian political leadership's vision of positioning Russia as one of the most politically influential and economically developed nations. As the coalition disbanded, the US continued its anti-terrorist military operations in Iraq in 2003, which faced fierce opposition from the leaderships of France, Germany and Russia. Similar operations took place in Libya in 2011 and in Syria from 2011 onwards, primarily without international support.

Since the early 2000s, the period has witnessed the rapid development of the four 'Asian tigers' —South Korea, Japan, Singapore, and Taiwan— alongside the rise of the Peoples' Republic of China as the world's second major economic power after the USA. China's economic ascent has made it an attractive model of development, sparking discussions about the connection between democracy and economic prosperity. In parallel, significant processes unfolded in Europe: in 1999, most Central and Eastern European countries, former members of the Socialist bloc, joined NATO. Just five years later, in 2004, these countries further expanded by joining the European Union (EU), constituting a major enlargement in EU history.

In reaction to these developments, beginning around 2005, a group of prominent emerging economies including Brazil, Russia, India, China, and later the South African Republic (SAR), emerged to counter the dominance of 'the West'. Their collaboration gradually gave rise to the BRICS bloc. Subsequently, there was a gradual shift towards authoritarian politics, reaching its peak in 2015 across post-socialist Europe, the UK, the Mediterranean, Asia, and even the United States (Skaaning, 2020).

Fourth, running parallel to violent conflicts, the global financial crisis of 2008-2009, commonly known as the Great Recession (Berend, 2012) impacted the global economy by causing the bursting of financial and real estate industry bubbles. This crisis was a direct and indirect outcome of the Washington Consensus (Farrar, 2013), raising further concerns about the efficacy of liberal policies and the aforementioned collective identities associated with liberalism. Fifth, sparked by the Great Recession, there was an anti-capitalist upraising in the USA as a response to bailouts that favored banks and company stakeholders over customers. This reached its peak in 2011 with the emergence of the "Occupy Wall Street" movement, which expressed opposition to capitalism and globalization.

Sixth, simultaneously with the "Occupy Wall Street" movement in 2011, the Middle East and North Africa (MENA) region witnessed a series of pro-democratic revolutions that gained global recognition as the Arab Spring. These events triggered the aforementioned invasion of Libya by the US and NATO, as well as a decade-long war in Syria and military interventions by Russia, USA and Turkey. Seventh, as a result of the Arab Spring and the NATO bombing of Libya in 2011, coupled with the outbreak of the war in Syria, the global migration crisis reached its peak in the summer 2015, when millions of refugees from the MENA region and Afghanistan arrived in Europe. This crisis coincided with the rise of democratic backsliding trends, particularly prominent in Central and Eastern Europe.

Eight, at the beginning of 2020, the world experienced the COVID-19 virus pandemic, which triggered unparalleled global lockdowns and an economic downturn that persisted until 2023. Lastly, the ongoing crisis that continues as I write, and the crisis that simultaneously ends the shortest 21st century is Russia's army invasion in Ukraine, which commenced on the morning of February 24, 2022. This invasion has already had significant repercussions for the global economy and order, but its ultimate outcome remains uncertain.

Overlapping with these numerous sequential and parallel crises are also two other underlying and escalating global crises. The first is the global environmental crisis, which encompasses pollution and global warming (Fraser, 2021). On the local and individual levels, these crises have been felt in various degrees, ranging from mere disturbance to slight fright and even horror, depending on specific geographies and individual circumstances. The second crisis, which overlaps with all the previously mentioned crises, is the crisis of ideology. In his book "21 Lessons for the 21st Century," renowned historian Yuval Noah Harari discusses the three major ideologies of the 20th century — fascism, communism, and liberalism — and argues that by 2018, the world was left without any of them:

> In 1938, humanity had a choice among three global ideologies ... In 1968 only two of them were left to choose between. In 1998, it seemed that we were left with only one. In 2018 we had reached zero options (Harari, 2018).

However, international relations scholar, Andrei Tsygankov (2022) has challenged this claim, emphasizing the persistence and significance of ideologies at the regional and local levels, at least within the Eurasian space. However, these ideologies seem to have been either overlooked, misinterpreted, or undermined globally.

This book aims to reveal the relationships between these global crises, the challenges they generate among individuals and communities, and the patterns of resilience they produce. It focuses on two broad groups: former Yugoslav citizens and former Soviet citizens. The book traces and compares the challenges that these two groups encountered before, during, and after the collapses of the two former socialist multinational federations. These challenges include the related wars of dissolution, citizens' emigration from their places of origin, immigration, and integration in their places of destination. It is important to note that the term 'place' of origin and destination is intentionally used here because, in the process of global crises and within the contexts of territories representing Yugoslavia and the Soviet Union, the concept of countries and states proved to be unstable.

The book examines whether and to what extent experiences of dissolutions have been utilized and applied to subsequent global crises, such as the Great Recession, the COVID-19 pandemic, and the escalation of the conflict in Ukraine. Building upon the literature on post-Yugoslav and post-Soviet migrations, this book provides insights from various geographical and politico-economic contexts. A major limitation of such study is simultaneously its major advantage: in their study that compared state-building processes in the Western Balkans and Ukraine, Bianchini and Minakov (2018, p. 292) correctly noted,

> what is particularly attractive in the implementation of comparative approaches is their inherent violation of disciplinary borders.
>
> Institutionally, comparison encourages invasion into others' disciplines, looking for new contextual analyses, decision making mechanisms, cultural and psychological mindsets, social and economic environments, external players' roles, and ideological and religious impacts. Methodologically, the incursion into a variety of fields potentially provides unexplored grounds for innovation.

Following this argument, in the remainder of this chapter, I will discuss key concepts and theories regarding the relationships between global crises and migrations, vulnerability, loyalty and resilience. This discussion will specifically focus on post-Yugoslav and post-Soviet migrants by reviewing the scholarly literature. The final section of the chapter will describe the set of inquiry methods and design used in the analysis.

Research Context: Global Crises and Migrants from former Yugoslavia and former Soviet Union

Depending on their source and nature, influences of global crises vary across places, time, and, most importantly, among people. The global crisis that marked the beginning of the shortest 21st century — the collapse of the Socialist bloc — had dramatic and profound effects on the population of post-socialist Europe. At the same time, the effects of the collapse also varied across this broad region. For example, in the Baltics, Poland, Czechoslovakia, Hungary, and to some extend in Russia and Ukraine, the collapse brought certain relief and liberation. However, in former Yugoslavia, it resulted in a series of civil wars, genocides, frozen conflicts, and poverty.

The interaction between crisis and migrations is complex and a few scholarly works have systematically addressed this relationship. For instance, analyses of post-Soviet and post-Yugoslav migrations not only represent two different area studies, but they also tend to focus on distinct aspects of migration and integration in diverse environments (Tepavcevic, 2022). Prominent scholars of post-Yugoslav migrations have predominantly discussed traumas related to forced migration, as well as the issues of changing identity and other psychological and cultural aspects of migration and integration in receiving environments (Halilovich, 2013; Kovacevic-Bielicki, 2017; Ramet & Valenta, 2011). On the other hand, while scholars of post-Soviet migrations also address cultural and psychological themes in their works, they tend to focus more on socio-economic and institutional aspects of migration and integration in host countries (Remennick, 2012; Ryazantsev, Pismennaya et al., 2018; Tepavcevic, 2017). Therefore, as I compare post-Yugoslav migrants with post-Soviet migrants, I maintain a profound awareness of the associated conceptual limitations.

One such limitation is the simplification in discursively constructing these two groups. As Dragana Kovacevic-Bielicki (2017, p. 44) correctly noted,

> [T]he labels do not signify clearly bounded or homogeneous groups. Any of these "groupist" terms may encompass people going through all kinds of identification and selfidentification processes and different feelings of (non)belonging. These are people with different ideas, preferences, life stories, ages, education, lifestyles, political views, social class, and many other possible lines of diversification.

Nevertheless, several similar features warrant the comparison of these two broad groups. Both post-Yugoslavs and post-Soviets are associated with socialist multinational federations that collapsed in 1991, either being born in them or in the remnants of those countries. For this reason, Heleniak (2017) considered the entire population of former socialist countries as post-Soviet. Additionally, both groups are typically native speakers of the majority languages in these two former federations: Russian in the case of the former Soviet Union, and Serbo-Croatian or Bosnian-Croatian-Serbian in the case of former Yugoslavia. However, in contrast to Heleniak (2017), in some of my previous studies, I defined post-Soviets as remnants of a political nation, who typically share Russian as a common language of communication or *lingua franca*. The shared experience of political, economic, and social transformations across the post-Soviet space, along with the resulting shared cognitive frameworks influenced by educational and social institutions, contribute to making post-Soviet people a relatively coherent unit of analysis (Tepavcevic, 2023). In this book, I consistently apply this definition of post-Soviets as a point of reference in the analysis of migrants and their communities originating from the post-Soviet space. Consequently, my inquiry encompasses Russians, Ukrainians, Belarussians, Armenians, Kazakhs, Uzbeks and Azerbaijanis, including both civic identities based on citizenship and individual identities based on self-perception.

Consequently, in defining post-Yugoslav migrants, I apply a similar principle as to post-Soviets. These are the migrants originating from the countries remnants of former Yugoslavia, whether they were former citizens of former Yugoslavia or citizens of the countries that emerged on the territories of former Yugoslavia. They either speak Bosnian-Croatian-Serbian as their first language or are bilingual (for example, Yugoslavia-born citizens of North Macedonia and Slovenia). As a result, my inquiry predominantly focuses on Bosnians (as citizens of Bosnia and Herzegovina), Serbians (citizens of Serbia), and Croatians (citizens of Croatia). This also includes people with Bosniak, Croat, Serb, Yugoslav, Jewish, Roma and other (self-)perceived local identities. Kovacevic-Bielicki (2017) has also emphasized the significance of the triple notion of 'former' in her analysis of the post-Yugoslav migrants in Norway: former Yugoslavs, former refugees, and former children. However, this does not overshadow their other ethnic, national, and professional identities. On the contrary, the notions of 'former' or 'post' as prefixes to Yugoslav and Soviet, as revealed throughout this book, usually strengthen or at least highlight other layers and aspects of the identities of these migrants.

Motives for Migrations

Migrations represent "a permanent or semi-permanent change of residence, usually across some type of administrative boundary. ... [a] person can migrate many times, for varied durations, and across numerous territorial divisions" (Wood, 1994). Since Everett S. Lee (1966) divided motives for emigration into positive and negative at home and host countries, migration studies have evolved around three axioms. The first axiom is that of forced versus voluntary migration. For example, Crawley (2006, pp. 58-59) points out:

> An economic migrant normally leaves a country voluntarily to seek a better life. Forced migrants, by contrast, leave because of the threat of persecution or other forms of harm that have affected, or will affect, themselves and their families should they remain. Unlike economic migrants, forced migrants are unable to return to their homes, because they do not believe that the government of the country from which they originate will protect them.

Simultaneously, many authors recognized that poverty, as an economic factor, could also compel migration. For instance, Wood (1994) demonstrated overlapping causal factors operating within national borders and juxtaposed them against international attempts to differentiate legally between refugees and economic migrants. Wood's model also highlighted the second conceptual axiom — internal versus international migrations — which remains consistently relevant in migration studies and migration-related legal frameworks (Samers & Collyer, 2016).

To some extent, authors proposing the transnationalism thesis in migration have bridged these backdrops. In contrast to the previous theories of migration, transnationalism recognizes the fact that migrants often represent economic and cultural 'bridges' between host and home countries, and in many cases, commute or frequently travel between them (Nazareno, 2018; Portes, 1997).

More recently, the themes concerning migrants' social classes have emerged as the third axiom in migration studies. Conditionally dividing migrants into the rich and poor categories, authors tend to associate forced migration with the lower social class, and voluntary migration with the wealthier class. The division originates from Michael J. Piore's (1979) seminal theory of the 'dual-labor-market,' which explains that high income economies are segmented into a capital-intensive primary sector that attracts high-skilled foreign employees, and a labor-intensive secondary sector that continues to rely on low-skilled migrant workers. On the supply side, Piore suggested that primary market workers emerged with increased unionization, while secondary laborers are constantly being recruited.

While Piore's study focused on patterns of integrating immigrant workers into the labor markets of receiving countries, Rath (2006) and Tepavcevic (2017, 2023) demonstrated that a number of immigrants from low-to-middle income countries immigrate to middle and high income countries with considerable savings. Furthermore, along with "highly skilled migrants and circulating students," these migrant entrepreneurs fell first into the category of "other" migrants. In one of the edited volumes, they were classified as "migrant professionals" (Meier, 2015), while in another, they were discussed as 'rich migrants' or 'lifestyle migrants' (Vailati & Rial, 2016). Their migration was framed within four parallel processes:

> First, intensified globalization processes and border-crossing flows; second, a general increase in formal qualifications; third, social and economic transformations in some regions due to crises; and, fourth, today's consideration

of migration as a necessary qualification and as a resource for a further career (Meier, 2015, p. 2).

Persistent examples of forced migrants are also found among middle class professionals and scientists escaping from oppressive regimes and seeking political asylum (Fomina, 2021). Overall, the proposition regarding the motives and structure of migrations proposed throughout this book is as follows: *migration is a transnational process taking place across countries of origin, the receiving countries, and beyond, and it is prompted by a set of factors. Therefore, most migrants do not fit into a narrow legal framework differentiating between forced and voluntary migrations.*

Global Crises

By following Karl Polanyi's concept of transformation to conceptualize global crises, Novy (2021) differentiates between two meanings of the concept. The first concerns "a certain political-economic moment of radical rupture, a type of political revolution and short-term change" (Novy, 2021, p. 60), while the second refers to ongoing long-term profound transformations that can be accelerated by the aforementioned radical rupture. As Novy (2021) correctly noted, the former cannot be understood without contextualizing it in a long-term profound one. Similarly, following Braudel (1980) notion of conjunctural temporality of the cycle and inter-cycle, Krasteva (2021, pp. 178-179) highlights that the later temporality represents "a precaution against allowing the theoretical attention to be usurped by the most dramatic events and the loudest actors, ensuring that it is evenly distributed". Therefore, as noted above, in this book, I analyze various global crises that occurred between 1989 and 2022 both as long-term profound transformation and radical ruptures constituting the peaks of the profound transformations that I conceptualized as 'the shortest century'.

Vulnerability and Resilience

Comparing vulnerabilities and coping mechanisms in Sarajevo during the siege in the early 1990s and during the COVID-19 pandemic, legal scholar Marina Velickovic, originating from Bosnia, keenly points out that "The crises, at their very core, are both about death, or, if one wants to be more upbeat about it—about ensuring survival. Different threats require different behavioural modifications to maximise chances of postponing death" (Velickovic, 2020). This statement reflects on the relationship between the vulnerability—roughly—being exposed to death, and resilience—an ability to survive and continue living. In migration studies, the concepts of vulnerability and resilience are profoundly interrelated. Human migration has been one of the most frequent adaptation strategies to various crises, from natural disasters (Ioneasco & Chazalnoel, 2015) to violent conflicts.

The Merriam-Webster dictionary defines vulnerability as "capable of being physically or emotionally wounded: open to attack or damage". The psychological definition of vulnerability—"a state of emotional exposure that comes with a certain degree of uncertainty"—is more complete as it tends to bridge vulnerability with resilience. For example, Brene Brown (2017) suggests that vulnerability is a significant measure of courage, which allows people to be understood by those who are important in their life.

Crises, in their turn, both reveal and generate vulnerabilities. In one of my previous works, I highlighted that migrations make migrants significantly more vulnerable than the non-migrant population, and that these vulnerabilities come in various forms, from physical and legal, to cultural and psychological (Tepavcevic, 2022). Global crises tend to increase these and reveal other vulnerabilities, but as Velickovic (2020) suggested, they also generate various forms and sets of resilience. Similar to vulnerability, resilience can be defined in various ways. For example:

- the ability to be happy and successful again after something difficult or bad has happened (Dictionary, 2022);
- An ability to recover from, adjust easily to misfortune, or change (Merriam-Webster, 2022).

Similarly, resilience theory is known in medical sciences as "the ideas surrounding how people are affected by and adapt to things like adversity, change, loss, and risk" (Hurley, 2022). Reviewing the social, behavioral and some natural science literature, I came across various use of the term resilience. For example, biologists have provided deep insights into the evolution of human kind and its' uneven biological, cultural, economic, and political development. Some books such as Jared Diamond's "Guns, Germs, and Steel" (1999) depict the biological-historical account on societies' resilience and prosperity, exploring the tools – guns, germs and steel – behind 'Western' civilizations' capability to develop the technologies and immunities that allowed them to dominate much of the world. Likewise, Daniel Brooks and his colleagues (2019) point out that each community, profession, and scientific discipline sees resilience in their own way, akin to 'blind men' each touching and addressing only "the part of the elephant" they encounter. On one hand, politicians and bureaucrats seek to "guarantee the future with no costs." On the other hand, evolutionists prioritize "survival." In response to these diverse perspectives, Brooks, Hoberg et al. (2019) propose the Action "Plan B," which they define through DAMA, abbreviating the sequence of required tasks: document, assess, monitor, act.

Behavioral scientists approach the term resilience as a psychological phenomenon. For example, by distinguishing concepts of 'moral injury' from post-traumatic syndrome disorder (PTSD) psychiatrists define resilience as the final stage of recovery therapies from these two forms of psychological traumas (Koenig H.G & Al Zaben, 2021; Williamson, Murphy et al., 2021). Similarly, psychologist Lucy Foulkes (2021) analyzes the definitions and recognition of mental illness, providing two concepts crucial to understanding the psychological resilience that she conceptualizes as "psychological immunization." She states, "the idea of stress inoculation is that (mildly) stressful challenges teach us ways to cope. When future stressors arise, we are then more likely to believe they are manageable" (2021, p. 203). Similarly, Eric Greitens (2016) defines resilience as "hard-won wisdom for living a better life", and asserts that resilience is the discipline to confront the brutal facts of the reality.

Other works demonstrate the relationship between psychological and socio-economic aspects of resilience. For example, sociologist Larissa Remennick (2012) contextualizes resilience within the ethno-political dividing lines. In her seminal exploration of the migrations of Soviet Jews, she drives an 'ethnic' division line between the resilience of Soviet Jews and Soviet Russians during the crisis of the late 1980s that led to the collapse of the USSR. Highlighting higher life expectancy statistics among the Soviet Jews in comparison to the Soviet Russians, Remennick demonstrated the advantage of Jewish men and women in this respect over Russians. She states that "one apparent conclusion from these statistics is that Jews as a group have adjusted much better than Russians to the drastic change in the economic and social environment of the post-communist years" (Remennick, 2012, p. 17). This finding confirms Diamond (1999) claim that resilience is not only individual, but also a collective phenomenon.

Remennick (2012) also emphasizes the socio-economic dimension of resilience in immigration and integration of Soviet and post-Soviet migrants in three countries of immigration — Israel, USA, and Germany — while observing two important trends. First, (post-) Soviet women exhibit greater socio-economic resilience than men because, in immigration, they take jobs at lower levels than those that they had in their home countries. Simultaneously, they express higher satisfaction with their new positions compared to their post-Soviet male counterparts. Second, Remennick finds that this socio-economic resilience varies depending on the host country: due to the dominance of liberal institutions and culture, it is higher in the USA and Canada than in Israel.

Furthermore, political scientists and anthropologists emphasize the significance of immigrants' national and geographical self-identities, along with their transformation, as crucial elements in understanding the socio-political aspect of resilience. For instance, in their exploration of the Bosnian diaspora across the globe, a group of scholars observed that mobility and the adaptation of old identities to new spaces were prominent integration and resilience strategies among Bosnian immigrants (Halilovich, 2013; Ramet & Valenta, 2011). Similarly, Munro (2017) discovered that factors such as the socio-political contexts of departure and arrival, the migrants' ongoing connection with their homeland, and the consideration of social and cultural elements played pivotal roles in shaping their migration experience in the UK, along with how they were received and represented in British media regarding Yugoslavia. Furthermore, Kovacevic-Bielicki's (2017) aforementioned study also highlights that despite being raised and socialized in Norway, many immigrants from former Yugoslavia still perceived themselves as "others," and this particular identity significantly influenced various aspects of their lives, including decisions related to choosing partners, professions, and other similar matters.

Likewise, one of my earlier studies found that social and economic resilience among former Soviet immigrants in Austria and Hungary is often interconnected. These immigrants typically achieve integration through the formation of a common-culture-based post-Soviet, Russian-speaking immigrant community (Tepavcevic, 2021 a). Having experienced poverty during the Soviet era, they perceive themselves as more motivated, and consequently, more resilient in facing challenges compared to their local Austrian and Hungarian counterparts. This observation aligns with the concept of 'psychological immunization' emphasized by Foulkes (2021).

Upon analyzing these definitions of resilience, I identified a direct relationship between the aspect of vulnerability and the type of resilience, leading me to conceptualize two types of resilience concerning global crises. The first type is what I term 'soft' resilience, encompassing cultural and psychological aspects of coping with a crisis, including psychological recovery from such events. The second type is 'hard' or tangible resilience, which involves physical and socioeconomic aspects (Tepavcevic, 2022).

In summary, resilience can manifest in both individual and collective contexts, taking on both 'soft' and tangible forms. As a result, this book is founded on the following proposition regarding vulnerability and resilience: *vulnerable to changes posed by crisis and migrations, migrants adapt to new environments by means of socioeconomic or 'hard' resilience – changing professions and accepting less qual-*

ified jobs than held back in countries of origin, and by means of 'soft' resilience such as adopting their old local, cultural, and 'ethnic' identities to new environments.

Analytical Framework: Bridging Political Science, Migration and Business Studies through Motives for Emigration, Forms of Resilience, and Forms of Loyalty

Lee (1966) was among the earliest scholars to propose the theory of migration and the framework for the analysis of motives to emigrate. This analytical framework, as presented in Figure 1 below, comprises of four major factors that shape motives for migration and volumes of migration: 1) factors associated with the area of origin, i.e. with home/sending country; 2) factors associated with the area of destination, i.e. with host/receiving country.

Figure 1.1: Analytical framework for motives for emigration

1. Factors at place of origin + -	2. Factors at place of destination + -
3. Intervening obstacles (immigration laws, physical barriers)	4. Personal factors (life-cycle related interests/motives, change of marital status)

Lee (1966) astutely observed that factors influencing decisions related to migration can be positive or negative in both home and host countries. Consequently, he outlined two additional groups of factors that influence migration decisions:

Intervening obstacles: These are factors that hinder migration and can include migration-restricting laws and physical barriers;

Personal factors: This category involves individual considerations such as life cycle-related interests or changes in marital status that may play a significant role in influencing migration decisions.

Indeed, the factors related to both home and host countries can be interpreted differently based on individual circumstances, falling into positive, negative, or insignificant categories under the group of personal factors. These motives for migration are closely connected to the concept of loyalty.

When negative factors in the home country outweigh the positive ones, loyalty to the home country tends to decrease. However, if positive or pull factors in the host country complement the negative factors in the home country, one can expect a higher level of loyalty to the host country, leading to emigration. Moreover, intervening factors, such as personal or legal obstacles, may also influence the levels of loyalty to either the home or host country. These complex interactions of various factors play a crucial role in shaping the decisions and loyalties of individuals during migration processes.

Analyzing decision-making mechanisms be it commercial organizations or states, Albert Hirschman (1970) proposed an influential framework for the analysis of emigration. According to Hirschman (1970), individuals who dissent, whether in political or economic matters, have two primary options: to voice their concerns or to exit. In the case of exit, which is often considered the easier choice, they decide to leave the political community or the company they are critical of (Hirschman, 1970). On the other hand, with the option of 'voice,' they express their dissatisfaction by criticizing the government or the company leadership responsible for the issues they perceive. Hirschman emphasized that an individual's loyalty towards the community in question plays a significant role in determining which option they will choose. The presence of loyalty influences the decision-making process between exit and voice. In fact, Hirschman views these two options as mutually exclusive to some extent. If the exit option is more readily available and convenient, the likelihood of individuals choosing voice diminishes.

Loyalty, as proposed by Hirschman (1970), arises from a complex interplay of rational and emotional factors that contribute to a customer or member's overall perception of an organization and their level of satisfaction with its products or services. When a customer or member perceives that the organization adequately meets their needs and expectations, loyalty tends to develop. This sense of loyalty can be reinforced when the organization offers high-quality products or services at reasonable prices. Additionally, emotional factors, such as a sense of belonging or identification with the organization, can also contribute significantly to the formation of loyalty (Hirschman, 1970). Therefore, Lee's analysis of the motives for emigration and Hirschman's exit, voice, and loyalty framework share some similarities in their focus on the reasons why individuals or groups choose to leave an organization or community. In both cases, the decision to leave or stay is influenced by a combination of factors, including rational considerations such as economic opportunities and emotional factors such as a sense of attachment or identity with the community or organization. Both frameworks highlight the importance of understanding the reasons why individuals choose to leave or stay and the potential consequences of those decisions.

In his later work, particularly when discussing the escalating emigration from Eastern Germany in 1989, Hirschman (1993) discovered an interesting phenomenon: mass 'exit' or exodus from the region triggered 'voice' among those who stayed behind. This means that as a result of the large-scale migration, individuals who chose to stay in Eastern Germany took to the streets to demand change, effectively expressing their dissatisfaction and advocating for improvements. This finding showed that 'exit' and 'voice' were working in tandem, and loyalty played a crucial role in this dynamic: those who wanted to remain in the country used 'voice' to drive change. Building upon Hirschman's framework, Hoffmann (2010) later reapplied it in the context of emigrants maintaining strong loyalty, or social ties, to their country of origin even after leaving. According to Hoffmann, transnational migration involves an overlapping and simultaneity of the categories of exit, voice, and loyalty. This suggests that in the context of transnational migration, these three categories are mutually inclusive options for individuals. Emigrants are found to maintain a level of loyalty to their home country and continue to engage in its public affairs through voicing their opinions and advocating for change even from abroad. Furthermore, Burgess (2012) contributed to Hirschman's framework by recognizing a third option: 'voicing after exit.' This refers to the engagement of individuals in 'home politics' to promote change in their country of origin after leaving. This type of action also indicates a certain level of remaining loyalty to the country they have departed from. These various arguments and findings suggest that loyalty is a more complex concept than it may have initially seemed in Hirschman's (1970) first study. The interactions between exit, voice, and loyalty are nuanced and require further examination, particularly in the context of transnational migration and authoritarian regimes.

Varieties of Loyalty

As the concept of loyalty is mainly explored in business literature, it becomes evident that loyalty manifests in various forms and can vary significantly in intensity. For example, examining the nature of loyalty among customers to a brand, Rowley (2005, p. 574) points out that

> There is agreement that loyalty is important for the future of the business... Since loyalty is key in customer development and profitability, it is important to understand the loyalty condition in more detail, and to use this understanding to develop further the relationship with customers in the loyal category.

Further differentiating between customers whose loyalty is inertial and those whose loyalty is positive, Rowley (2005) identifies four types of loyal customers, each representing a distinct form of loyalty: captive, convenience-seekers, contented, and committed. Building on this classification, founder and entrepreneur McGinn

(2015) briefly explains the variety of loyalty as follows: Captive Loyalty: McGinn associates this type of loyalty with a "coercive" nature, where customers feel compelled to choose a particular product or service due to its dominance in the market. Convenience-Seekers Loyalty: This form of loyalty refers to customers who choose products or services primarily based on their ease of accessibility. Cost Loyalty: Referring to Rowley's (2005) contented customers, this type of loyalty is characterized by customers who perceive the value for money as balanced and satisfactory. Commitment Loyalty: Considered the most important and desirable type of loyalty among businesses, commitment loyalty refers to customers who remain loyal to a brand, service, or organization despite potential costs or challenges. Expanding on these concepts, I propose further categorization, distinguishing between weak, strong, positive, and negative forms of loyalty, as demonstrated in the following table.

Table 1. 1: Forms of loyalty

	Strong	Weak
Positive	Commitment	Convenience and Low Cost (adequate value for money)
Negative	Coercion or Captive loyalty	Contended or High Cost

It is worth emphasizing, as pointed out by McGinn (2015), that these different forms of loyalty are not rigidly separated; they can and often do overlap in various situations. In this book, I delve deeper into these loyalty concepts, specifically in the context of migrant communities and their role as sources of resilience during global crises. I explore how loyalty plays a significant role in shaping the experiences and responses of migrant communities in times of challenges and uncertainties.

Overall, while underlining social and economic aspect of emigration, Hirschman's framework may serve as the basic tool for analyzing forms of resilience in global crises: as exit, voice and loyalty interplay, their interactions vary depending on the context. For the purposes of this book, Lee's positive and negative factors in home and host countries, and Hirschman's and his followers' exit, voice, loyalty, voice because of exit, and voice after exit serves the analysis of this book to evaluate (post-) Yugoslavs' and (post-)Soviets 'hard' resilience in global crises. Similarly, Foulkes' (2021) concept of 'psychological immunization' serves to evaluate 'soft' resilience. The next section analyzes the research methods applied in the process of data collection for the present book.

Narratives as Data and Methodological Approaches to Its' Collection

The study of migrants' resilience inherently involves exploring questions of identity and analyzing discourses and narratives. For instance, in her examination of Mexican immigrants in the US, Anna De Fina (2003) recognized the increasing use of narrative analysis as a revolutionary method in qualitative research across various social science fields. De Fina emphasized the importance of narrative analysis, referring to the influential linguist Labov (1972), who utilized narratives in his study of vernacular language in urban settings. Labov observed that when people narrate their experiences, they become more engaged and less self-conscious about the way they speak. Expanding on Labov's insights, De Fina (2003) noted that narratives are central to the encoding of human experiences because they constitute a temporal sequence, making these experiences comprehensible to individuals only when they are narrated. By employing narrative analysis, researchers gain valuable insights into the lives of migrants and their experiences, allowing for a deeper understanding of their resilience in the face of challenges and adversities. It provides a powerful lens through which to explore the complexities of identity formation and the narratives that shape the migrant experience. Throughout this book I refer to Hinchman and Hinchman (1997) definition of narratives as storied ways of knowing and communicating. With regard to the notion of 'knowing', Kovacevic-Bielicki (2017, p. 41) argues that

> It is very useful to have "knowing" in the definition, in order to point out that narrative does not have to be expressed explicitly to be a narrative, but it does need to have a certain storied and temporal form to be a narrative.

Building on the insights of De Fina (2003), Hinchman and Hinchman (1997), and Kovacevic-Bielicki (2017), this book views narratives as textual representations that arise from the context of personal notes, informal conversations, and interviews. These narratives serve as prototypical stories that highlight the vulnerabilities and resilience of migrants during times of crises. In this book, among the narratives analyzed that pertain to migrant experiences during global crises, I include my personal notes. Analytical method that allows for such analysis is autoethnography, which Adams, Ellis et al. (2017, pp. 1-4) describe as follows:

> Autoethnography uses personal experience ("auto") to describe and interpret ("graphy") cultural texts, experiences, beliefs, and practices ("ethno"). … Given the focus on personal experience, autoethnographers also describe moments of everyday experience that cannot be captured through more traditional research methods. … Autoethnographers offer accounts of personal experience to complement, or fill gaps in, existing research.

Applying autoethnography as a method of analysis, my positionality as the author is of great significance. Being born as a Yugoslav citizen during the late years of the Cold War, I observed and noted the distinctions between Yugoslavs residing in the country of origin (of which I was a part back then) and Yugoslav migrants, including members of my family, family friends, and my friends. Although these groups shared similarities in terms of citizenship, origin, culture, education level, and background, the experience of working abroad — professional mobility, in other words — was highly valued as a soft skill in my social circles. The children of these professionals — my peers and friends — were a significant source of knowledge about life abroad for me, even before I became an emigrant myself. Many of them had fluent or even near-native foreign language skills. I distinctly remember envying them for having friends from abroad, as it was considered a privilege in a country where foreigners were mainly tourists from Western Europe or Arabic and African students, who were mostly adults.

In the early 1990s, when war tore Yugoslavia apart, I, as a teenager, was compelled to move with my family to post-Soviet Russia. During my time in Russia, I underwent all stages of integration into post-Soviet Russian society. This journey ranged from starting with learning Russian from a beginner level to eventually working as a reporter and anchor at a Russian television channel nine years later. As both a migrant and a journalist, I naturally became integrated into migrant communities in Moscow. Later, upon emigrating from Russia to Hungary, my work led me to become deeply involved with post-Soviet and post-Yugoslav migrant communities, primarily in Hungary, Austria, Germany and Spain, but also spanning across the European Union (EU) and worldwide. My native knowledge of Bosnian/Croatian/Serbian and close-to-native proficiency in Russian positioned me as an insider and equal member within both post-Yugoslav and post-Soviet migrant communities. This deep understanding and familiarity with their cultures and languages were recognized as a form of loyalty to these communities, and reciprocally, they embraced me as one of their own. Having this unique connection allowed me to gain a comprehensive insight into the motives behind migration and the selection of countries for immigration, the boundaries of these communities, and their internal dynamics. Additionally, I could better grasp their perspectives on the relationship between space and time, which together contribute to the simultaneous production and consumption of elements that constitute resilience.

As a result, I documented over two hundred first-hand insights and close to a thousand second-hand insights from representatives of Yugoslav and Soviet migrant communities across geographic sites as diverse as Germany, Switzerland, Austria, Russia, Ukraine, Azerbaijan, Armenia, Vietnam, India, South Africa, USA, Canada, and Mexico. Among classical ethnographers and other social scientists, this approach would automatically imply multi-sited ethnography as a necessary research method or approach. As George Marcus, the 'founding father' of the term 'multi-sited ethnography' pointed out, it treats the study of social phenomena as its objective that cannot be accounted for by focusing on a single site (Marcus, 1995). Following Marcus, Mark-Antony Falzon (2009, pp. 1-2) pointed out that

[P]reviously, the 'world system' was seen as a framework within which the local was contextualized or compared; it now becomes integral to and embedded in multi-sited objects of study. The essence of multi-sited research is to follow people, connections, associations, and relationships across space (because they are substantially continuous but spatially non-contiguous). Research design proceeds by a series of juxtapositions in which the global is collapsed into and made an integral part of parallel, related local situations, rather than something monolithic or external to them. In terms of method, multi-sited ethnography involves a spatially dispersed field through which the ethnographer moves — actually, via sojourns in two or more places, or conceptually, by means of techniques of juxtaposition of data.

Equally important, with the emergence first, of low-cost travel opportunities, and second, of Internet and social media, the distances were virtually shortened and the meaning of these geographical sites became to certain extent blurred. Therefore, as Gallo (2009, p. 89) correctly noted,

the importance of multi-sited ethnography is rooted in the recognition that the 'field' of ethnographic inquiry is not simply a geographical place waiting to be entered, but rather a 'conceptual space' whose meanings and confines are continuously negotiated by the ethnographer and their informants (Gupta and Ferguson, 1997) ... the meanings of what the site will be are never predictable. ...However, multi-sited ethnography... requires the researcher to put into question previous sites of ethnographic inquiry in light of new ones.

Even in multidimensional and ambiguous ethnographic settings, in-depth interviews remain a crucial method of inquiry and a primary source of information about migrant communities and their connections. Therefore, interviews with post-Yugoslav and post-Soviet migrants were also utilized for narrative collection. Interviewees were selected based on their origin, either from former Yugoslavia or the former USSR, and then divided into two generational groups. The first group consisted of migrants born in the Soviet Union and Yugoslavia between 1945 and 1965, while the second generational group included interviewees aged between 1970 and 1990. A semi-structured questionnaire was employed to guide the conversations and focus on reasons for migration, vulnerability, and resilience. However, in practice, the interviewees predominantly narrated their life stories and personal experiences. Last but equally important, especially during COVID-19 pandemic, I extensively engaged in digital ethnography, defined as systematic participant observation of social media discussions, mostly through Facebook, LinkedIn, and Telegram and thematic migrant, cultural, professional groups. I used two approaches: first, I analyzed digital materials as artifacts; second, I participated and observed social media discussions in post-Yugoslav and post-Soviet migrant groups. The methods of inquiry are summarized in Table 1.2 below.

Table 1.2: Methods of inquiry referred in the text

Method of research	Reference in the text
Participant observation of post-Yugoslav and post-Soviet immigrant communities, including face-to-face interviews, informal presence and conversations	personal communication, a time when conducted (month and year)
Personal notes made either in writing, or recorded and then transcribed	personal notes, a time when conducted (season or month and year)
Interviews and personal communication conducted via telephone, email, or online applications	online communication, a time when conducted (month and year)
Digital ethnography and virtual immigrant groups in social networks	social media group discussion/ communication, a time when occurred (month and year)
Surveys created online and shared in social media groups to receive responses anonymously	online survey response, a time when received (month and year)

Regarding the ethical and legal aspects of the research, given the sensitivity of the research topic and in compliance with the EU General Data Protection Regulation (GDPR), I carefully selected my informants based on three principles. Firstly, following the consent of my interviewees and seconding it to informal conversations and personal notes, I ensured that all personal data remained anonymous. Secondly, I made sure that all my respondents were older than 18 years of age. Thirdly, I recruited interviewees on a purely voluntary basis. By adhering to these principles, I collected direct narratives from over two hundred respondents across the world with their consent to use their testimonies anonymously. This consent and the way that narratives are used in the analysis is also directly related to the concepts of vulnerability and resilience. The fears—retained from traumatic experiences of state collapses and some of the global crises that followed—conditioned their consent to the anonymous use of these narratives for the analytical purposes. At the same time, most of my interlocutors sought these conversations as an opportunity to reveal challenges that they faced and express their views—in other words, arguing their own legitimacy related to the global crises—without being directly exposed to negative criticism, judgement or even physical threat. Some of the most illustrative narratives are directly quoted in chapters that follow.

Structure and Outline of the Book

The present book is structured into three thematic parts, spanning across six periods, and covering three broad regions. As mentioned earlier, following Remennick's (2012) argument that the level of socio-economic resilience depends on the institutional system present in a host country, and that it is higher in host countries with liberal institutions and culture, as noted above, the host countries are analytically divided into the three broad clusters. The first cluster consists of countries formerly referred to as 'the West' or the 'First World'. The second broad cluster comprises former socialist bloc countries, including post-Soviet republics, and Central and Eastern European states, which were conditionally characterized as the 'Second World' during the twentieth century. The last cluster encompasses developing countries and former European colonies, which were previously commonly referred to as 'the Third World'.

   In addition to the present introductory chapter, the first part also includes Chapter 2, which analyzes the drivers of migration flows from Yugoslavia and the Soviet Union during the Cold War. This chapter delves into the formation of Yugoslav and Soviet migrant communities and diasporas, revealing the distinct drivers, patterns of emergence, and forms of loyalty that bind these communities. The second part of the book consists of two chapters.

Chapter 3 examines the emergence of division lines during the collapses of Yugoslavia and the Soviet Union, and how these factors influenced stay or migration decisions. This analysis reveals that the crises of these collapses were inherently multi-exclusive in nature. Chapter 4, on the other hand, delves into the reasons and modes behind the trajectories of migrations related to the collapses of the former Yugoslavia and the former Soviet Union. The roles of existing Yugoslav and Soviet migrant communities and diasporas in these migration flows are also explored. Consequently, this chapter contributes to the migration literature by presenting a more nuanced, source of resilience-based typology of migrant communities, in contrast to the existing three types. It also establishes connections between these typologies and the various forms of loyalty displayed within these migrant communities.

The third part of the book is centered around lessons drawn from collapses and their application, which is conceptualized as resilience, among post-Yugoslav and post-Soviet migrants during subsequent global crises. Chapter 5 analyzes influence and outcomes of the Great Recession on lives, geographical and professional trajectories of post-Yugoslav and post-Soviet citizens. Chapter 6 reveals challenges encountered by post-Yugoslav and post-Soviet migrants and their communities, and their resilience during the COVID-19 pandemic. Chapter 7 provides an analysis of the reactions to and challenges posed by Russia's ongoing invasion in Ukraine. It also offers insights into the emerging forms of resilience among post-Soviet migrants, with a comparative reflection on post-Yugoslav migrants. Chapter 8 concludes by situating the findings into existing literature, real world implications of the analysis, and suggesting avenues for further research.

Chapter 2
Challenges and Resilience in the Times of the Cold War: Motives and Geography of Yugoslav and Soviet Migrations in 1946 – 1989

We usually went to Trieste for shopping. Once I bought one pair of Levi's jeans for me, and two more I wearied over to smuggle and sell when I return to Yugoslavia. When I came back home, I sold these two other pairs, and covered the costs of my own pair (personal conversation, Germany, winter 2000).

We could not travel abroad, but we travelled all across a huge country. We believed that we were so happy and satisfied, and we had no clue how unfortunate we actually were (personal conversation, Russia, summer 2007).

As a young journalist, I found these statements particularly intriguing, and I took notes on them. The first statement caught my attention because it reflected on a sense of freedom that was not available to my generation of citizens from the countries comprising former Yugoslavia and the former Soviet Union during the time of the conversation. The second quotation left a strong impression on me as it revealed that a lack of awareness could lead people to feel happy or at least believe they are happy. Both statements arose during my informal conversations about traveling during the Cold War with my friends' parents who belonged to the same generation, born in the mid-1950s. One person was born and raised in Yugoslavia and later moved to Germany after the collapse of Yugoslavia. The second person was born and raised in the Soviet Union and relocated from Soviet Ukraine to Soviet Russia about a decade before the collapse of the USSR. These two statements strikingly illustrate the differences in private freedoms, including the possibilities for the mobility of citizens in the two former socialist multinational federations. Much later, I came to understand that the concept of loyalty to the state of origin underpinned these two statements. In the process of writing this book, I further grasped that the first statement reflected loyalty of convenience to Yugoslavia as a state that

allowed freedom of mobility. On the other hand, the second statement exemplified loyalty based on ignorance, stemming from coercion within the former Soviet Union. While the first form of loyalty
aligns with the initial framework proposed by Hirschman (1970),
the second form initially appears in business studies as loyalty of
coercion, referring to the domination of a product in the market.
However, in the case of an authoritarian state, it goes beyond mere
loyalty to a dominant entity; it represents a vacuum of choice, an
absence of options.

The two statements further motivated me to explore several
key issues: How did the motives for emigration of Yugoslavs and
Soviets influence the trajectories of their migrations? In what ways
did Yugoslav and Soviet migrant communities differ from each
other? And how did (e)migration relate to the resilience of Yugoslav and Soviet citizens? Through my inquiry, I discovered that the
paths of emigration from Yugoslavia and the Soviet Union differed
significantly in both form and nature. Emigration from Yugoslavia
during various periods of the Cold War was seemingly largely
driven by opportunities, often taking on a temporary character. Despite facing administrative and physical obstacles, Soviet citizens
also found ways to emigrate in diverse forms, ranging from legal
ethnic group emigration to even extreme cases like terrorist hijack-
ing of planes. As a result, the Yugoslav and Soviet migrant communities that emerged during the Cold War were driven mostly by
different motives and faced distinct challenges, leading to the development of varying forms of resilience. The following section
starts with a brief overview of the main propositions regarding
global migration during the Cold War. Then it analyzes the patterns
and geography of Yugoslav migrations and Yugoslav migrant communities in several national sites. Section 3 analyzes geography and
patterns of Soviet emigration and Soviet migrant communities
abroad. The last section provides comparisons of Yugoslav and Soviet modes of migration during the Cold War period, the types of
their migrant communities and forms of loyalties to them, and
forms of their resilience.

Major Forms of Migrations during the Cold War

Analyzing immigration in Europe, Baycan and Nijkamp (2006) found that since the end of World War II up to the end of the Cold War it proceeded in three phases. The first phase — the post-war adjustment — happened between the late 1940s and early-1950s. It encountered mass refugee flows and decolonization with around 15 million people forced to transfer from one country to another because of boundary changes between Germany, Poland, and the former Czechoslovakia, and return migration and the inflow of workers from colonies to Great Britain, France, Belgium and the Netherlands. The second phase that took place between the early 1950s and 1973 was characterized by the labor migration prompted by the reconstruction of Europe and the average economic growth rate around five per cent per year and consequent a huge demand for workers. Western European and Scandinavian countries recruited unskilled workers from the Southern European countries, thus net immigration for Western Europe reached around 10 million in this period. The third phase that lasted between mid-1970s and mid-1980s was marked by the oil shocks and the related increased social tensions and fears surrounding recession that prompted Western European governments to decrease labor immigration. As a result, the immigration was limited to family reunion and humanitarian immigration. In the same period Southern European countries became attractive for immigration as a result of relatively successful reforms of their political and economic systems (Baycan & Nijkamp, 2006). These migration inflows led to the formation of two main types of migration that resulted in the emergence of new, ethnically distinct populations in economically advanced countries. These migrations also serve as key examples that exemplify the main propositions about migrations during the Cold War.

The first form included a migration of workers from the European peripheries to Western Europe usually through the guestwork system: free movement of workers within the European Community became increasingly significant. The global oil crisis of the early 1970s brought economic recession soon followed by the period of the global economic restructuring, and, consequentially, by organized recruitment of manual guest workers by advanced industrial countries;

Secondly, the immigration of populations from the former colonies to the European power centers. Starting from Germany and ending in the UK, the timing of these movements varied, but they both were followed by family reunion (Castles, Haas et al., 2019).

The world migrations during the Cold War period also included mass movements of refugees from Europe, most significantly from Germany and Poland to North America, and former European colonists' return migrations to their countries of origin. Exploring Yugoslav and Soviet migrations during Cold War, following sections situate them to the broader context of global migrations.

Motives and Geography of Yugoslav Migrations

In the late 1940s, collaborators with the forces of the Nazi Axis — Germany, Italy, and Spain — representing the Independent State of Croatia, which emerged on the territory of the Kingdom of Yugoslavia and existed during World War II as a protégé of the Axis, faced arrests and prosecution for war crimes (Subotić, 2019). Notably, these individuals were remnants of Croatia's fascist Ustasha regime, which operated the concentration camp in Jasenovac, known as the "Auschwitz of the Balkans." Approximately 600,000 Serbs, Jews, and Roma were killed there between 1941 and 1945 (Rotella & Wilkinson, 1998). Consequently, many of these collaborators and their supporters sought to immigrate to countries where they could find protection (Molnar, 2014). For example, Argentina, under Juan Perón's regime, invited them to settle there, offering support to ease their passage from Europe. The Argentine government provided travel documents and, in many cases, covered their expenses (Minster, 2021). At that time, Argentina already had the most numerous German, Italian, and Spanish immigrant communities, making it an appealing destination for these collaborators seeking refuge.

Defeated in World War II, these remnants of Nazi governments' protégé were forced to emigrate — in Hirschman (1970) terms, to opt for exit—to avoid prosecution, and this emigration represented their political, social and physical resilience. Their position in the new emerging system of socialist Yugoslavia left them with no other option but to be seen as war criminals, leading to a complete absence of loyalty towards the country. Paradoxically, these Croats, lacking loyalty to Yugoslavia, constituted the first post-World-War-II community of emigrants from the country. Writing about the commander of Jasenovac, Dinko Sakic, journalists of Los Angeles Times gave a general characteristic of this community:

> Sakic, the retired former owner of a textile factory, has left his home in the beach resort of Santa Teresita and apparently traveled to Buenos Aires, but technically he is not a fugitive ... Rather than keeping a low profile after he came to Argentina 50 years ago, the reportedly outspoken Sakic has been active in the sizable Argentine Croatian community. He traveled to Europe to espouse Croatian nationalist causes and boasted about having clout with Argentine politicians, according to Argentine officials and Jewish activists (Rotella & Wilkinson, 1998).

As this excerpt from the Los Angeles Times article suggests, he was a significant representative of the Yugoslav-era Croatian far-right migrant community activists, remaining loyal to radical right ideas. He maintained close contact with other geographically distant Croatian emigrant communities that shared his views. Similarly, the remnants of the Serbian King's Army, while having fewer crimes on their accounts during World War II compared to their Croatian counterparts, did not see a future under the socialist regime. Consequently, many of them moved and settled in the South African Republic.

Starting from 1948, when the Yugoslav government, under the leadership of Josip Broz Tito, refused to join the socialist bloc led by Joseph Stalin, Yugoslavia was the only country in Europe with a socialist regime where its citizens could move freely across borders until its collapse in 1991 (Archer, Bernard et al., 2023; Molnar, 2014). Apart from remnants of the Nazi collaborators, emigration from Yugoslavia in this early aftermath of World War II was significant due to devastations that the country faced: destroyed infrastructure, poverty, and political reconstruction. As Bubalo Zivkovic,

Ivkov et al. (2010) point out, "around 200,000 people who went to western European countries crossed the ocean" further and went to the countries of traditional immigration of the 'new world' (27). Therefore, these early post-WWII Yugoslav migrations were one of the forms of Yugoslav citizens' post-war socioeconomic resilience. This Yugoslav emigration wave ended by the 1950s, with the beginning of the country's industrialization and economic restructuration. Table 2.1. displays reported numbers of this further emigration of Yugoslav citizens from Europe.

Table 2.1. Reported numbers of emigration of Yugoslav citizens from Europe 1945 - 1985

Receiving country	USA	Canada	Aus-tralia	Argen-tina	Brazil	New Zealand
Reported number of Yugo-slav im-migrants	84000	30400	23350	15000	5000	560

Source: Bubalo Zivkovic, Ivkov et al. (2010)

These examples place early post-World-War-II Yugoslav migrations in line with what Castles, Haas et al. (2019) characterized as mass migrations from Europe to North America, simultaneously contributing to insights in emigration to the countries of South America and Africa.

In the later post-World-War-II periods, Yugoslav citizens continued to enjoy visa-free borders, allowing them unrestricted travel to both Western Europe and countries within the Socialist bloc. Later, this privilege expanded to include newly decolonized African and Asian states as well. On the one hand, the political leadership of the most of decolonized countries together with Yugoslavia's political leader Josip Broz Tito founded the Non-Alignment Movement. In practice, the Movement represented the third weak bloc in the bipolar world system, revealing also the loyalty of coercion to both major blocs and simultaneous balance between them.

However, in contrast to other non-aligned countries during the Cold War,

> Yugoslavia's non-alignment was neither a product of anti-colonial revolution nor of post-colonial defiance to former masters. It was a direct outcome of inter-bloc dynamics, where a country performing an authentic communist revolution—striving for independence and equality from both blocs—had completed an arduous political journey from the fringes of European bloc politics to the forefront of world politics where it was shaping a new ideological and foreign policy response to the existing dominant currents in international relations (Cavoski, 2019).

As a result, during the post-Second-World-War period of economic and political restructuring, Yugoslavia stood out as the economically most developed and the only European member of the Non-Aligned Movement for other partners. In the 1970s, Yugoslavia played a crucial role as a key source of knowledge and technologies for developing industries in recently decolonized countries, contributing to the building of their industrial and military infrastructures (Jovanovic & Stojmenovic, 2023). Consequently, many Yugoslav engineering companies signed the project-based contracts with third world countries and sent their professionals there. For instance, Iraq was Yugoslavia's most important trade partner among the third world countries (Serbia, 2022). In the mid-1970s, Yugoslav and Iraqi governments signed a large contract for building the deep-water port, Umm Quasr Port in Iraq (Gatarić, 2003). Similarly, in the 1980s, during Iraq's invasion on Iran, Yugoslavia was a major exporter of weapons to Iraq (News, 2013). Therefore, it was quite common among Yugoslav engineers, architects, and economists to move temporarily for work to Iraq for several consecutive years, and often to bring their families with them. As a result, at the beginning of Iraq's invasion on Iran, about 100000 Yugoslav citizens were evacuated from Iraq (Gatarić, 2003). Therefore, Yugoslav citizens' decisions to temporarily move to third world countries were generally opportunity-driven. Yugoslav professionals were enticed by significantly higher salaries offered for conducting these infrastructure projects abroad compared to what they earned by working at home. Additionally, being paid in hard currency was another crucial benefit for these professionals. All these factors enabled them to experience socioeconomic upward mobility upon their return to Yugoslavia.

Similarly, as the only socialist country outside the socialist bloc, Yugoslavia represented a relatively free market and became the place with the easiest access for many governments and citizens of other socialist countries to some otherwise unreachable Western products and technologies. As a result, Yugoslav construction, trade, and technological companies, along with their employees, saw these opportunities as a means not only to earn better salaries than available at home but also to enjoy upward social mobility simply by being foreigners in places where the local currency was weak. Earning in hard currency allowed them to boost their savings. Moreover, since not many Yugoslavs could afford long trips abroad, temporary migration was also regarded as a certain status symbol or prestige (Jovanovic & Stojmenovic, 2023). Starting from 1964, when Yugoslavia became a member of the Council for Mutual Economic Assistance (CMEA or COMECON), an organization facilitating development among eastern European socialist countries, Yugoslav students also took advantage of student exchange programs to study in some of the other socialist countries.

Simultaneous Yugoslav emigration to the countries of the Capitalist bloc presented somewhat contrasting picture: these Western European nations, including militarily neutral states like Germany, Austria, and Switzerland, were in need of labor due to their rapid economic development. As a result, in the late 1960s, these countries signed bilateral agreements with several Southern European countries, including Yugoslavia, for sending guest work force (Bernard, 2019a; Molnar, 2014). Based on these agreements signed between Yugoslavia as the sending country and Germany, Austria, and Switzerland (Bonifazi & Mamolo, 2004; Kraler, 2011) as host countries, Yugoslav medical doctors and nurses, blue-collar service providers, mostly construction workers, massively migrated as guest workers (Fibbi, Wanner et al., 2015; Fotiadis, Ivanovic et al., 2019). Within Yugoslav mainstream society, they became the class called *Gastarbeiter*, after the German expression meaning the guest worker (Karabegovic, 2018). Over the 1960s, emigration — or temporal migration — from Yugoslavia to Western and

Northern Europe reached around 1150000, but in the 1970s, the number of Yugoslav guest workers decreased to 650000, while the number of their family members joining them abroad increased (Bubalo Zivkovic, Ivkov et al., 2010).

In the 1970s and 1980s, as the countries of the Western bloc entered a phase of technological revolution, Yugoslav high-skilled workforce, including scientists and researchers were in high demand, much like in third world and socialist bloc countries. Each year, approximately 30,000 Yugoslav workers were employed across the countries of the Western bloc (Bubalo Zivkovic, Ivkov et al., 2010). In some contrast to the latter, they received their salaries in local currencies as foreign guest workers from a less developed country than the receiving one (Bernard, 2019a). As such, they enjoyed less favorable conditions than their fellow citizens working in third world countries. Finally, in the 1980s, some top managers from Yugoslav production companies, particularly those from relatively well-developed industries like furniture and car manufacturing, represented these companies in the USA, UK, France, Italy, and the Netherlands.

Yugoslav migrant communities from Western Europe to the Third World

Concurrently, migration flows between Yugoslavia and countries of the Socialist and Capitalist blocs, as well as the Non-Alignment member states, were influenced by the broader interests of their respective members. Additionally, these migration flows also reflected the professional and personal motives of Yugoslav citizens to migrate. There were relatively significant migrations from Yugoslavia to Great Britain, with the 1991 census recording 13,846 residents of England, Scotland, and Wales who were born in Yugoslavia (Munro, 2017). With exception of remnants of the Nazi-collaborative Ustaha regime, who escaped from the Yugoslav socialist government to Germany and formed nationalist Croatian community of emigres (Molnar, 2014), in Western Europe and the USA, Yugoslav labor workers created temporary communities, interacting with local professionals. The differences in identity and attitudes towards the socialist regime in Yugoslavia sometimes led to tensions and conflicts between remnants of Croatian Nazi-collaborators and labor workers, who by default of Yugoslav citizenship were identified with the socialist Yugoslavia. Nevertheless, as Duranovic (2020) demonstrated citing one of his Bosnian interviewees living in Berlin, in the late 1970s and in the 1980s there was not always clearly visible distinction between these Yugoslav migrant communities:

> I complained to a man from Herzegovina, from Ljubuški, (that a German doctor would not give me a sick leave); I didn't even know that Ljubuški existed in Bosnia then, and he gave me the address and said, go, there is a doctor, he is our man, speaks our language, he is a Yugoslav, do not tell him anything hurts you, just tell him 'I need a sick leave' and he will give it to you. And I accepted that. ... I found the address, it read 'Dr. Jelić' ... In the end, he said to me 'here you are, my son' and he gave me two books. Read these in peace. And I took the two books...there were interesting things, and then some of their propaganda, like 'Tito is not the Tito at all; ... This Tito killed a number of Muslims and Croats after the war, partisans killed a number of people after the war'. ... I could not understand it because I had come from Yugoslavia where Tito was, almost, *astagfirullah* [May God forgive me], we were to swear by Tito, and these people here wrote such things (Duranovic, 2020, p. 255).

While revealing insider's view of being a Yugoslav labor migrant, this lengthy citation from Duranovic's study stresses the relevance of labor migrant experience in recognizing cultural clichés that constituted this hybridity of simultaneous similarities and differences among Yugoslavs living in Yugoslavia, Yugoslav temporary migrant workers, and Yugoslav long-term emigres. However, their 'hybridity' significantly differed from multicultural communities existing for examples in Vojvodina (Agardi, 2022; Schwartz, 2018) and in Transylvania (Agardi, 2022). As Karabegovic (2018, p. part I) explained, this difference appeared even in informal titles of Yugoslav labor migrants.

> Within both German and Yugoslav circles, members of these populations were referred to as *Jugovići* and *Jugošvaben*, respectively, connoting their combined identities. *Jugovići* typically denoted guest workers from Yugoslavia, while *Jugošvabe* implied a certain level of assimilation into Germany society. Second-generation Yugoslavs became *Jugošvaben*, combining the

words Yugo and Schwabe, a colloquial Yugoslav term used for German peoples. Comparatively, in former Yugoslavia, they were often referred to as '*Švabe*' or '*Gastarbajteri*'.

Concerning the viewpoints of the governments and populations of the receiving countries, according to Molnar (2014), coming from a country with a communist regime, Yugoslav migrants in West Germany were initially suspected of inoculating communist ideas among the Germans. They were thus regarded as a significant — communist — 'other' among the native population. However, as Molnar (2014, p. 140) also emphasized,

> Yugoslavs were far less active in leftist or communist politics than every other sizable immigrant group on West German soil ... The rapid growth of German tourism in Yugoslavia beginning in the early 1960s also suggests that for many Germans, Yugoslavia came to be seen more as land of sunny beaches than a menacing communist state.

As the number of immigrants increased in these countries, Yugoslavs gained reputation as skilled and reliable workers, who easily adapted to life especially in West Germany. For these reasons, Yugoslav migrants became preferable over other foreign guest workers, particularly Turks (Molnar, 2014). As a result, in Western Europe and USA, Yugoslavs created temporal communities, which were immersed with local professionals. Claiming the emigrants in distant places as "their own", Yugoslavia's government engaged in as Brunnbauer put it "transterritorial nation building" (2016, p. 321).

While Yugoslav labor workers in the countries of the Western bloc were "a consequence of inequality and alienation in the country" (Brunnbauer, 2019, p. 413), due to the specificities of political regimes and cultural norms in third world and socialist bloc countries, Yugoslav highly skilled and educated workers constituted "a privileged part of the working class" (Jovanovic & Stojmenovic, 2023, p. 7). As third world and socialist bloc countries pursued "East-South" globalization as an alternative to the Western bloc processes (Calori, Hartmetz et al., 2019), Yugoslav migrant communities across Africa and the Middle East evolved mostly around business endeavors of Yugoslav corporations in the construction and metallurgical industry (Baker, 2018; Bernard, 2019b; Jovanovic

& Stojmenovic, 2023). Recent research has demonstrated that their managerial practices facilitated capitalist ventures and economic liberalization instead of providing an alternative to the Western bloc economic hegemony (Archer, Bernard et al., 2023). For example, examining Yugoslav highly skilled temporary labor migrants in the field of copper mining in Iran during the 1980s, Jovanovic and Stojmenovic (2023, p. 1) found that their "everyday practices of managerial bureaucratic improvisations and improvisations at work" led to silent acceptance of the capitalist reproductive relations. Most interestingly, these managerial improvisations seemed to appear as a socioeconomic form of Yugoslav labor migrants' resilience to excessive and rigid bureaucracy of Yugoslav socialist public companies.

Following the aforementioned bilateral agreements between Yugoslavia and several Western European countries for guest labor force, in Western Europe, Yugoslav communities were the highest in West Germany, Austria, and Switzerland. These agreements primarily served to send relatively cheap Yugoslav labor force to the rapidly developing countries of Germany, Austria, and Switzerland. While in West Germany alone "in 1960 there were 8,800 Yugoslav labor migrants, in 1968 there were 1 19,100; and by 1973 they reached a peak of dependents are included, there were just over 700,000 Yugoslavs residing in FRG in 1974" (Molnar, 2014, p. 146). As a result, working-class migrant ghettos emerged in some of the key European cities. For instance, Vienna's Ottakring, a typical working-class quarter, became one of the most populous districts with a clear segregation between the city's bourgeois and aristocratic center and the peripheral districts, even dating back to the beginning of the 20th century. In the 1960s and 1970s, many Yugoslav guest workers moved into substandard dwellings in and around *Ottakringer Straße* (Mijic, 2019). My post-Yugoslav interlocutors, who also settled in Vienna, told me that this area is still represented by migrants of a lower social status and known as a notorious place of troubles. "Every now and then you can hear that there was some fight between some former Yugoslav workers in Ottakringer. We never go there and try to stay away from these groups" (personal communication, April 2023). The aim of these guest workers "was not to emigrate but to quickly earn desperately-needed money" (Ivanovic, 2019, p. 138).

Similarly, for Yugoslavia, remittances from these guest workers, especially for households in economically less developed regions of the country, were one of the important sources of income. It was quite common for families to plan major purchases, such as a car or a house, by sending one of the adult family members to West Germany or Austria to earn the needed amount over the course of a year or two. Therefore, the primary if not the only motive to migrate was the positive economic opportunities in the country of destination. The first wave of immigration from the Balkans to West Germany, Austria, and Switzerland brought highly qualified professionals, including engineers, doctors, and dentists. This wave was quickly followed by an influx of seasonal workers (Jorio, 2005). As the number of economic emigrants was significant and held economic importance for Yugoslavia (Le Normand, 2021), the Yugoslav government organized cultural-entertainment tours, generating additional lucrative income from the Yugoslav economic emigration (Bakovic, 2015). Therefore, Yugoslav migrants simultaneously enjoyed social upward mobility in their home country not only on return, but also already as guest workers, which acted as an important additional motive to migrate. Yugoslav emigration to Western Europe had also significance for the Yugoslav internal and foreign policies, and in each decade, it followed certain political goals, as Bakovic (2015) correctly noticed,

> In the 1960s, the Yugoslav state, together with national radio stations and *Matica iseljenika* institutions, supported large and financially lucrative music tours based on folk music, the content and staffing of which were in accordance with the federal and multiethnic structure of the country. However, in the early 1970s, the state support shifted towards smaller-scale activities, in order to fight accusations of commercialization and to facilitate migrants' amateurism as a form of Yugoslav self-management being transplanted to a capitalist soil, presenting it as an inherently transnational phenomenon (Bakovic, 2015, p. 354).

Furthermore, migration experience opened the new perspectives to Yugoslav guest workers in the Western Europe attracting their attention to ethnic business opportunities in and across the countries of their temporary residence. As Ivanovic (2019, p. 139) pointed out,

> There were over 800,000 Yugoslav "guest workers" in West Germany in 1972, making them the largest community of foreign workers. Most of them were qualified workforce. A lot of them worked in the restaurant business before going abroad. Many wanted to open their own restaurants. The outcome was the popping up of Yugoslav restaurants during the mid-1960s, which was met with excellent response from the German public. As Yugoslav papers reported, there were more than five thousand restaurants and fast food kiosks offering Yugoslav food at the beginning of the 1970s.

As a result, these guest workers became the creators of Yugoslav cuisine, primarily in West Germany. At the same time, this phenomenon was their first attempt in entrepreneurship, emerging independently from the Yugoslav government. This entrepreneurship, in turn, had an enormous impact on Yugoslav migrant communities in Germany, Austria, and Switzerland. Coming from a self-governing socialist country, many of them felt the need to be independent and venture into private businesses. As a result, they played a significant role in shaping the economic landscape of these countries and contributed to the development of Yugoslav migrant communities. As a result, they were leaving their workplaces in factories where they had pay and job security, and higher prospects of remaining in West Germany. Neither did most of them know the system and the language, nor did they have any previous entrepreneurial experience.

> They could not estimate whether their business would be profitable. It was a kind of adventure ...The restaurants were also often named after tourist destinations—"Dubrovnik", "Opatija", "Dalmacija", "Makedonija Grill"—which was in accordance with Yugoslavia's image as a "touristic paradise" (Ivanovic, 2019, p. 140).

This means that the Yugoslav guest workers exploited the positive image of their country of origin for building their own small businesses. As a result, not only did the Yugoslav migrant community emerge in West Germany, Austria, and Switzerland—aligning with Castles, Haas et al. (2019) argument about the emergence of ethnically distinct populations in economically advanced countries representing guest workers—but it also formed a new transnational social class of entrepreneurs. This new class was diverse in terms of regional and gender composition, consisting of Croats, Serbs, Macedonians, Bosnians, and Montenegrins, with a third of Yugoslav guest workers being women (Ivanovic, 2019). For these women, starting their own businesses — such as opening small shops or restaurants — represented a form of further socioeconomic resilience.

> I came to Germany as a guest worker. I married a German and, since my German was and still is very good, I decided to continue my studies there. ... The marriage did not go well, so I decided to leave my husband. Through the student employment service, I found a job as a cab driver, and it was sufficient to be financially independent while studying (personal communication, September 2017).

In this way, for Yugoslav women, emigration turned into a resilience response to double vulnerability — facing challenges as both women and migrants. These factors, when taken together, shaped Yugoslav citizens' migration experience in Western Europe and gradually influenced a change in their mentality, leading to the formation of a better-organized and more resilient group of individuals. At the same time, their fellow citizens in Yugoslavia perceived these changes as different, or non-Yugoslav and regarded them as a rather inconvenient set of informal norms and culture. For example, in Yugoslavia's socialist system, the social norm was for people from villages or provinces to stay and eat for free at the place of their urban settled relatives when visiting major cities for study or medical check-ups at major urban clinics. In the capitalist system of Western Europe, this free-lunch culture was rather fluctuating, as anecdotal experiences of one former Yugoslav musician exemplified:

> We were touring around Germany giving concerts for Gastarbeiters, but there was the last minute cancelation, and we were left without promised lunch and accommodation. Then one of the band members recalled that his relative owns the restaurant in the neighboring city, so we went there expecting that she will provide us with a dinner for free. When we arrived, the band member told that he was her relative, and — as we expected — we were offered very nice table and food. However, after we finished the dinner, the waiter brought us an ordinary bill. As a result, we spent almost all our earnings for that dinner that was supposed to be free (personal communication, July 2016).

For some Yugoslav migrants application of social norms different from the ones widely accepted in the home country made them and their small businesses economically resilient. On the other hand, the Yugoslav government attempted to use them as a positive projection of the state abroad as well as an important source of economic growth through their individual investments in home country local communities (Bernard, 2019a). Simultaneously, in Western Europe they were perceived as Yugoslav migrants — guest workers from a different — communist — institutional and political system and as potential communist activists, therefore, threatening German capitalist system. However, as Molnar (2014, p. 140) pointed out,

> By the late 1960s, Germans ... had more encounters with Yugoslavs than with the citizens of any other communist state in Eastern Europe, and these experiences simply did not confirm the suspicions that Yugoslavs, because they came from a communist state, represented a security threat.

As a result, as they lived in German-speaking countries, or — in the case of Switzerland — in German-speaking cantons, these Yugoslav emigrants were coined as *Yugo-Schwab* — the title derived from Yugoslavia and the German word for Germans in Austria and Southern Germany.

In sharp contrast to Yugo-Schwabs, Yugoslavs who temporarily migrated to other socialist countries and third world countries formed migrant communities usually based on diplomats and representatives of foreign companies. For example, as Jovanovic and Stojmenovic (2023, p. 7) found,

> The task of the skilled workers from Yugoslavia in the Sarcheshmeh Copper Complex in Iran was to complete the copper assembly and start the smelter. ... The Yugoslav project was related only to the mine, the flotation plant, and the smelter, and other companies from Belgium and Germany were simultaneously present to finish the job around the electrolysis.

These workers' migrant communities also included their kids, who usually attended international schools or Yugoslav schools organized in embassies. Through personal communication with my Yugoslav migrant peers, I realized that feeling privileged as foreigners, Yugoslav youth in other socialist and third world countries unconsciously adapted a 'colonizer' approach towards the locals. In third world countries, this approach was a product of a long colonial history and the attitude of the locals towards foreigners as privileged by default. In response, Yugoslav professionals and their families usually behaved as good 'colonizers'. Describing her experience, one of my peers, who lived in one of the newly independent countries of East Asia, shared with me: "I came home from the school, and I see our gardener in my old favorite t-shirt. Being surprised, I looked at my mom, and she calmed me down saying that he needs that t-shirt more than I did" (personal communication, July 2001).

With certain exceptions of Yugoslav metallurgic giant RTB, whose workers were located in camps close to lead and zinc ores in Zambia, Angola, Libya, and Uganda (Jovanovic & Stojmenovic, 2023), Yugoslav migrant communities were usually concentrated in diplomatic areas of the third world countries' capitals, where both their offices and residential houses usually were located. Unlike in Yugoslavia, where it was safe to let kids to go to school alone, in emigration in the third world countries, Yugoslav migrant professionals' kids were either picked from homes by specially organized school buses or escorted by company or embassy specially allocated staff.

Communities of Yugoslav migrant professionals in the Soviet Union had much in common with their fellow Yugoslav professional communities across the third world. They also lived in specially designated blocks of residential buildings, called 'diplomatic corpuses' or '*dipkorpus*,' named after their major purpose—to accommodate diplomats. These residential buildings were surrounded by security fences, and one could access them only with an invitation by a resident and by demonstrating valid personal documents. Mini parks and playgrounds were usually located within the residential fence zones. There were also chains of supermarkets called *Beryozka*, where only foreigners and Soviet diplomats were allowed to purchase products.

Being raised under influence of brotherhood and unity, ideology of equality and social inclusion heavily propagated among the Yugoslav society in Yugoslavia, when I arrived to early post-Soviet

Russia, I was shocked to hear complains about 'the Russians' — usually meaning the sum of the Soviet population — from the Soviet-time Yugoslav migrant community peers:

> We are so unlucky to be brought here to live among the Russians. They are so grey, so boring. Those whose parents went to work in Spain or in Cyprus are much luckier to live among Spaniards and Greeks, who are always friendly and warm. Actually, anyone is more interesting than the Russians. We are so unlucky to have to tolerate them (personal communication, August 1994).

Finally, but importantly, one of their most notable and most numerous Yugoslav immigrant communities emerged in the South African Republic. Leaving the country with — for them — an inconvenient and hardly acceptable socialist regime, the group of remnants of officials and soldiers of the Serbian King's supporters settled mostly in Johannesburg. In the 1970s, they founded the Serbian Orthodox Church of Saint Thomas (Dragovic, 2016). While integrating into the wider society of the Europe-originating colonists in racially segregated South Africa, these immigrants retained strong loyalty to Serbia and consequently Serbian — and similarly to Croats in Argentina, strong anti-Yugoslav — component of their transnational Serbian-African identity (personal communication, spring 2019). Most of them have resided in the central so-called 'cluster' of Johannesburg, Sandton, where until the end of Apartheid — the sociopolitical system that segregated citizens according to their race and lasted up until the early 1990s — was reserved exclusively for the privileged 'white' population. As a result, along with their transnational identity, this 'whiteness' made up a significant — privileged — component of the identity of this Serbian migrant community in South Africa: living in luxurious villas with swimming pools, large gardens, and servants to take care of it was a typical lifestyle for them (personal communication, spring 2019). Table 2.2. summarizes motives for emigration from Yugoslavia during the Cold War and this typology of Yugoslav migrants community.

Table 2.2. Motives for (e)migration from Yugoslavia, geography of emigration, and Yugoslav migrant communities during the Cold War

Motive of (E)migration/type of (e)migrants	Escape from prosecution/ Croats Nazi-collaborators; Serbs remnants of the king's supporters	Search for better life conditions/ former peasants, manual/industrial workers, and traders	Higher salaries in hard currency than available at home and upward social mobility	Student exchange within the framework of COMECON	Rapid earning as guest workers, upward social mobility after return to Yugoslavia	Upward social mobility by representing the company abroad
Period of (e)migration	1945 - 1947	1945 - 1950	c.ca1968 – 1985	Since 1964	Since 1968	Since late 1970s
Geography of (e)migration	Argentina/ South African Republic, Brazil	USA, Canada, Australia, New Zealand	Iraq, India, the Soviet Union	Countries of the socialist bloc	Western and Northern Europe, mostly West Germany, Austria, and Switzerland	USA, Great Britain, France, Italy, Netherlands
Characteristics of the migrant community	Retaining anti-Yugoslav sentiments and national identity tied with religion, integrating among other European migrant communities, entrepreneurial	Retaining national identity tied with the religion, integrating with other immigrant communities, weakening ties with the country-of-origin	Temporal professional communities, building professional relations and friendships with other foreigners, having strong ties and dependence on the country of origin, mostly closed communities	Individuals, building professional and personal relations with local population and students	Mass migration guest workers – professional, but mostly blue-collar workers, many turning entrepreneurs	Business professionals

Overall, these insights into the emergence of Yugoslav migrant communities in countries of socialist bloc and third world countries adds a new dimension to Castles, Haas et al. (2019) proposition about migration flows between newly decolonized third world and economically advanced former power centers. This aspect has been overlooked by mainstream migration theories, and the findings shed light on the unique dynamics and factors that shaped Yugoslav migration patterns during that period.

Geography and Forms of Soviet Migrations

In sharp contrast to Yugoslavs, during the Cold War, Soviet citizens were not allowed to leave the country without the Soviet government's permission (Remennick, 2012). Indeed, as Byford and Bronnikova (2018, p. 9)

> emigration from the Russian empire and the Soviet Union has been consistently political in nature. It was mostly governed by political decisions and events, irrespective of whether those migrating were explicitly engaged in political action, embroiled in it by default (e.g. because of class or ethnic belonging), or randomly affected by large-scale political upheavals.

Simultaneously, the Soviet government carried out massive repressions on the social and ethnic grounds, prompting the rise of anti-Soviet dissenting groups. These included mostly Soviet Jews, Germans, Crimean Tatars, and Meskhetian Turks — whom the Soviet authorities were relocating from their places of origin to other parts of the Soviet Union to working camps (Polian, 2003). In response to these repressions, these groups required restoration of their ethnic minorities' rights. However, as Polian (2003, pp. 222-223) wrote, they

> have been carrying on a peaceful, organized and generally — regarding the fulfillment of key tasks — unsuccessful struggle. ... As far as Soviet Germans are concerned ... they see their total emigration to the FRG as the only alternative to restoration of the Volga German ASSR ... emigration to Turkey represents no feasible alternative for either Crimean Tatars or Meskhetian Turks.

When translating this situation into Hirschman's (1993) voice-or-exit framework, it becomes clear that the 'voice' option, represented by peaceful protests, did not soften the Soviet authorities' repressions. However, in contrast to Hirschman's theory, their 'voice' was not a sign of loyalty. Quite the contrary, the exclusion through repression of these groups made them entirely disloyal to the regime. These Soviet citizens opted for the 'exit', however, it was also heavily restricted. Thus, simultaneous ethnic repressions and restrictions to emigrate resulted in informal linkages of solidarity among these ethnic groups (Remennick, 2012) as a source of 'soft' resilience, loyalty of commitment to them motivated by repressions, and in further clearly defined trajectories of emigration as both soft—psychological and physical—hard resilience. Once allowed to travel abroad, Soviet Germans relocated to Germany, while the Soviet Jews immigrated initially to Israel. Particularly, starting from the late 1970s, the Soviet Jews and their non-Jew relatives sought to immigrate to Israel as the first available option to leave the Soviet Union. However, arriving to historical homeland, many of them encountered unexpected discrimination that prompted them to explore other opportunities.

> When we still lived in Tajikistan... Jews were regarded there as a minority. Thus, by moving to Israel, we hoped to become decent citizens of that country. However, it turned out that we are second-class citizens, because there is a division in Israel to 'whites' and 'blacks', and we turned to be 'blacks'. So the 'whites' are European Jews, Ashkenazi, and we—Central Asian Jews—we are so-called Sephardi—in Hebrew it means "Spanish", so we originate from Spain and Morocco. As a result, there is a major rabbi of Ashkenazi, and major rabbi of Sephardi—this division is already unpleasant. So these divisions also influenced my decision to move forward (online communication, March 2020).

Thus, according to my interlocutor, ethnic divisions and social segregation, which were the major motives for most Soviet Jews to immigrate to Israel, continued and, to a certain extent, sharpened in their historical homeland. This further exclusion generated loyalty of convenience to Israel as a 'gate' to the world, but it rarely turned into loyalty of commitment. In turn, encountering another exclusion in Israel, Soviet Jews sought further migration as a form and channel of tangible resilience. As Remennick (2012) and Toltz (2019) also point out, many Soviet Jews first moved to Israel, and then to Western Europe and North America. Most Soviet Germans 'repatriated' to Germany in the early 1990s (Polian, 2003; Remennick, 2012). Therefore, although taking similar directions — to 'historic homelands' — these migration processes represented the opposite form from Castles, Haas et al. (2019) general proposition about the return of colonialist from the former colonies to economically advanced power centers.

Apart from such ethnic emigration, there were also other forms of emigration from the Soviet Union. On the one hand, within the socialist bloc, there was a controlled but widespread exchange of students and professionals.

> In 1987, my childhood friend called me and said that his friends Hungarians came to Baku to work for three years. They work at the fridge factory; they construct some equipment. They asked someone's phone number to help them adopt there, to show where to go to eat, where to take a walk. My friend (name) asked me whether he can give them my number, and I agreed. They lived in the factory's dormitory, but the flat in which they lived had five rooms, tapestries were all over the flat, they had all then modern equipment such as washing machine — not all Soviets had it in our homes — everything was unusual to me. ... They came in September, they came by Volkswagen Passat, it was the only one of its sort in Baku. Their salaries were 2000 rubles, and she had 1500 rubles, these were huge money in those times. One could not spare that money even in the most expensive restaurant. They were buying vodka and Champaign in boxes. They had a lot of money!
> At the time of Christmas, they asked me about my plans. I was a musician, and the holidays were always the best time to earn additional money by playing, so I told them that I have concerts. They offered to travel with them to Budapest ... I stayed in Budapest for three months. I did not need to hurry back to Baku because it was winter, there were no concerts, there was no urgency to get back (personal communication, January 2020).

Student exchange among socialist bloc countries was extensive, so was and marriage-based immigration from the USSR to the Central and Eastern European members of the socialist bloc was quite spread phenomenon during the Cold War. Another interlocutor, who came to Hungary in the late 1970s, recalled,

[B]ack then, there were many Hungarians, who studied in the Soviet Union and returned to Hungary, so did my husband and I went with him. ... Hydrology was very close to my expertise, and I got a job in the geological institute ... where I was very welcomed. Everyone spoke Russian there; I got a salary higher than my husband, who is Hungarian (online communication, April 2020).

Therefore, student exchange and marriage-based migration during the Cold War as motives for emigration represents significant contribution to the literature on migration.

On the other hand, after World-War-II, Soviet troops were located across the European members of the Socialist bloc. In Czechoslovakia their number included about 85 000 Soviet citizens, while in Hungary this number was about 60,000, while in (East) Democratic Republic of Germany there was 500000 Soviet troops. The motives of Soviet citizens to work abroad were similar, though not the same, as for Yugoslav citizens. "Money was source of constant worry, hurt, and envy. Soviet citizens viewed long-term foreign posting as an incomparable source of income, often enough to lay the foundation for a lifetime of good living back home" (Gessen, 2012, p. 64). In this respect, the Soviet citizens did not regard the countries of the Soviet bloc as a 'real abroad':

East Germany ... was viewed as not quite foreign enough, by ordinary people as well as by Soviet authorities: salaries and perks there could hardly be compared with those in "real" foreign land, which is to say, a capitalist country. ... the government finally authorized small monthly hard-currency payments (the equivalent of about a hundred dollars) as part of the salaries of Soviet citizens working in Socialist bloc countries (Gessen, 2012, p. 64).

Similar to Yugoslav engineers, between the late 1970s and the late 1980s, Soviet engineers were also temporarily employed on industrial and infrastructural projects in the socialist bloc countries of South-East Asia. The Tri An Hydro Power Plant in Vietnam was one of the significant projects completed with Soviet assistance in Asia (Ray & Balasingamchow, 2010). As one of the Soviet engineers employed there explains,

I was a member of the large team of Soviet engineers, who built the Tri An Hydro Power Plant, which so far remains the most powerful hydro power plant in Asia. I worked there between October 1985 and September 1988, almost three years. I was an engineer of instrument of trust bundling (online communication, April 2022).

Thus, this Soviet migrant community, particularly in Vietnam, had a mid-term professional character. Being temporary, these communities held the kind of loyalty of coercion towards their country of origin. Thus, these migrations were overlooked by the mainstream literature on migration during the Cold War, and — similarly to student exchange and marriage-based migration — that fits the personal motives category in Lee (1966) analytical framework — represents another additional explanation of the global migration flows during the Cold War.

In contrast to the migrations between the Soviet Union and other countries of the socialist bloc, migrations between the USSR and the Western bloc were even more strictly controlled and much less frequent. Due to these strict restrictions and extensive repressions by the Soviet authorities not only on the ethnic, but also on the social and political grounds, Soviet migrations to the West were typically permanent, and they came in a whole set of forms that were hardly imaginable to citizens of most other world countries.

The first form of Soviet emigration seemed like voluntary emigration: it took the form of non-return. The Soviet emigration committee often allowed famous artists, sportsmen, and scientists to travel abroad for participation in international tournaments and research. However, after completing their research or sport tasks, they simply stayed abroad and applied for political asylum or accepted invitations to work, expressing their disloyalty to the Soviet regime in this way. Therefore, the Soviet government labeled them 'non-returners' and declared them 'homeland traitors' (Krasnov, 1986). These, for example, included famous cellist Mstislav Rostropovich and his wife, the equally famous soprano opera singer, Galina Vishnyevskaya. Rostropovich was inconvenient for the Soviet government as the famous musician, who believed in and fought for democratic values, including art without borders and freedom of speech (Wilson, 2007).

The second form of emigration was individual escape by the sea. Examples include oceanologist Stanislav Kurilov, whose escape was so dangerous and unusual that even the Radio Voice of America reported it. According to some journalists, Kurilov's sister, who was married to an Indian citizen, went with her husband to India. From there, they immigrated to Canada. Having a relative abroad was the official reason given by the Soviet emigration ministry to refuse Kurilov's request to travel abroad. Despite this, Stanislav Kurilov, who worked as an instructor of deep-water swimming at the Institute of Oceanology in Vladivostok, found out in 1974 that the *Sovetsky Soyuz* cruise would travel from Vladivostok to the equator and back. Kurilov decided to join the cruise. When the boat approached the coast of the Philippines, Kurilov jumped into the ocean and swam 100 kilometers over the next three days without food, water, and sleep until he reached the Filipino island of Siargao. Filipinos, whom he met on the coast, took him to the city of Cagayan de Oro in Mindanao, after which his escape was extensively covered the international media. The Philippine authorities deported Kurilov to Canada, where he reunited with his sister and her family, and later received Canadian citizenship. Simultaneously, Kurilov was sentenced in absentia for 10 years for treason (Krasnov, 1986). In Canada, Kurilov learned English working as a handyman in a pizzeria. His skills and knowledge later paved him a way back to marine research in Canadian and American companies. Later, he met his wife, a Soviet Jew, who lived in Israel, and moved with her to Israel, where he continued his scientific marine research (Gomberg, 2018).

Similarly, in 1979, an 18-year-old waitress named Lilia Gasinskaya escaped from another Soviet cruise liner in Sydney Harbor "in the red bikini" and swam for forty minutes to the Australian coast. There, she sought political asylum (Krasnov, 1986). Soon after, Gasinskaya became known as the 'red bikini girl', and her escape was dubbed "swim for freedom" by the Australian press, gaining her instant fame and political asylum. However, this almost instant political asylum fueled debates over queue-jumping refugees in Australia, where refugees from conflicts in Asia with greater fears of persecution than Gasinskaya were not extended the same welcome. Despite these debates and the simultaneous appearance of Gasinskaya on the KGB's wanted list (Krasnov, 1986), she was allowed to stay in Australia and build her career as a model and DJ (Edwards, 2009).

The third form of emigration from the Soviet Union was a political exile prompted by the Soviet authorities. Finding the work or publicly expressed views of famous Soviet artists and poets unpatriotic or otherwise dangerous to the Soviet political system, the Soviet government deprived many of them of Soviet citizenship and expelled them from the country (Polian, 2003). Though not particularly large, this group of Soviet emigrants included famous names such as the natural scientist and Nobel laureate Andrei Sakharov, novelist Alexander Solzhenitsin, and the poet Joseph Brodsky (Azrael, Brukoff et al., 1992). Particularly, Brodsky was expelled from the Soviet Union in 1972 for his poems that were in defiance of the Soviet regime. This harsh exclusion from the home country was compensated by immigration to the US, which became possible with the support from senior colleagues poets, most notably of British-American poet, Wystan Hugh Auden (McFadden, 1996).

The fourth form of an attempt to escape the Soviet Union was the most radical one: there were several cases when individual Soviet citizens or a small group tried to hijack passenger planes on their inter-Soviet flights and force pilots to fly to countries outside the socialist bloc. The most striking example of such a form of escape was the Ovechkin family—Ninel Ovechkina and her ten children—a famous Soviet music ensemble. On March 8 1988 on their flight from Irkutsk to Leningrad, by sending the message through the stewardess to the pilot, they tried to force their flight to change the trajectory and fly to "any capitalist country, most preferably to England". When they realized that, nevertheless, the pilot landed the aircraft on the Soviet military airfield, the Soviet army assaulted the plane, resulting in the death of all the family members and several other passengers (Lenta.ru, 2018). Putting this example along with cross-sea escapes into Hirschman's framework of political dissent, these forms can be categorized as a radical exit, or escape from repression, and simultaneously the only form of physical resilience.

Putting this example along with cross-sea escapes into the Hirschman's framework of political dissent, these forms can be categorized as a radical exit, or escape from a repression, and simultaneously the only form of physical resilience.

The last form was legal and a mix of professional and ethnic principles: starting from the late 1960s, Soviet scientists and artists were invited to US universities. The late 1980s and early 1990s were characterized by significant migration outflows of Soviet Jews, Armenians, and Germans from the USSR to Western Europe, the USA (Aron, 1991), Canada (Remennick, 2012; Shvarts, 2010), and Israel (Remennick, 2012). Obtaining permission from the Soviet government's emigration ministry to travel to these countries required not only the submission of all existing Soviet documents provided to citizens by the state but also long periods of waiting and uncertainty about the government's decision for every individual applicant (Remennick, 2012). Therefore, those, who were lucky to receive such permission, had only the option to relocate permanently. Overall, for Soviet citizens the Cold War period turned into the time of continuous crisis prompted by the threat of repressions and resilience through informal communities and social networks.

Soviet Migrant Communities Abroad

These motives and paths of Soviet emigrations generated three general types of Soviet communities abroad: the first type comprised of the Soviet occupying troops across the socialist bloc countries of Eastern Europe, including army and KGB officers, procurement servicers, community schools' teachers, and their families. These communities held the mix of loyalty of convenience and coercion to the Soviet state as international actor, and the loyalty of coercion to the Soviet regime. The second type comprised mostly of the Soviet intellectuals dissenters, who were dispersed across Western Europe and North America and were openly opposing the Soviet regime. The last type to certain extent overlapped with the second one: these were mostly ethnic-based communities of the Soviet Jews and to a lesser extent of the Soviet Armenians.

The first type of Soviet migrant communities—those located in the countries of the former Soviet bloc—usually represented introverted and locally concentrated groups. In the second half the twentieth century, they organized hospitals, schools, clubs, and shops, where officers' spouses were working to fulfil its own needs (Tepavcevic, Molodikova et al., 2020). As famous Russian-American journalist and author, Masha Gessen (2012) points out, one such community was in Dresden, East Germany, where the long-standing Russia's political leader, Vladimir Putin served.

> The Putins, like five other Russian families, were given an apartment in a large apartment bloc in a little Stasi world: secret police staff lived here, worked in a building a five-minute walk away, and sent their children to nursery school in the same compound. They walked home for lunch and spent evenings at home or visiting colleagues in the same building. Their job was to collect information about "the enemy" which was the West, meaning West Germany and, especially, United States military bases in West Germany, which were hardly more accessible from Dresden than they would have been from Leningrad. ... Ludmila Putina liked Germany and the Germans. Compared to the Soviet Union, East Germany was a land of plenty. It was also a land of cleanliness and orderliness: she liked the way her German neighbors hung their identical-looking laundry on parallel clotheslines at the same time every morning. Their neighbors, it seemed to her, lived better than the Putins were used to. So the Putins saved, buying nothing for their temporary apartment, hoping to go home with enough money to buy a car. ...KGB staff in Dresden had to scrimp and save to ensure that at the end of their posting they would have something to show for it. Over the years, certain conventions of fragility had set in—using newspapers instead of curtains to cover the windows, for example. (Gessen, 2012, pp. 63-64).

In such conditions, wives of the Soviet secret agents usually did not work. Their husbands also never talked to them about their work. However, according to some of my interlocutors, there were rare exceptions:

> I adore my job of being a teacher of the Russian language, because I could always work everywhere. My husband was a secret agent of KGB in East Germany, and I was the only wife, who worked there, because I was a teacher at the community school. All other women, who all were highly educated and smart could not find their professional mission abroad, and remained only housewives and mothers. I remember simultaneous admiration and envy in their eyes, when I was passing by them on my way to the school (personal communication, October 2021).

Thus, both migrant community structures and professions appeared as key sources of both soft and tangible resilience for Soviet migrant women. The largest Soviet troops-based migrant communities in Hungary were located in Budapest, Paks, and Debrecen; in Czechoslovakia, they were located in Milovice, Mlada Boleslav, and Bruntal, and in Germany, they emerged in Dresden, Wunsdorf, and Magdeburg. Their livelihood activities were community-based and community-self-sustaining. However, the contacts with the local communities also brought them to a certain level of integration into the local societies and the definition of their own national identity.

> I came to Hungary when I was seven. ... In the 1980s, I moved to Budapest to study ... I never could become the Hungarian because of the Hungarians: they were constantly teasing me because I am Russian ... When I graduated, I got a job in a Russian logistics company and I travelled a lot between Hungary, Russia and Ukraine (personal communication, May 2020).

Therefore, despite immigrating to Hungary as a child, some of the representatives of the Soviet migrant communities in the countries of the socialist bloc have never felt completely socially integrated. In comparison to Soviet communities in the European socialist countries, Soviet professional migrant communities in Asia were composed majorly of male engineers, while their families stayed in the USSR. As my interlocutor, who worked as an engineer in Vietnam recalled,

> Occasionally, we were travelling home to USSR to visit families. My work was a major income for the family. ... In Vietnam, we lived close to the construction site, 80 km from Hanoi. ... We went to Hanoi twice to see the city. The rest of the time, we spent at the construction site. Our contacts with Vietnamese were limited to professional communication. I learned several key words in Vietnamese, and earned enough to have above the average comfortable life back home (personal communication, July 2011).

At the same time, similarly to both Soviet migrant communities in countries of the socialist bloc and Yugoslav professional migrant communities in socialist bloc and third world countries, this Soviet professional community in Vietnam represented a rather small and closed community.

In Western Europe and North America, Soviet migrant communities mostly emerged from the Soviet no-returnees intellectuals
and sportsmen, exiled Soviet artists, and Soviet ethnic communities—Jews, Armenians, and Germans (Azrael, Brukoff et al., 1992).
For example, when Joseph Brodsky was exiled from the Soviet Union, Mstislav Rostropovich and Galina Vishnyevskaya accommodated him in their place in New York City (Wilson, 2007). This solidarity with compatriots expelled from the country-of-origin along
with non-return turned to be one of the major forms of resilience of
these Soviet migrant communities composed of the Soviet intelligentsia. Similarly, Soviet ethnic-based migrant communities followed the family reunion paths, as was the case with Yugoslav
guest workers in Western Europe.

> After seven years in Israel we moved to Vienna, because we had a lot of
> relatives here. At the same time, the climate, friends, relatives—everything
> was much closer to us here in Austria, than in Israel. … In Vienna, where—
> despite wide-spread narratives about Austrian anti-Semitism, I have never
> saw and felt it—and I have been living here for almost forty years (online
> communication, March 2020).

However, as my interlocutor explained, in contrast with Yugoslav and other European guest workers in Western Europe, the
Soviet family reunions emerged as further relocation, mostly from
Israel to Western Europe or to North America. All these findings
are summarized in Table 2.3. below.

Table 2.3. Motives for (e)migration from the Soviet Union, geography of emigration, and Soviet migrant communities during the Cold War

Motive of (E)migration/type of (e)migrants	Economic motives in a form of representation of the Soviet army or engineering company abroad	Search for professional, social, and ethnic freedoms in forms of non-return and escape	Ethnic discrimination and ethnic-based repressions
Period of (e)migration	Between early 1960s and late 1980s	1970s	Starting from early 1970s on (with periods of restriction)
Geography of (e)migration	Socialist bloc	Capitalist bloc countries	Israel, Germany, USA
Characteristics of the migrant community	Closed professional communities, living in small localities, where the life was organized around inter-community activities	Geographically dispersed professional communities of Soviet intellectuals, artists, sportsmen; to some extend overlapping with Soviet ethnic communities	Ethnic-based communities — Soviet Jews, Germans, Armenians

Comparisons and Conclusions: Yugoslav and Soviet Migrations and Migrant Communities

Despite the striking differences between Yugoslavia's and the Soviet Union's migration policies, purposes for temporary migration, and treatment of their citizens abroad that generated different attitudes and forms of loyalty to their countries of origin and political regimes in them, the analysis of emigration from the two former socialist multinational federations reveals certain commonalities. They simultaneously provide important theoretical contribution to the global picture of migrations during the early aftermath of World-War-II and the Cold War. Both Yugoslavia and the Soviet Union were temporally sending their citizens—engineers, trade managers, soldiers, and intelligence and procurement services providers abroad—to other socialist countries, some of which—like Vietnam—overlapped with third world countries. Simultaneously,

Yugoslav and Soviet citizens' temporary emigration to these countries was driven by socioeconomic motives. These included search
for higher salaries and consequentially prompter available savings
than even imaginable in their home countries. Temporary labor emigration also provided Yugoslavs and Soviets with almost immediate upward social mobility, both in the countries of temporary residence, and back in the countries of origin. Additionally, temporary
professional relocations abroad were also important resource of remittances for both Yugoslav and Soviet families. Another similarity, though much smaller in its scale among Yugoslav citizens in
comparison to the Soviets, was student exchange within COME-
CON member states.

Further theoretically and empirically significant similarity in
temporary Yugoslav and Soviet migrations to other socialist and
third world countries analyzed in this chapter was in separation —
though not the segregation — of these migrant communities from
the mainstream societies in host countries. As revealed through this
chapter, both Yugoslav and Soviet migrant communities in socialist
and third world countries perceived themselves as different from
local societies. As their assignments were temporal, these migrants
were not making any efforts to immerse, let alone to integrate into
these societies. As a result, they lived in their migrant community
'bubbles'. Still, being immersed in communities of other foreigners
from the countries of the capitalist bloc, Yugoslav migrant communities differed from their Soviet counterparts. Therefore, while
overall this type of motive for migration corresponds to Lee's (1966)
positive factors in the country of destination, it sheds light on the
migration flows within the less researched former socialist bloc and
migration flows between the Soviet bloc and third world countries
during the Cold War. Due to its transnational nature, these migration flows provide a new historical dimension to later-emerged migration theories of ethnic enclaves and transnationalism, whose
first proponents were Portes and Wilson (1980) with their study of
immigrant enclaves in the USA.

Although the differences in motives for migration from Yugoslavia and the Soviet Union are more visible, they also deserve to
be discussed for their conceptual contributions. While 'exit' — in

Hirschman's meaning — was the only option for remnants and supporters of the defeated World War II political regimes existing on the territory of Yugoslavia in the mid-1940s, it remained a major vision — though not always an available solution — for survival and a form of political and social resilience for many Soviet citizens during the long Cold War decades. This led not only to differences in forms of emigration that were particularly radical on the part of Soviet citizens as described in Section 3 of the present chapter, but also resulted in very different forms and types of Yugoslav and Soviet migrant communities, especially in the countries of the former capitalist bloc. In general, escaping the tyranny at home, the Soviets usually immigrated to the countries of the capitalist bloc by applying for political asylum or ethnic repatriation visas and accepting professional contracts in US and Canadian, but also Western European and Israeli research institutes and companies.

On the contrary, starting from 1968, Yugoslavs migrated mostly as legal and invited guest workers to Western Europe in masses, and later, in the late 1970s and 1980s, as representatives of Yugoslav companies. As a result, they emerged as significant in numbers, socioeconomically-motivated migrant communities, perfectly fitting the opportunity-driven positive factors in Lee's (1966) analytical framework for the receiving country. Their experiences as migrant workers in rapidly economically redeveloping countries of Western Europe influenced changes in their mentality and culture, particularly in its economic aspect. Many of them became entrepreneurs and started to envision interpersonal relations through the prism of economics, which was in striking contrast with their compatriots and family members who stayed in Yugoslavia. Due to this feature, Yugoslav migrant communities in Western Europe, predominantly in West Germany, Austria, and Switzerland, emerged not merely as a Yugoslav diaspora (as in other Western European countries) but as the so-called "Yugo-Schwabs," an entirely new concept of mid-nation: no longer Yugoslav, but not yet German, Austrian, or Swiss.

Table 2.4: Similarities and differences in Yugoslav and Soviet motives for (e)migration and migrant communities

	Yugoslav citizens (Yugoslavs)	Soviet citizens (Soviets)
Similarities between Yugoslav and Soviet motives and forms for migration	Socioeconomically motivated temporary migration to other socialist countries and the countries of the third world – mostly Soviet Union and Iraq	Socioeconomically motivated temporary migration to other socialist bloc countries – mostly Eastern Europe and Vietnam
Differences between Yugoslav and Soviet motives and forms for migration	Opportunities-driven legal temporary/guest-worker mass migration to Western Europe; loyalty of convenience towards country of origin and its' political regime	Necessity-driven sociopolitical ethnic and social emigration mostly to USA, Canada, Israel, and Germany; disloyalty towards the political regime in the country of origin
Similarities between Yugoslav and Soviet migrant communities	In socialist bloc and third world countries – introvert communities	In socialist bloc countries – introverted communities
Differences between Yugoslav and Soviet migrant communities	Relatively large, geographically concentrated, well-connected, and coexisting with other migrant communities, usually connected with Yugoslav state institutions abroad	Locally concentrated 'ethnic' communities, sometimes overlapping with geographically dispersed dissident/professional migrant communities, disconnected with any Soviet institutions

Finally, while this finding confirms the general propositions regarding migrations during the Cold War – mass migration of workers from the European peripheries to Western Europe usually through guest-work system (Castles, Haas et al., 2019), this concept of mid-nation represents major conceptual contribution for further studies of global migrations. Similarly, the concept of loyalty of coercion and loyalty of ignorance through coercion are notable for the research of Yugoslav and Soviet communities during and in the aftermath of the collapses of Yugoslavia and the Soviet Union, which is the topic of the next part of this book. It explores how Cold-War-times Yugoslav and Soviet migrant communities, their experiences, and obtained skills served Yugoslav and Soviet citizens in the times of collapses of their multinational states.

PART II

Chapter 3
Exclusions and De-Territorialization: Collapses, Vulnerabilities, and First Available Solutions

> Mom told me to pack up some basic clothes and shoes, and that I am leaving for ten days, until the situation calms down in Bosnia ... I never thought that these ten days will turn into years, and that I might not return home. Actually, moving to Australia turned more realistic (personal conversation, June 1997).

> [W]ith imperceptible suddenness, things changed. We stopped whispering. Camp survivors returned home. Elections came to matter. ...In August 1991 I was crossing the Atlantic ... for a year-long high school exchange on Long Island, New York. The world opened up. The country I left behind was the Soviet Union; the country I returned to was independent Ukraine. It was destitute but hopeful. Whatever the hardships, my generation now had the opportunities our grandparents and parents could never have dreamed of (Budjeryn, 2022, p. 2).

Collapses as Vulnerability and as Resilience

These two citations are among strikingly different examples of personal experiences of the collapses of former Yugoslavia and the former Soviet Union. They also reflect almost opposing attitudes towards the collapses: the first, expressed by a citizen of Yugoslavia who was a teenager at the time of collapse reflects on the war and trauma of displacement, and emigration as the only source of resilience. The second, expressed by a citizen of the Soviet Union, who also was a teenager at the time of collapse reflects hope and even certain excitement because of the changes; these changes appeared as major source of resilience, while possibility to travel abroad emerged as an opportunity, not necessity.

Historians, political scientists, and sociologists have extensively discussed the collapses of Yugoslavia and the Soviet Union and their underlying causes. The explanations for the collapse of the USSR have varied, encompassing factors such as institutional incapacity of the centrally administered state and economic decline (Csaba, 2007), failure of ideologies (Hough, 1997), opportunism of bureaucracy (Solnick, 1998), and the rise of nationalism (Beissinger,

2009). Similarly, the explanations for the collapse of Yugoslavia have included the absence of a common cultural identity (Baruch Wachtel, 1998), the Yugoslav political leadership's commitment to the Marxist ideology of 'withering the state away' (Jovic, 2008), demobilization of political and economic reformists, and challenges to the existing regime (Gagnon, 2004), as well as the influence of nationalism (Kovacevic-Bielicki, 2017). Arguably, all these explanations for the collapses of two multinational socialist federations are plausible as they represented interrelated rapid transformations within the underlying process of global decline of centrally planned economies under one-party political systems. This chapter explores the vulnerabilities that the collapses posed to the citizens of Yugoslavia and the Soviet Union, as well as their responses to the crisis. It makes a significant contribution to the existing literature on the collapses of Yugoslavia and the Soviet Union by revealing an additional factor that influenced the course of events. The analysis of this chapter suggests that social divisions that contributed to violent breakup of Yugoslavia and short-term looking relatively peaceful breakup of the Soviet Union emerged from varying forms of loyalty to the state among their population, which stemmed from the level of their inclusion, or exclusion thereof, from the system.

In Yugoslavia the peak of collapse was followed by the first multi-party elections held in 1990s. These elections brought to power forces that used nationalism and called for independence and separation as a mobilizing principle in most of the republics. The clashes of interests among the political elites and their reflection on various groups of citizens resulted in a series of violent conflicts that lasted until 2001. These included the "Ten-day war" following the Slovenian declaration of independence in June 1991; the Croatian War of Independence that lasted between 1991 and 1995; the Bosnian War that lasted between 1992 and 1995; the violent conflict in Kosovo that culminated with the Kosovo war in 1998 and continued throughout the NATO intervention against Serbia and Montenegro in 1999; and the armed conflict in Macedonia known as the Insurgency in 2001 (Kovacevic-Bielicki, 2017). The violence often spilled over to Serbia and Montenegro, republics that were not formally engaged in a particular conflict but had participated in it without formal admission or had been influenced, most notably, by the large inflow of refugees from violence-torn Yugoslav republics and international sanctions posed because of their involvement in the conflict.

In the Soviet Union, democratization started in 1985 during the political leadership of Mikhail Gorbachev through his policies of *glasnost* — translated from Russian as transparency or freedom of speech and *perestroika* — meaning reform or transformation. In the realm of foreign policy, the USSR gradually reproached with the US, Western Germany and the West in general, which in turn put an end to the Cold War. Although there were social and military uprising across the USSR, such as the Azerbaijani-Armenian conflict over control of Nagorno-Karabakh in 1988 and 1989, the Baltic states' request for independence from the USSR in 1989, and the *coup d'etat* in Russia in August 1991- the dissolution of the world's second superpower initially seemed more peaceful than the dissolution of Yugoslavia. The internal economic and social crises generated conflicts among Soviet political elites and pushed the first elected President of the Soviet Russia, Boris Yeltsin and the leaders of Ukraine — Leonid Kravchuk, and Belarus — Stanislav Shushkevich, in December 1991 to sign the Belovezhskaia agreement, which ended the USSR and heralded to the Commonwealth of Independent States (CIS).[1]

Despite some differences, the overall situation in the former USSR was not vastly different from the former Yugoslavia. During the period between 1989 and 1995, the Soviet space experienced violent local conflicts. Apart from the war in Nagorno-Karabakh, there were also strong secessionist movements in Abkhazia and South Ossetia, which sought independence from Georgia. Similarly strong secessionist forces sought independence of Transnistria from Moldova. These movements resulted in internationally unrecognized sovereignty of these post-Soviet-republics' separatist regions and the conflicts were 'frozen'. Similarly, in Northern Caucasian region, Chechnya sought the independence from Russia first

---

[1]   Symbolically, they both passed away during the spring of 2022, and the war — Russia's invasion in Ukraine.

in 1994, and later in 1999, both attempts resulted in Russia's military operations that suppressed these attempts.[2] In Central Asia, Tajikistan experienced civil war because of power struggles.

For all these reasons, the dissolutions of the USSR and Yugoslavia profoundly affected the population of both former Yugoslavia and the former USSR, generating a global crisis. Focusing on the vulnerabilities and resilience of the citizens of these two multinational federations during their collapses, the present chapter aims to answer the following questions: What challenges did the citizens of Yugoslavia and the Soviet Union experience during the disintegration of their countries? How did they adapt to the changes? Through the analysis of their narratives about these events, the chapter compares the impact of the disintegration of Yugoslavia and the Soviet Union on their citizens and examines their decisions to stay home or move further. Thus, this chapter directly responds to scholarly calls to further debate the dissolution of Yugoslavia (Bieber, Galijas et al., 2014) delving into experiences of ordinary people through their narratives and comparing them with those of citizens of the former Soviet Union. In addition to the general analytical framework combining Lee's (1966) motives for emigration with Hirschman's (1970) relationship between options of exit and voice depending on a form of loyalty, I found significant two interrelated concepts: the concept of exclusion in its broad meaning, and the concept of de-territorialization proposed by Alioua (2014) referring to the start of emigration process.

(Post-)Yugoslavs' Experiences of the Collapse of Yugoslavia

Kovacevic-Bielicki (2017) pointed out that "the Serbian leadership in Belgrade and the majority of Serbs outside Serbia proper did not support the separation and dissolution." While this statement illu-

---

[2]   The Kremlin gained a stronger control over Chechnya, and became its' devoted sponsor. In turn, under Putin's regime, Chechen political leaders became substantially integrated in the political structures of Russia.

minates some general trends of the period, such as the more frequent loyalty of commitment to Yugoslavia as a state among Serbs,
it overlooks the complexity of the discussed situation. Reflecting on
my own experience of the day when Slovenia declared its independence, I noted this event as follows:

> In the bay, we officially opened the new swimming season, and afterwards
> we went to play billiards. The TV was on in the cafe and there were news.
> ...Someone turned up the sound on the TV and the buzz in the cafe suddenly
> stopped. We stopped the game and turned our faces to the screen.... Slove-
> nia declared independence and the television showed tanks going through
> the streets of Ljubljana. ... The pool cues slowly dropped to the table and the
> game remained unfinished and abandoned. ... We went out to the terrace in
> silence and watched the darkness fall on our little old town. We looked at
> each other through the tears. "What will happen to us?" said (name) quietly.
> As usual when I felt danger and fear, I felt the urge to calm my friends down
> and cheer them up, I said that everything would be fine, but my anxiety did
> not leave me (personal notes, June 1991).

The place referred to in the notes is a small town on one of the
Dalmatian islands, where the group of children to which I referred
as 'we' in my notes resided in our second homes. Most members of
the group went to schools in central Yugoslav cities, including Split,
Zagreb, Sarajevo, and Belgrade, while having origins and spending
all school holidays with their grandparents, who lived in island-lo-
cated second homes. Apart from the initial shock provoked by the
news, the event of Slovenia's declaration of independence generated a sense of anxiety among my friends who were with me at that
moment for several reasons. First, the war that, until then, we had
only heard about from our grandparents and hoped to be a distant
past, became a reality. Second, at least half of us from that small
group of friends had either some origins or relatives in Slovenia,
which added a personal connection to the unfolding events. At the
time, we were teenagers raised in the families of third generation
Yugoslav citizens, with developed sense of belonging to Yugoslavia
as a geographical and cultural unit, or inertial loyalty of convenience. Hence, we took for granted Slovenia as an equal part of our
homeland, and learning about its independence we unconsciously
felt excluded from where we believed that we belong. Therefore,
Slovenia's secession felt like losing a part of ourselves and a part of

our home. Being together and crying brought us some comfort, helping us cope with the fear and accept the new reality. Soon after, this new reality approached us directly in our second homes. As I noted several days later,

> I woke up in my bed, in my home, but in a different country. I went to (names) to arrange for the beach, and there (names) were standing in front of the house and yelling at each other. One defended (the actions of) Yugoslav People's Army, the other complained about the fact that the Army is shooting around Zagreb where her parents and grandfather are, while her grandfather was a retired Army's general. I did not hold back, I knelt down, cried, and begged them not to fight about it. (Name) came from the waterfront and was confused when he saw us crying (personal notes, July 1991).

This note refers to the day when Croatia declared independence from Yugoslavia, and the quarrel happened between two out of six friends who had cried together days before when Slovenia declared independence. This time, they had different perspectives on the situation, as parents and relatives of one of them were in Zagreb, and therefore, they were physically vulnerable under the threat of gunfire. Their vulnerability translated into their child's psychological anxiousness, which manifested in different ways within the entire group of children. For one child, the Army turned from a source of security into a source of threat. Another child, who had previously lived in Belgrade and still viewed the Army as a defender of the state and its people, found it difficult to accept the conflicting narratives. As someone who felt a strong bond with both of them and the entire group, and identified with a Yugoslav geographical and citizenship-based identity, I struggled to take sides in the conflict. Instead, I tried to pacify my friends and maintain a sense of belonging to the community we shared. This loyalty of commitment to both my immediate environment and the larger state-based community helped me cope with the situation and supported my friends. However, the situation also marked a radical change in the statuses of group members, transforming them from 'insiders' or included into the larger community, to 'outsiders' in a broad sense, excluded from the community. This, in turn, affected our friendships. In contrast to our confusion with the events, our grandparents, who experienced World War II as teenagers, saw Yugoslavia as a symbol of inclusion and defense. For them, the declarations of independence of Slovenia and Croatia were signs of a larger threat. They feared that the disintegration of Yugoslavia could lead to instability and conflict, which brought back memories of the hardships they endured during the war. As we grappled with the changing political landscape, their perspective provided us with a deeper understanding of the historical context and the complexities of the situation. They became more cautious themselves, and they alerted us to be quieter and more attentive to avoid any conflicts with peers who, in the views of our grandparents, could become radicalized. Depending on their personal experiences from World War II and based on their geographic, professional, and material positions, most of them seemed to believe that the capital cities of the republics might be better places to hide and stay safe — in the sense of remaining part of the society — than the provinces. Most of them also found dangerous the new situation for anyone generally loyal to some if not most of ideas on which post-WWII Yugoslavia was built including antifascism, economic self-management and social equality that, as noted in the previous Chapter, were extensively promoted in the country through the popular and broad inclusive slogan of 'brotherhood and unity'. However, in examining the social distance between Slovenians and Bosnians working in Slovenia, Mežnarić (1986) proposed that ethno-nationalism was a consequence of social and existing class inequalities between the two 'ethnic' groups (Vezovnik, 2018). As a result, our grandparents were cautiously exchanging opinions on the situation, alerting each other about potential assaults by the pro-secession right-wing politicians and their active supporters.

At the same time, the Army that by June 1991 most of them considered as a defending force was also falling apart following the lines of political divisions into three general groups. The most visible group was the hardliners — loyalists (of commitment) to the regime — who chose to defend the territorial integrity of Yugoslavia by all means, voicing their dissatisfaction with the situation through military actions. The second stream consisted of soldiers with a more liberal approach — their loyalty was conditioned by the

convenience of broad inclusion and the high cost of exclusion—
they preferred peaceful solutions to violence. The last group comprised members with moderate to radical right political views.
Among the majority of Slovenians, Croats, and later Bosniaks, this
resulted in the exclusion of non-majorities and minorities in particular republics, and their exit from the Yugoslav Army. This led to
the emergence of regional military groups that later transformed
into the armies of post-Yugoslav independent states. The remaining
Yugoslav Army was gradually taken over by excluded moderate
and radicalized right-wing Serbs from Croatia, Bosnia, and later
from Serbia. According to Posen (1993), the radicalization of Serbs
in Croatia resulted from a fear for security as a minority in a new
state, and a similar argument could hold for Serbs in Bosnia.

Although the vast majority of my grandparents' generation
shared various aspects of loyalty to the ideas of building Yugoslavia—a mixture of loyalty of convenience and loyalty of commitment—they found themselves without a clearly defined political
leadership to either align with or oppose. As a result, they lacked
the option of 'voice' in the face of significant changes and challenges
during the dissolution of Yugoslavia. At the same time, they were
already pensioners with profoundly 'territorialized' lifestyles and
usually with limited foreign language skills. In the absence of both
a unifying political agency and options for physical exit, such as
emigration, they sought various internal exit strategies. Some of
them gradually limited their contacts with the rapidly changing environment by focusing on their homes in provinces, using gardens
to grow vegetables and fruits, and minimizing their spending. They
relied on their pensions to fulfill the rest of their basic needs. Those
who lived in the capitals similarly limited their contacts to what
they perceived as the least dangerous ones, attempting to continue
their routines. Their loyalty to the collapsing state and system transformed into a focus on and loyalty to a very limited territory and a
small group of people. Therefore, Gagnon's (2004) argument about
Yugoslav citizens' demobilization seems correct. As the conflict
raged on, these Yugoslav pensioners increasingly encouraged their
children—the generation of my parents—to move temporarily to

quieter parts of what remained of Yugoslavia, such as Bosnia, Serbia, Montenegro, and Macedonia, or to relocate abroad.

Towards late 1991, in Sarajevo, the capital of Bosnia and Herzegovina and simultaneously the geographical center of Yugoslavia, I met several peers who had escaped from the conflict-torn Croatian region of Slavonia. My family shared clothes and food with these less fortunate compatriots at that time. By then, Vukovar, where most of them came from, had already been turned into ruins, and their experiences felt like a personal loss. Showing solidarity with them and assisting in their social integration in Sarajevo provided some psychological and social relief to both them and the local population. Simultaneously, some of my parents' friends alerted them that the conflict could escalate to Bosnia. One of them even brought an application for emigration to the South African Republic, which at the time still lived under the racially divisive Apartheid system. To me, the thought of emigrating there seemed adventurous, as I read a lot about the history of South-African diamond mines and dreamt of distant travels. However, when I showed the application form to my father, he looked at it and then put it aside. When I asked him why he did not want to even consider it as an option, he responded, "I don't want to live in a system where I have to hate someone just because their skin color is different from mine" (personal notes, April 1992). His response clearly reflected his rejection of the idea of social exclusion.

As a rule, the initiators of emigration as a reaction to the looming breakup of Yugoslavia were women. These women either already had experience as temporary workers abroad or had close ancestors who were themselves immigrants in Yugoslavia. It was precisely these women with such backgrounds who anticipated an escalation of the crisis and prepared to emigrate. For example, one family friend, who previously worked in the MENA region, announced that they were moving to France and organized a small farewell party in December 1991. She mentioned unfavorable economic situation as a key to her decision to relocate, humorously noting that she can earn more by working less in France. Long after these events, another one of my parents' generation peers recalled that

In the 1991, the war in Croatia started and my family and I were already experiencing some economic difficulties. As I spoke some German and my uncle lived in Austria, I wrote letters to several factories inquiring whether they are interested in employing me as a foreign specialist. Only one of them responded asking for a meeting. Since I lived and worked in Yugoslavia, my aunt went to represent me at the interview and she persuaded the employers that she can represent me well at the interview, and that I could be a good employer for their business. I arrived soon after to talk to them personally, and in February 1992, I relocated to Austria and started to work. The outbreak of the war in Bosnia happened only a month later. My husband's colleague evacuated my kids to Serbia, where I picked them up and took to Austria (personal conversation, April 2023).

The described experience of emigration confirms the long-standing chain-migration theory, postulating that existing migrant networks prompt further immigration (Castles, Haas et al., 2019). The challenges that the war brought to Sarajevo were numerous and overlapping. After the third day of shelling that we spent in a corridor as a shelter, I told my father that I would rather be in the South African Republic than in Sarajevo. He nodded affirmatively and said sadly, "At least there we could determine from whom we should keep away. Here, even that is impossible" (personal notes, May 1992), referring to the population of Sarajevo and Bosnia, among whom there were no physically visible differences. This response reflected that, if choice was between two sorts of social discrimination or exclusion, he preferred the one that is more physically visible. Bosnia's capital experienced the longest siege recorded in the twentieth century — it lasted three and half years, and was extensively analyzed by many local and foreign writers and scholars. For example, young legal scholars, who was born in Sarajevo during the siege, Marina Velickovic made very concise illustration of the survival under siege based on her mother's memories.

> During the siege one was to seek shelter during shelling, to avoid areas that could be seen through a sniper scope (which as it turns out, are most areas in a surrounded valley), and to secure sustenance (which was often in conflict with the first two principles) (Velickovic, 2020).

The extent of these challenges left permanent traumas on all, who experienced the siege, and they still represent a specific community of survivors, while the siege remains one of almost regularly discussed topics in private conversations and in social media public groups. At the same time, these virtual conversations revealed coping strategies constituting the most tangible — physical — forms of 'hard' resilience. Several following excerptions from these discussions are deeply revealing, thus I found them useful first-aid guidance in such extreme situation as the war and the siege.

> My son and his friends brought parts of the glass from the shop window, and we spent the whole day to rebuild the glass out of small parts. In the evening, the bomb fell to the top of the building, and the completely repaired window collapsed again. Instead of repairing it again, we put the UNHCR foil over and it stayed there until the end of the war (social media discussion, February 2022).

This example describes the relationship between physical and psychological resilience. On the one hand, it demonstrates the attempt to continue the previous mode of existence by fixing the glass back to the window. On the other hand, when the physical inconvenience of a broken window repeated, it generated a change in both psychological and — as a result — physical approach to it — the use of foil instead of glass. It served the further step to adaption to what Brooks, Hoberg et al. (2019) marked as suboptimal conditions and the consequent physical-psychological resilience. Such suboptimal conditions became the norm as violence escalated across Bosnia and Herzegovina. Much of the other public infrastructure was bombed and, therefore, dysfunctional. Water, including drinking water, soon became scarce. The lack of sources to fulfill such basic needs made my fellow citizens more sensitive to nature and the weather than they used to be prior to the conflict. "With the first drops of rain, we were running out with washbowls to pick up water. It was important to hear the rain pouring so to run as fast as possible to pick up as much water as possible" (personal communication, July 1997). Otherwise, one had to go several kilometers to pick it up and bring it home, so the use of trolleys from destroyed supermarkets and hotels increased significantly. As one participant in social media group discussions recalled, "I brought the trolley from a destroyed supermarket. The whole wartime we used it to bring water from the other parts of the city" (social media discussion, February 2022). In a way, such vulnerabilities influenced Bosnians to be among the first relatively large communities who actively practiced the reuse of metal and plastics. During the winter months, when food was even scarcer, my close family members told me that they applied unconventional health-controversial strategies to ease their hunger.

> There was never enough food for all in the household, so some of us had breakfast, others had lunch, and sometimes some even had a dinner. To trick the sense of hunger, we kept several cigarettes and smoke a bit, and the hunger disappeared (personal communication, June 1997).

Later, whenever some of them were criticized for smoking, they would recall how cigarettes helped them to avoid feeling starvation. Many people who survived the siege have told these stories many times, including my grandparents, who until the end of their lives time after time were recalling some of the hardest memories of the siege.

> We mastered cooking in scarce of food: we learned how to make and enjoy rice pie, yeast pate, to hunt for pigeons and to prepare soups from their meat, and salad from dandelion … When the existing clothes became overused, to make ourselves warmer, we took some remaining sleeping bags and made the new jackets for us. We gave all your remaining clothes to kids in neighborhood, who grew out of their old clothes (personal communication, June 1997).

These memories revealed collective form of hard resilience, but also suggests that solidarity increases between the people who encountered similar challenges, simultaneously turning into soft resilience. At the same time, specific to Bosnians, their sense of humor, for which they were known and respected among other former Yugoslavs, became the best source of soft — psychological — resilience even in the most dramatic situations during the 1990s war.

> I was injured during a shelling, and at that moment, I thought it might be the end for me. However, a neighbor passing by noticed that I had fallen and quickly rushed me to the shelter, providing much-needed relief before we could get to the doctor. In that moment of distress, I jokingly asked him to cremate me if I didn't make it through. He turned his face to me as if he was surprised and asked "are you mad? Do you know that we do not have

enough electricity for the cremation?" And we both laughed (personal communication, November 2009).

In many cases, these situations remained a source of dark humor, even long after the events had passed. Whether it was in individual conversations or within groups, my interlocutors emphasized the role of humor as the most applicable psychological strategy during the most critical moments. Bosnian participants in some
public groups on social media fondly recalled these instances of humor and resilience during challenging times.

> We laughed about the things that probably no one else would find funny.
> For example,… The bomb felt and cut off a neighbor's ear, and he looked for
> his ear all around. "Why are you looking for your ear? It's gone, forget it"
> said another neighbor. "I don't care for my ear, but I look for the cigarette
> that was hidden behind it" replied a neighbor (social media discussion, Feb-
> ruary 2022).

Yet, though facing similar physical obstacles, those, who appeared to be an 'ethnic' minority in their locality quite often, were
the target of discrimination by some representatives of 'ethnic' majorities.

> When the war started in Bosnia, I was close to sixteen, and armies tried to
> mobilize all male population. I lived in a majority Bosniak town, so, once
> Bosnia became independent and the war started, I became a minority, be-
> cause it turned that I am a Croat. As a Croat, I was suspicious to the Bosnian
> army, as they did not trust in my loyalty, which was good for me. … As a
> Croat, I tried to get the Croatian passport, but I was told that first I have to
> become a Catholic officially. As it seemed as my only solution to escape from
> Bosnia, I went to the local Catholic Church and learned theology. Six months
> later they told me that I am ready to be baptized, and six months after I was
> baptized and accepted as a Catholic. Only with these official documents, I
> could finally apply for the Croatian citizenship. I was sixteen when my mom
> hided me into one track and we went throughout war-torn Bosnia toward
> the Croatian border. When we got to the territory controlled by the Bosnian
> Croatians, I thought I was safe. However, then they tried to mobilize me into
> the Bosnian Croatian army. After mom's long requests and explanations that
> I was sixteen, they finally decided to let me go. That is how mom and I went
> to Germany (personal communication, June 2017).

Owning a Croatian passport was beneficial as soon as Croatia's independence received recognition from several key European
states, including Germany. Ownership of the Croatian passport

provided an opportunity to travel across Europe without visas and gain "inclusion into the kin-state, type and the extent of opportunities kin-states provide, as well as the routinization of citizenship practices" (Subasic, 2022, p. 335). Therefore, obtaining a Croatian passport represented the legal aspect of tangible resilience, combining loyalty of coercion and convenience for many residents of Bosnia and Herzegovina and Serbia. At the same time, as one of my conversers who left Croatia during the war explained that

> applying for the documents issued by the newly independent Croatian state, Croatian Serbs were under double threat. On one hand, they were recruited to the Croatian Army and sent to the war immediately. On the other hand, they were suspicious in the Croatian army for being Serbs, and it was not a rare case that they were sent to the first frontline and were killed earlier than other soldiers were. Many Croatians were also brave in words, but not in deeds when it came to the question of defense, but they still received passports without much questions. To receive the Croatian passport as a Croatian citizen, my husband had to pay the considerable fine for living Croatia as a refugee. They considered him as a deserter, and fined him for 3000 German marks, All that just because he did not want to kill his neighbors or to be killed by his neighbors. It was all deeply hippocratic and so disgusting (personal communication, September 2016).

Furthermore, in the opinion of one of my conversers, suspicion towards representatives of the groups taking an opposite side in the conflict was the characteristic of people with lower level of education.

> There was frequent shelling of our building and the surrounding ones. While others were given guns and ammunition, my dad had to defend the building without the gun and any weapons. *Nacionalnost* – the 'ethnicity' was not important to us, but it was important to others. Hatred was equally life-threatening as bombs. People were manipulated by media and by politicians, especially people with low level of education. They thought to defend someone and some interests … My dad was an engineer, and he kept some copies of his previous projects in his own home archive. When they came to check him, they did not know what the official document was, let alone a project for construction. I can only imagine what they were doing to the people who were interpreters for example (online communication, March 2023).

Similarly, as one of my Bosniak peers, who also experienced the war as an early teenager, recalled in one of numerous informal conversations about the Bosnian war,

> There was bombing in the nearby town and we were sitting in the shelters waiting and frightening that the Serbs can soon come to our town and kill us. Among us, one neighbor was a Serb. He was silent all the time, keeping his hand on his left ear. Some of the men asked him what is he doing, but he seemed so involved in keeping his hand on his ear that he did not react to the question. Other men were Bosniaks, they came to him and started to beat him until he moved his hand away from his ear. At that moment, a small old radio transistor felt from his left hand and the Bosniak neighbors took it. Now they listened and realized that he was trying to hear the news. I was so desperate when I realized that they beaten poor neighbor for listening the news, but if I said something in his defense, they would beat me too (personal conversation, September 2017).

Therefore, as this example demonstrates, the discrimination was taking form of physical oppression, while representatives of majorities could encounter oppression themselves if they stood to the defense of their minority peers. Besieged, people also learned which public spaces were more dangerous than others, and which army or fighting group was occupying a particular position. Since Bosnians were on all sides in the conflict, and there were neighbors and cousins fighting on different sides, one could guess about the target of a sniper coming from a certain direction. As one of my former Serb neighbors from Sarajevo, after he escaped from the city, described one of the episodes from the besieged city.

> [My] Bosniak friend and I went to pick some water and flour from the local humanitarian station. We walked across the Kosevo Street when the sniper started to shoot. We hid behind the wall. (Name) looked to the direction from where the sniper shot. "This one was not directed at me, but at you" he said. "Stand beside me, and he will not hit you" (personal notes, May 1995).

Many explained such behavior as a pragmatic interest. Namely, defending their neighbors, who were increasingly excluded from the remaining mainstream society, conscientiously could be long-term beneficial: if the other day they turn to be in the 'minority', the neighbors whom they defend now will defend them later. This seemed like a strategy for long-term resilience. It appeared again in one occasional conversation that occurred a year after the war ended with the person who, as a Bosniak, spent the entire war under the siege in Sarajevo.

> You can hear now everywhere how Serbs are terrible, they are oppressors and so on, but then everyone will mention 'their Serb' who is kind and nice and good, unlike the majority. This is so disgusting to me, because it is so hypocritical (personal notes, July 1997).

Therefore, the people who represented an 'ethnic' or, as it was usually referred to, 'national' minority in certain war-torn localities experienced dual exclusion, regardless of what minority they were considered by the majority or even by themselves. My own note illustrates the extent of confusion: "The shelling stopped, and it became quiet outside. I finally went to the bathroom and looked at myself in the mirror and I thought whether I see an ally, or an enemy" (personal notes, April 1992). Therefore, feeling increasingly uncertain in all local communities especially across conflict-torn Bosnia, people were searching for potential allies among their peers who found themselves in similar situations.

> Going to work through one of those more secure from bombs and snipers streets, I met my old friend that I have not seen for several years. We hugged and talked for a while. I asked him how his family is, and he said that they are safe in Belgium. He asked about my family, and a little quieter, I told him that I managed to send my wife and children to Belgrade for the time being. His expression suddenly changed, and he immediately asked me if I had any connections to help him transferring 'there'. I told him I did not have any – I really did not. He approached me closer and said that his wife and children were actually in Belgrade, and he began to persuade me to try to run away together. Of course, I was suspicious and told him that it might be better for Croats to go to Croatia. He looked at me and said: "What am I going to do as a Serb in Croatia now, are you kidding?" Even more confused, I said, "Since when are you a Serb?" It turned out that he also thought that I was Croatian! Therefore, we figured out that we could try to escape to the other side together, and then try to reunite with our families and emigrate further (personal conversation, December 1992).

This story told by my acquaintance provides anecdotal evidence supporting Wimmer's (2004) argument about ethnicity and ethnic divisions as social constructs and Malešević''s definition of 'ethnicity' as "a politicized social action" rather than "a synonym for cultural diversity" (2010, p. 71). At the same time, the narrative reveals that 'taking the side' was not a predetermined choice, but rather a 'voice' option, a process in search of an available solution to social exclusion. Though taking the side has been perceived predominantly as a psychological process, in besieged Sarajevo, Bihac, and other places where the conflict took a variety of violent forms, taking sides or remaining neutral represented the means of physical survival, a form of hard resilience. For the people who, sometimes surprisingly even for themselves, turned into 'ethnic' minorities among the emerging 'imagined communities' in their places of residence, physical escape—exit—became a major survival strategy.

> There was no life back home anymore and I wanted to make sure that the kids are safe. I sent them to Belgrade because my relatives who lived there offered so. We expected the crisis to be short. However, when I realized that it would last long, I tried to run away and to get to my children. I escaped besieged city running zigzag over the bridge to avoid snipers' fire. Finding the operational bus line, I arrived to Belgrade and accommodated at my relatives' place. I planned to wait there until the war stops. We expected to return home anyway (online interview, March 2022).

My personal notes, written several days after escaping Sarajevo, still vividly recall a dramatic event that I experienced together with my sister and two cousins.

> We spent three days in the airport waiting in a queue to the military plane that evacuated mothers and children from the city. There was no more food left in the airport. One boy, who stood in front of us, had several sandwiches left in his bag, and he shared them with us. That was the first time that I heard my dad saying thank you to someone for sharing food with us. It was a devastating experience.
> My dad could always provide any kid with food and shelter; he always could play with and talk to the kids. My dad, who always was smiling and strong, in that moment looked completely discouraged. Even then my dad rubbed the boy's head and warmly said "thank you, son". Oldest cousin said that we should catch the next flight whatever it takes. Four of us were the last who entered the plane. I turned once again to wave to dad to ensure him that everything is ok. I sat to the only left unoccupied spot in the huge plane without seats and windows and I covered my face with hair and hand from the Japanese journalist's photo-camera. In another hand, I kept my sister's hand. I closed my eyes. Babies cried loudly. It was my first flight by plane

ever and—as it turns—the last evacuation flight from besieged Sarajevo. How lucky we were to get to get on that flight (personal note, April 1992).

The self-reimagining of existing and the emergence of new communities in Bosnia and the rest of the former Yugoslav territories continued during the conflict. Until 1992, all Bosnians shared the same language and dialect (Maleševic´, 2010), but the Bosnian population divided along confessional lines (Stipić, 2022). They consist of Bosniaks (those whose ancestors converted to Islam during the Ottoman rule, and the Balkan Slavic Muslims), Serbs (those whose ancestors belonged to one of the central and western Balkan Slavic Orthodox nations), and Croats (those whose ancestors were among the Balkan Slavic Catholics). Equally importantly, the division lines also went through Bosnians' own self-perception and sense of belonging, as many families consisted of members who followed more than one or, during Yugoslavia most often, none of these confessions, as was the case with my family. There also were other lines of divisions, such as regional, local, and level of education-based ones. As a result, some of those adult Bosnians (as noted in Chapter 1, the citizens of Bosnia and Herzegovina) who were mostly or partially perceived or self-perceived as being in majority in particular areas, such as Croats in central Bosnian town Kiseljak, Serbs in Sarajevo's area Ilidza, and Bosniaks in Sarajevo's city center, usually felt less endangered by their neighbors. In fact, they sought the neighbors rather as the source of social resilience. Therefore, in the beginning of the war, they usually did not try to escape immediately: though they might not had loyalty to the local community, they neither were disloyal. However, as the war was continuing, they had fewer possibilities not to be involved in the conflict at least psychologically, and to remain safe at least physically. "Emigration was the solution to physical safety in the first place. Physical danger and the lack of electricity, water, food, bombs— that is the worst danger ever" (online communication, February 2023).

In addition to war, and as a side effect, criminal underworlds emerged on the territories of the collapsing countries (King, 2001) as one of the most significant sources of threat. Many of these criminals were used as warriors (Vivod, 2009). My acquaintance, who witnessed and escaped from the war in Bosnia, recalled that

> bombs and shelling were just part of the problem, and not the biggest one. Much bigger problem were gangs of newly emerged warlords, who were marginal in peaceful times and the war seem to be their only chance to become 'someone'. These people could flourish only in such terrible circumstances (personal communication, June 1998).

By the time when the situation reached the stage defined by the UN as a humanitarian catastrophe, corridors to escape shrank in numbers, directions, and safety. Still, despite the worsening conditions, most of them succeeded in escaping. Particularly in Sarajevo, the most frequent and tragically famous escape route was the tunnel that locals dug below the Sarajevo's airport runaway. The tunnel was between one meter and one and a half meters high and about one kilometer long. As my converser whose parents came from all three major Bosnian national-confessional communities recalled,

> I was sick, tired, and deeply depressed because the war and the siege. I said to all my family that I leave. They were afraid to let me go, because for one it takes exceptional accuracy, luck and courage to get to the tunnel. Nevertheless, my boyfriend and I decided that it is better to die trying to escape, than to die of hunger and of bombs. Our eyes have already been adapted to the dark, so during one night, we crossed the spaces between the buildings and by the morning, we were at the tunnel. From there we went to my relatives in Kiseljak, where the life seemed completely peaceful in comparison to Sarajevo (personal conversation, December 2007).

One outcome of these migrations was that many from the former republic of Yugoslavia exchanged their population. With the movement of refugees from Slovenia and Croatia to Serbia, there was also the reversed migration: Croats from Serbia exchanged property with Serbs from Croatia.

> Wars in former Yugoslavia produced huge number of internally displaced persons (IDPs) and refugees in neighboring countries and in Western Europe: 300,000 to 350,000 Croatian Serbs were displaced between 1992 and 1995 and 2.6 million citizens of Bosnia were displaced between 1992 and 1995. In 1999, 450,000 ethnic Albanians fled Kosovo for Albania, 250,000 for Macedonia, and 70,000 for Montenegro (Krasteva, 2010, p. 9).

However, despite being officially uninvolved in wars by 1998, Serbia was negatively affected by a mixture of factors, including UN trade sanctions, a skyrocketing inflation rate, cities flooded with weapons, and the return of local criminals plying their trade in Western Europe to take advantage of the chaos (Knezevic & Tufegdzic, 1995). Over the 1990s, these factors also contributed to the escalation of the conflict in Kosovo between Serbian authorities and ethnic Serbs on the one side and ethnic Albanian population and political forces on the other. Making personal notes during my visit to Kosovo in 2003 as part of a documentary recording crew, and through my communication with the locals, I found certain similarities between the vulnerability of social exclusion encountered by the Kosovo population with those that I noted back in Croatia and Bosnia. Similar to Bosnia, in the conflict in Kosovo, the most vulnerable appeared to be local minority civilians: Albanian population in northern Kosovo areas predominantly populated by Serbs, and Serbs and other Slavic groups such as Kosovan Slavic Muslims in areas predominantly populated by Albanians, most notably in the capital of Pristina, and the town of Prizren. Their legal statuses and physical safety have constantly been in question. Due to the presence of the UN peacekeeping forces English was the major language of communication in Pristina, making it impossible to differentiate visually between local Albanians and Serbs. Most conversations with regular population took place in a British expat-owned café in Pristina downtown and were informal. All the Albanians that I met were very friendly and open to talk about their experiences of the war and its aftermath, expressing mostly gratitude for the US support and the presence of UN forces, saying that this meant quite a relief for them. Their expression of loyalty to the US and the UN peacekeeping forces seemed like loyalty of commitment to the defenders as a major source of resilience. This loyalty was visible even through naming the largest street in Pristina after US President, Bill Clinton, who was seen as playing a crucial role in taking control over Kosovo away from the Serbian political leadership. A very small number of my Kosovan Albanian conversers were expressing radically right political views, openly complaining about the UN presence, portraying it as "another occupation force," referring to Serbian authorities as the first one, and aspiring for Kosovo's full-fledged independence from all sorts of non-Albanian forces.

At the same time, Kosovan Serbs (as they introduced themselves to me) and Slavic Muslims that I met were much more cautious to talk about their experiences, and I did not insist. They, however, were demonstrating more openness when I explained that I am originally from Sarajevo and turned to Serbo-Croatian, or Bosnian-Croatian-Serbian, which despite the difference in dialects was native both for me and for them. I learned from them that most of their relatives and friends left Kosovo. They either went to Serbia or further abroad. Those who stayed continued either to live in the majority Serb enclave, Grachanica, and travel every day to work in the UN office in Pristina, or in one of two residential buildings in Pristina still partially populated by Serbs. They commuted by the special UN bus and it was the mean of physical security, as if they used personal cars they believed that they could be attacked by Albanian radicals: they talked about several precedents. Others in the group showed me these two residential building close to the center of Pristina, where they lived. Most of them cautiously expressed dissatisfaction with the outcome of the conflict as it decreased their citizen rights from dominant majority to oppressed minority; however, they seemed to adjust to the new situation. While all of them seemed calm, only one remained open to express that he understands that he lives under constant danger of being attacked, but that he is accustomed to it and plans to remain in Kosovo. He also expressed that his work at the UN provides him with certain physical and economic safety, which may be characterized as a loyalty of coercion. Through these conversations at the time of my visit to Kosovo, I got the impression that the presence of UN peacekeeping forces overall balanced the interests among the Kosovan population.

In summary, the resilience of Yugoslav citizens during the conflicts of Yugoslavia's collapse appeared in several forms. While hard resilience—physical and socioeconomic aspects—proved to be mostly collective or communitarian, soft resilience such as response to social exclusion were mostly individual and shared with very small communities. While mostly radical right political forces among the society prompted the collapse, the search for particular republics' sovereignty was their way to express dissatisfaction with certain exclusion from the mainstream political processes. These groups built their resilience by opting for a collective exit from the system that marginalized them towards a smaller system that would prioritize them over those who represented the majority in the previous system. Thus, they demonstrated loyalty restricted to certain geographical and community boundaries, while either excluding or marginalizing the former majority by political and physical coercion. In turn, this coercion radicalized Yugoslav center political forces to use army and weapons against their opponents. Gradually other far right forces trying to prevent exclusion and consequent exit joined them. In this way, their bounded loyalties made vulnerable themselves and the rest of population of former Yugoslavia, living them with fewer options: either to 'voice' by joining conflicting factions, or to 'exit' by emigrating.

The third — left-wing group sought its resilience in protesting against violence from both the aforementioned political forces and suggesting reforms within the existing state, making it overall more inclusive to accommodate conflicting interests of both right-wing and center forces. However, this group had little influence over the first and the second ones and found resilience either through internal exit — mostly in the case of pensioners — or through emigration in the case of middle-aged and young generations. In turn, the far-right forces used their voice to discredit the central forces' voice by characterizing it as aggression. These conflicts between republics of former Yugoslavia during the 1990s resulted in the largest migration flows in the period between the end of the Second World War and the beginning of Russia's government invasion in Ukraine in 2022: during the 1990s, about ten million people in the former Yugoslavia were displaced (Krasteva, 2010).

Post-Soviet Experiences of the Collapse of the USSR

Numerous conversations with my friends and colleagues from the former Soviet republics largely reflected situations that citizens of former Yugoslavia experienced during the country's violent breakup. Depending on self-perception and perception by others, people could interpret the same situation completely differently. The contrast of these perceptions was particularly striking among the residents of the Ukrainian city of Lviv in the early 1990s. On one hand, as my postgraduate classmate wrote in the prologue of her recently published monograph,

> Lviv became the staging ground for Ukraine's independence movement. In September 1990, fifty-one years after the city was occupied by the Soviets, the statue of Lenin in front of the Lviv Opera came down on the orders of the city council... a chance to shape Ukraine's future, to transform it from a post-Soviet mutant into a well-governed and prosperous democracy (Budjeryn, 2022, p. 2).

On the other hand, as one of my colleagues told me once over a lunch break of a Moscow-based TV-production office, where I worked as a reporter,

> We lived in Lvov and when the Union collapsed my family as Russian speakers experienced many inconveniences, starting from the school. ...We are Ukrainians, but we are not nationalists, and ...once they attacked our house, and we sat inside for several hours waiting for the police to defend us (personal communication, April 2004).

Already having experiences of being a refugee and emigrant, I sympathized with her. "Do you miss your home in any way?" I asked. She stared at me, nodding negatively. "After all the experiences that I had there, I do not want even to visit it ever again" (personal communication, April 2004). These very different views on the effects of the demise of the USSR on life in Lvov—expressed even in pronunciation of the city's name—demonstrate that loyalty to the Soviet Union and to Ukraine as states differed along the lines of language-related identity, which varied from one person to another.

For this reason, Heleniak (2017) noted that with the dissolution of the USSR, the Russians became the world's second largest 'ethnic' diaspora after the Chinese, changing their legal status into an ethnic minority in all former Soviet states except Russia. This development prompted large-scale migrations initially between post-Soviet republics. For example, Ukrainians residing in the republics of Central Asia, Russia, and the Baltic states also constituted a large minority; however, they were mostly considered as larger Slavic Russian-speaking Soviet majority. Therefore, despite living in vibrant multinational capital of Uzbekistan, Tashkent, one of my conversers, who at the time was already a mid-age adult felt endangered by this change and envisioned emigration to post-Soviet republics with Slavic majorities, where she expected to have more rights and possibilities.

> After the dissolution of the Soviet Union, we could not stay in Uzbekistan. Our way of seeking the safe place to live was long and hard. It started in Russia, where my husband has an extended family. However, we could not get the citizenship and a sustainable employment there (online communication, April 2020).

As this description of my converser's decision to relocate after the collapse of USSR suggests, most of the post-Soviet states encountered socioeconomic and legal challenges — a lack of sustainable jobs and a lack of legal framework to address sudden and increasing statelessness.

It also reveals that these new challenges resulted from exclusion from the processes in the place of residence, and therefore led to the loss of loyalty to local institutions. In the case of my converser from Uzbekistan, her vulnerabilities primarily resulted from her Slavic ethnicity. On the contrary, my conversers from Southern Caucasus, some of whom turned into ethnic minorities with the collapse of the USSR, expressed rather strong local identities. "It may sound strange, but I am a *Bakinets*. There was such a 'nation' — *Bakintsy*. No one asked whether you are a Jew, Azerbaijani, Russian, we all are *Bakintsy*. ... It was a kind of emblem, the city-based identity" (personal communication, December 2019). The term *"Bakinets"* in Russian refers to a citizen of Baku, the capital of Azerbaijan. Such a strong local identity during the crisis that preceded the collapse of the USSR translated into a relatively long-retained sense of safety and, consequently, considerable loyalty to local communities, and simultaneously relatively low resilience. Nevertheless, when talking about the collapse of the USSR, most of my Armenian conversers portrayed it extremely negatively in general and for themselves in particular.

> I returned from my second travel abroad in the end of March 1988, and one of my friends a musician, met me at the airport. We sat into the car and he gave me the newspaper. I wondered why he took a newspaper, as he never read newspapers before. He told me to open and read. I opened the newspaper and I read: "*pogrom*, Armenians, Azerbaijanis, war". I could not understand what is going on. I asked him what happened while I was absent from home. He was very sad and serious. He said: "do you see, can you imagine that this is happening?" He was Azerbaijani and his wife was Armenian. He said "I even don't know what to do. I think that we should get away from here." I could not believe my ears. "Are you serious?" I asked. He was serious. "You have just arrived. Now you go to the downtown and you'll see what is going on". What I saw from the car were tanks on the streets, there was curfew. I came from Europe in a great mood, and what I saw at home is curfew, the war, Nagorny Karabakh.
> What could I do? I came home. In Baku, it was still more or less calm. The conflict in Karabakh was echoing in Baku, there was pogrom in Sumgait by radical right Azeri. The longer I spent time in Baku, the more people were leaving: Armenians, Russians, Jews, because the process that started was somehow nationalistic. The topic of Armenian-Azerbaijani conflict in Karabakh seemed to serve to destruct the attention from full-fledged nationalization of Azerbaijan. People started to walk in the Islamic green clothes, they were protesting all around the city. We from Baku could not understand who are these people, and where do they come from. It was unclear, who brought them to Baku. By then, Baku was very quiet city. And throughout 1988 it remained quiet. There were tanks around, but there were no *pogroms*. I continued to work, I traveled with the orchestra, we were playing in Ukraine, in Belarus, we were returning to Baku (personal communication, January 2020).

As this narrative of personal experience reveals, in the perception of my converser, Soviet Baku was a quite multiethnic city, with Azeri, Armenians, Russians, and Jews living together. The narrator's reference to a "friend, also a musician" and mentioning his ethnicity more in the context of his family life suggests that communities formed among inhabitants were based on professional principles rather than ethnic ones. The narrative also highlights that ethnically mixed marriages were common in Baku. Furthermore, the story depicts Azerbaijan as the Soviet republic where the collapse was evident through the conflict in Nagorno-Karabakh much earlier than in some other parts of the Union, such as Ukraine and Belarus. In contrast to his friend, who considered leaving Baku early in the wake of the crisis, one feature that my Armenian converser had in common with most of my Yugoslav interlocutors is an attempt to continue the previous routine despite the radical changes. This routine became a way of socioeconomic coping with the escalating crisis, in which local multiculturalism and multilingual skills played a fundamental role in building hard resilience.

For this reason, as the narrative suggests, he retained an inertial loyalty to the local community on one hand, and to the wider Soviet one, while becoming disloyal to the republic of his origin as the unit that generated exclusion, turning him into a minority. The collapse of the USSR brought about complex changes in identities, loyalties, and perceptions of belonging for many individuals, and this personal experience sheds light on the diverse ways people navigated through the challenges of the time.

> Sometimes, I was even working in restaurants, when some of my colleagues, who played in restaurants, were ill, so I was substituting them as a pianist. I worked all the time. I worked with Azerbaijanis, even with those, who did not speak Russian. I spoke to them in Azerbaijani language, I learned it in the school, though my native language is Russian. I went to the Russian school, we spoke Russian at home. My parents spoke to their parents in Armenian, but they spoke to each other and to me only in Russian. Only my grandpa did not speak Russian well, he was a turner, and he and my grandma spoke in Armenian (personal communication, January 2020).

As a result, many Armenians from Azerbaijan migrated to Russia slightly prior to the official dissolution of the USSR and in its early aftermath. Similar to Baku, in Armenia, the collapse of the USSR was initially felt through the war in Nagorno-Karabakh. However, unlike their counterparts in Azerbaijan, Armenians in Armenia remained the majority, and due to the virtual absence of other ethnicities, they were more insulated from interethnic conflict. During the crisis that preceded the collapse of the USSR, they focused on managing the technological and natural disasters that occurred, as well as dealing with the challenges posed by the war.

> There was a war in Karabakh and we felt it in Armenia through electricity and water cuts, but it did not change the life too much. No one from the family left Armenia. Earthquake in 1988 and the Karabakh war had much worse consequences than the USSR collapse itself. ... My relatives from the region that was mostly affected by the earthquake moved to Yerevan. Many

Armenians from Karabakh also moved to Yerevan (personal communication, January 2020).

In that way, for Armenia both the earthquake and war in Karabakh generated more socioeconomic hardship than ineffectiveness of the Soviet system. In turn, Armenians in Armenia perceived the collapse of the USSR as a public threat. "The most negative effect of the collapse was the lack of the border with Russia, which is seen as a guarantor of Armenia's security" (personal communication, January 2020). Informal economy combined with corruption (Rekhviashvili, 2017), and debt-based exchange were the most frequent households' responses to these increasing socioeconomic challenges all across the former Soviet republics (Turaeva, 2022).

> If there was not enough money for covering the salaries, the workers were receiving food. In other enterprises, they received talons that served as a currency for obtaining hardly available products. We always had a plenty of food at home, but there was scarce of hygiene products. Thus, we exchanged food for other products that we needed (personal communication, December 2019).

In contrast, from the perspective of Moscow's population who were underage children at the time of the collapse, the memories of those times seem less dramatic.

> I remember the collapse through the pictures of humanitarian aid conserves received in the school and the parents receiving talons to get the food products — there were products, but the choice was limited. Because of the collapse, my parents changed the place of work — went to the private sector and started to earn more (personal communication, July 2022).

As this quotation demonstrates, depending on the particular location and even individual situation, the collapse of USSR brought sense of hope along with uncertainty and fear. It signified that there was an opportunity for change, and many people hoped that the new political regime and newly independent states would bring greater freedom and democracy. As reflected in one of opening quotations to this chapter, most important positive aspect of the collapse was the opening of the borders and possibilities to travel abroad. Many representatives of generations, who were teenagers when the USSR collapsed aspired to study abroad.

> I studied it in the school, and together with my parents, we tried to make the strategic decision. In the 1990s, it was very popular profession to be a lawyer, so many people went to the legal studies. However, soon I realized that there are enough lawyers, who work as sales persons in various shops, even without myself, so I wanted to study interpretations from the foreign languages—to see the world, to travel abroad, and I thought that should I speak several languages, I would not be left without a bread. Thus, the entire accent was on the languages. However, since I come from Chelyabinsk, I could not receive a good quality of English teaching back then, and I learned German. My level of German knowledge was more than sufficient for studying in Russian universities, however, since I was preparing to study abroad and that was my dream, I had to study for another year in the Russian university to get to the level of German that I needed for studying in Austria (personal communication, February 2020).

Simultaneously, as described in the previous chapter, the Soviet citizens who came as providers of services to the Soviet military troops located in Czechoslovakia, Hungary, and Democratic Republic Germany have fewer options to survive by returning home, than to stay in the countries previously occupied by the Soviet troops.

> When the Soviet Union collapsed, I worked for the Southern Soviet troops in Hungary for already several years. I already spoke some Hungarian, I knew quite some people. Prior to coming to Hungary, our home was in Moldova. We had beautiful vineyards viewing the Dnistria's waterfront... My parents resided there until the collapse, but then the conflict in Transnistria started. Being from Moldova, my family has Ukrainian, Lithuanian, and Jewish origins ... Our native language is Russian. It became unsafe for my parents to stay in and for us to return to Moldova, so we brought them to Hungary and we all settled here (personal communication, January 2013).

In this way, the temporal service of my converser in the Soviet Army in Central Europe turned Hungary into a permanent destination for him and practically three generations of his family. Relocating to Hungary became a major channel of their resilience during the crisis of collapse, and their loyalty of convenience towards the country of residence replaced their previous loyalty of coercion and convenience to the Soviet Union. This shift in loyalty allowed them to adapt and find stability in Hungary, making it their new home.

In sum, the experience of the collapse of the USSR varied greatly among Soviet citizens, depending on the particular combination of their individual circumstances, including geographic location, ethnicity, social class, age, and, as a result, the degree and form of loyalty to the Soviet system. These diverse factors contributed to the different perceptions and responses to the momentous event, shaping the way people navigated through the uncertainties and challenges of that transformative period. While Soviet citizens were accustomed to the insufficiency of the Soviet economy and repression, their hard resilience embodied in informal social networks and economy. During and in the aftermath of the collapse, these coping mechanisms proportionally grew to compensate for increasing physical threats, job losses, and the uncertainty surrounding legal statuses. Simultaneously, the collapse and its aftermath led to the creation of new job opportunities, possibilities for travel, and a broader range of lifestyle choices, which offered some compensation for the losses caused by the profound transformation of the system. As a result, individuals and communities adapted to the changing landscape, finding ways to navigate the complexities and challenges of the post-Soviet era. While significant numbers of Soviet citizens residing by the collapse in Central Asia and Caucasus relocated to other more prosperous post-Soviet republics, others sought to leave the post-Soviet space for less troubled regions. As a result, from the mid-1990s onwards, post-Soviet emigration waves included Chechens, Russians, Kazakhs and Ukrainians (Molodikova, 2017; Ryazantsev, 2015). Many host countries official statistics, in particular Germany, Israel and Hungary, have accounted citizens of post-Soviet countries as "citizens of the former USSR" long after the dissolution of the Soviet Union, with the definition continuing to be used within Israeli official statistics today (Ryazantsev et al., 2018).

Comparison and Conclusion: Yugoslavs' and Soviets' Resilience during the Collapses

As demonstrated throughout this chapter, the processes of systems' collapses generate the lines of new social divisions. Based on these social constructs, processes of collapse implied exclusion on multiple levels. In turn, resilience in the crisis of collapses appeared in two major ways. For citizens of Yugoslavia, soft—in this case political-cultural—resilience emerged as loyalty revealed through one of the three following forms of national-regional-local identity. First, liberal leftists—the group loyal to Yugoslavia as a country and the Yugoslav identity based on citizenship—were pro-reform and preferred avoiding secessions. As a result, they were left without political representation. These groups initially were numerous and most vocal 'voicers' in the beginning of the conflict. However, being demobilized—as Gagnon (2004) correctly noted—by conservative elites in Serbia and Croatia, but also in other Yugoslav republics, they were choosing two different exit options. One was emigration, or classical 'exit' in Hirschman's terms. Another resilience strategy observed was a 'soft exit' through disengagement, a strategy similar to that employed by Soviet Jews and noted in Chapter 2, as described by Remennick (2012). In this manner, Hirschman's concept of loyalty is connected to resilience, as both concepts involve a willingness to persist despite exclusion and adversity. Both loyalty and resilience require a sense of commitment and determination, proving crucial in navigating challenging situations and achieving long-term survival during periods of collapse. By collapse, Jared Diamond meant

> a drastic decrease in human population size and/or political/economic/social complexity, over a considerable area, for an extended time. The phenomenon of collapses is thus an extreme form of several milder types of decline, and it becomes arbitrary to decide how drastic the decline of a society must be before it qualifies to be labeled as a collapse (Diamond, 2005, p. 3).

The narratives of former citizens of Yugoslavia and the USSR, as presented in this chapter, align with Diamond's definition of collapse, with an important social aspect added: the collapse led to the exclusion of all citizens from their previous communities, statuses, and positions. However, for some post-Yugoslav and post-Soviet citizens, the collapse also brought positive changes, perceived as access to more rights and opportunities. Examples of this can be found among Croats in Croatia, Albanians in Kosovo, Russians in

Russia, and Ukrainians in Ukraine. When we analyze their responses in Hirschman's (1970) framework, which offers exit or voice options depending on loyalty to an existing system, we see that the exits of Yugoslav and Soviet citizens represented both their voicing against multiple exclusions and the vulnerabilities that these exclusions created. As a result, emerging challenges decreased their loyalty to the previous system.

In a certain way, exclusion also meant coercion towards two radical choices: to choose a side in conflicts as soft resilience, or to escape as hard resilience. In some cases, 'voice' was only attainable through 'exit,' meaning that taking a side or expressing dissent was possible only through leaving the situation or place. The prevalence of social discrimination or 'othering,' which involves the cultural exclusion of certain groups based on external characteristics, was a common vulnerability experienced by cultural and ethnic minorities, ranging from mild forms of discrimination to the most extreme cases of physical violence. In such situations, loyalty to the community, which shared similar experiences of collapses, between both Yugoslav and Soviet citizens narrowed down to emerging smaller social groups.

For both Yugoslav and Soviet citizens, these differences were initially rooted in the system of values with which each person was raised. During the collapse, new differences emerged around self-perceptions, perceptions of other people, and consequential self-perceived individual vulnerabilities among both Yugoslav and Soviet citizens, whose places of residence happened to become zones of violent conflicts. The intersections of these factors, combined with the level of physical danger and options for relocation, shaped the challenges faced by citizens of these two former socialist federations during their collapses, leading to a range of resilience strategies. A significant response was to connect with people who shared similar experiences of the collapse. This finding aligns with Kovacevic-Bielicki's (2017) notion of identity boundaries, which, as this chapter has demonstrated, were challenged and blurred throughout the collapse process. While seconding Connerton (1989) thesis that everyone's perception is unique, and that it enables individuals to connect with their own truth and identity from the past, this finding echoes the community ties theory postulating that a community emerges around a specific cause (Barabasi, 2014; Kim, 2014). This theory is addressed in further detail in the next chapter in the context of migrant communities. Here it is important to re-state one of the findings of this chapter, namely that Yugoslav and Soviet citizens, who during collapses of Yugoslavia and the Soviet Union appeared to be in a majority in their localities usually did not emigrate. In war-torn areas, they built their resilience by reconnect-ing with the nature and through communitarian activities. As a re-sult, they formed communities of, in the words of Kovacevic-Bielicki (2019), "those who stayed". Moreover, the present chapter demonstrated that young population of post-Soviet citizens ap-peared rather optimistic in the light of demise of the USSR, detect-ing more opportunities for travel, study, employment and earning than was available in the Soviet system. This finding points toward emergence and nature of post-Yugoslav post-Soviet migrant com-munities, which is the topic of the next chapter.

Chapter 4
Re-Inclusion through Re-Territorialization and De-Re-Territorialization: Diversity of Post-Yugoslav and Post-Soviet Migrant Communities

> The violent breakup of Yugoslavia changed all the plans and all flow of life... My parents were very strong and brave, so they helped me to overcome the loss of home.... Luckily, it turned better than expected: I received international higher education and diverse life experience (online communication, February 2023).

> The identity became somehow more striking and important for me, when I moved here... I needed to make boundaries of myself... Then I became a patriot... it became important for me to give the answer to myself, who am I, and I am Russian (personal communication, January 2019).

Types of Migrant Communities and Community Ties

Exploring trajectories of migrations prompted by demises of Yugoslavia and the USSR, the present chapter traces emergence and content of post-Yugoslav and post-Soviet migrant communities. The chapter is, therefore, guided by the following questions: What kinds of challenges, if any, did post-Yugoslav and post-Soviet citizens encounter when they emigrated? Why and with whom did post-Yugoslav and post-Soviet migrants form new relationships and communities? Did these communities differ across receiving countries, and if so, to what extent? In answering these questions, the chapter draws upon two major strands of literature. Alongside migration literature, which discusses the dynamics of migrations, the chapter also reflects on propositions from related literature concerning community ties. The first strand of literature distinguishes between concepts of migrant communities and diasporas, as the following quotation demonstrates.

> If migrant communities are known to be unstable, transient, and unincorporated, diasporic communities are characterized by the extended organizational infrastructure, sustained participation in other diasporic networks around the world, the presence of two or more generations in a host country,

and permanency in settlement and employment. The transition from one to another is not instant and accompanied, and inspired, by growing personal and eventually corporate, or organizational, reflectivity (Khanenko-Friesen, 2017, p. 49).

In addition to the concepts of diaspora and migrant communities, which are seen as two opposing concepts in the context of migration, there is a third concept widely present and discussed in migration studies known as transmigrants. Transmigrants represent an intermediate stage between migrant communities and diasporas. According to Glick Schiller (1997, p. 155), these are immigrants who live their lives across national borders, participating in the daily life and political processes of two or more nation-states. Therefore, transmigrants usually overlap between population of sending countries, emerging migrant communities, and diasporas. As noted in Chapter 1, more recent migration literature recognized also a class of 'rich' or 'life-style' migrants (Vailati & Rial, 2016). Seen as wealthy cosmopolitan, they, in fact, represent the new generations of post-World-War-II Northern American and Western European 'jet-set', who, were rather rich frequent travelers, than relocators or migrants. For these reasons, this group is treated rather as individuals, than the type of migrants. Table 4.1 below summarizes characteristics of three concepts.

Table 4.1: Classification of migrants in existing migration literature

Type	Characteristics
Diasporic communities	organizational infrastructure, sustained participation in other diasporic networks around the world, the presence of two or more generations in a host country, and permanency in settlement and employment
Migrant communities	unstable, transient, and unincorporated
Transmigrants	immigrants who live their lives across national borders, participating in the daily life and political processes of two or more nation-states

Throughout this chapter, these three types of migrant communities recognized by existing literature serve as analytical benchmarks for exploring post-Yugoslav and post-Soviet migrant communities. The chapter aims to demonstrate how these communities emerged or evolved, either integrating around existing Cold War-time migrant communities and diasporas or forming as distinct and separate communities and groups.

The second strand of literature that underpins the analysis of this chapter is the emergence of communities and community ties. This multidisciplinary literature offers two competing propositions, and one complementing proposition concerning the emergence of migrant communities. The first proposition is that the emergence of networks and communities are random (Barabasi, 2014, p. 17). The competing proposition suggests that the emergence of networks and communities are predetermined, as seen with network or chain migrations. The third, complementary proposition suggests that communities emerge around a specific cause: once the cause is exhausted or a problem resolved, communities shrink, and their ties weaken or even disappear over time. In the context of emigration, Kim (2014, p. 352) discussed "[t]he concept of 'cumulative causation,'" and pointed out that

> prior contacts serve to lower the costs of transnational movement by providing tangible and intangible resources to would-be migrants, thereby facilitating and channeling cross-border migratory flows. The key causal factor here is network-mediated social capital that resides between the members of the immigrant community in the country of destination or the people with prior migratory experiences in the country of origin and those interested in moving abroad.

Combining these propositions with the multiple concepts of loyalty and resilience, the present chapter demonstrates that post-Yugoslav and post-Soviet migrant communities emerge around various forms of loyalty. In this context, the concept of emergence is crucial to understand migrations, both mid-term and ad hoc (Krasteva, 2021), because it "implies selforganization from below through adaptation to the internal and external environment and co-evolution or the ability to transform with the environment" (Kavalski, 2007, p. 440).

The formation of communities is primarily influenced by the loyalty individuals have towards a major source of safety and resilience. This can manifest through informal groups of people who bond over shared traumas or through employees working in the same or similar companies. In the following chapter, I will begin with an auto-ethnographic analysis of post-Yugoslav refugees, specifically focusing on Bosnians who relocated to Serbia, which has been one of the most frequent first destinations for refugees within the former Yugoslavia. The section addresses the ways in which post-Yugoslav refugees responded to multileveled exclusion and their resilience strategies that determined emigration paths. Section 2 traces further migrations and the ways of post-Yugoslav communities' formation in several distinct geographical sites and their contacts with Yugoslav-time migrants and communities in these sites. Section 3 traces the ways in which vulnerabilities influenced trajectories of post-Soviet migrations after the demise of the USSR and analyzes the formation of post-Soviet migrant communities in several geographical sites and their contacts with Soviet-times migrant communities. The last section compares findings about post-Yugoslav and post-Soviet migrant communities that emerged in the aftermath of the socialist federations' demises contributing to Wimmer (2004, p. 4) plea for more research on 'the everyday praxis of group formation' and 'its variability and context dependency', and draws some conclusion concerning their community ties as resilience.

Post-Yugoslav Migrations: Refugees' Communities in Serbia

Initially, many Yugoslavs, particularly Bosnians, sought security by relocating to safer regions within their own republics or to neighboring Yugoslav republics such as Serbia, Croatia, Slovenia, Montenegro, and Macedonia. These regions were perceived as comparatively safer during that time of turmoil. However, as the previous chapter has demonstrated, their legal statuses varied, depending on many factors, including their age, gender, profession, geographic and religious origins, existence of additional homes, and even on existence of personal connections with local and republic authorities of the time. As mentioned in the previous chapter, between 1945 and 1991, many individuals from war-torn regions, including Bosnians, owned summerhouses on the Adriatic seacoast in Croatia and Montenegro. In some cases, these individuals chose to relocate to these second homes if they were deemed safer during times of conflict. Consequently, strictly adhering to legal definitions, these individuals could hardly be characterized as internally displaced persons. However, such instances were relatively rare. The majority of the population from war-torn areas either sought refuge in calmer regions within their own republics or became refugees within other Yugoslav republics or abroad. The trajectories of their escape depended largely on the availability and relative safety of transportation corridors.

After escaping besieged Sarajevo, many teenage children, including myself, found themselves without parents among unfamiliar temporary receiving families and adults mostly across Serbia, less in Montenegro and in calmer parts of Croatia. In Belgrade, the capital of former Yugoslavia and Serbia, where most of foreign embassies were located, the inflow of Bosnian and Croatian refugees was evident even on the streets. For example, the monument to the Serbian Prince Mikhailo riding a horse at Belgrade's central square — The Republic Square — was refugees' focal meeting point. Interestingly, the devotion of the monument to the prince was neglected as everyone referred to it as *kod konja*, literally 'around the horse'. Teenage refugees sought ways to connect with each other and spend time together as an unconscious attempt to retain a sense of continuity and familiarity with their hometown routines. Due to the rapidly rising living costs, only a few Bosnian children who had escaped to Serbia were allowed to use their host's phones to make calls to their peers. As an alternative means of communication, they would gather in public spaces where they could meet familiar faces from their home places. In these gatherings, teenagers engaged with one another, sharing their impressions and confusions about adapting to local customs different from their own. They would also exchange stories about their general daily experiences, finding solace in the company of peers who understood the challenges of being in a new environment. These interactions helped them cope with the difficulties of displacement and fostered a sense of community and belonging during their time as refugees. The gatherings of teenage refugees also served as an opportunity for them to hope for news from their parents and relatives who remained in besieged cities like Sarajevo and other parts of Bosnia. As the war raged during 1992, and in early 1993, almost every day there was someone 'fresh' from home. Adults, mostly refugee children's mothers also were gathering 'around the horse' in the evenings to reconnect with fellow *Sarajlije* – citizens of Sarajevo, refugees to learn about potential new routes to escape besieged city, and possibilities of employment and rent of accommodations in Belgrade and Serbia, as they were trying to avoid bothering their hosts by their presence for long. As one of my peer Bosnian teenage refugees recalled, "the longest plan was a week: we knew where we would be accommodated for the next seven days maximum. Only where to stay overnight, and where to take a shower" (online communication, February 2023). For many adults it took quite some time before they realized the depth of the crisis.

> I am a type of person who does not react in a moment, and who needs more time to realize what is happening. For me the most important goal was to find a safe place. I escaped to Belgrade to my relatives until the war stops. We expected to return home soon (online communication, March 2023).

Additionally, during these early evening gatherings at the central square, the refugees discussed the possibilities and procedures for their children to enter local schools, despite lacking the necessary documents. The violent conflicts in Croatia and Bosnia had fundamentally interrupted their education, and they were now seeking ways to continue it in their new surroundings. These discussions provided some comfort and a sense of shared understanding before they returned to their accommodations, which often presented mutual inconveniences for both the hosts and the refugees. Unlike the situation in war-torn Sarajevo, where division lines between people were drawn along religious and confessional origins, as discussed in Chapter 3, the refugees from Sarajevo, wider Bosnia, and Croatia in Serbia formed a community bound together by similar or close geographical origins, shared traumatic war experiences, and the common goal of survival and prosperity. However, their shared experiences also set them apart from the local population and even from their fellow citizens of Sarajevo who had arrived in Belgrade earlier under different circumstances, not directly linked to the ongoing war.

In the early summer of 1992, the square seemed to be a place of hope, as teenage refugees shared their relief with peers regarding the news about the escape of some of their parents and friends from besieged Sarajevo, and to a lesser extent, from other war-torn Bosnian and Croatian cities. However, with the ongoing mass mobilization in Croatia and Bosnia, mothers and wives were primarily preoccupied with finding ways of escape for their male family members. As the war continued and more refugees arrived, they brought with them negative, often blood-chilling news from their homes. Consequently, the central square, which had initially served as a convenient public space for gathering, soon transformed into a place of loss and pain. As the frequency of shocks and pain increased, Belgrade's central square evolved into an informal symbol of simultaneous vulnerability, representing the spontaneously emerged community of post-Yugoslav refugees in Serbia and the embodiment of their soft resilience.

At the same time, the square became a symbol of crisis and irritation for many locals, illustrated through the following anecdote that one local peer told me in the winter of 1992-1993: "Do you know what happens in the Republic square when the tire on the trolleybus bursts? Everyone immediately lies down on the floor" alluding to refugees' traumas of shelling. Such jokes were rare, but their mere existence generated previously invisible dividing lines between locals and refugees. In attempts to avoid escalations and further inconveniences, refugees spontaneously built collective resilience through cooperation within the refugee community, confirming Kontos' (2003) argument that the more discrimination a community faces, the tighter becomes the community and the more support it has from the inside.

Before the war, the majority of adult refugees were full-time employees in their home country. After seeking safety in Belgrade and its vicinity, they actively searched for jobs and opportunities to continue their work there. Many of them perceived Belgrade as the capital of their home country by default. Some of these job-seeking attempts proved relatively successful, offering a glimmer of hope amidst the challenges of displacement and starting anew.

> I started to work for a local multilevel marketing company immediately af-ter I left Sarajevo. However, the income from that job was not salary-based, but depended on the percentage of sales. I worked as much as I could. That was an available job, but not a secure one. Therefore, I found an additional job. The refugees from Sarajevo — employers of the Sarajevo-based newspa-per, opened the representative editorial office in Belgrade. I worked in the marketing service of this newspaper. My job was to search for advertisers and for the subscribers. It was also percentage-based job, so it was also not completely secure one. Neither of these jobs were related to my profession and my previous employment (online communication, March 2023).

To a certain extent, this example resembles Hoffmann's (2010) thesis about migrants' voice after exit with loyalty of overlapping coercion, convenience and commitment that on the one hand nar-rowed to colleagues who happened to escape from the same place of origin to the same place of destination. On the other hand, they created opportunity for income for other fellow refugees, who pre-viously had no experience in the field, making them resilient through inclusion to this smaller emerging community and gener-ating new loyalty- or the community tie — to the relatively small group of people, who experienced similar obstacles.

One of the rarely available and, therefore, most frequently used economic coping mechanisms during the crisis — demonstrat-ing hard resilience — for both refugees and locals was opening de-posits in one of the two newly founded private banks in Serbia. The first private bank, Jugoskandik, was founded by Jezdimir Va-siljevic, a Serbian quasi-businessman who had previously been a convicted criminal. The second bank was Dafiment, and both insti-tutions offered favorable interest rates for citizens' savings. Infor-mal conversations revealed that in most cases, these savings did not exceed 1000 German Marks, which was the most commonly used hard currency in Europe at the time (personal notes, March 1993). Despite the challenges of the crisis, people sought to safeguard their resources and maintain a degree of financial stability through such banking options. Money obtained in this way was used to bypass internationally imposed sanctions and import oil, which was sold in Serbia, while savers were paid rates from the profit (Vasic, 2010), for most refugees, these interest rates were the only source of income (personal notes, October 1993).

Constant night queues in front of Dafiment bank — ironically located on the other side of the same Belgrade's central square, opposite the monument to Prince Mikhailo — also bore witness to the rapidly increasing poverty among the local population. However, even this source of income was short-lived. In 1993, thousands of tons of oil were confiscated from the Montenegrin seaports, leading to the collapse of both banks, leaving depositors without their savings (Vasic, 2010).

Moreover, as one after another, other states recognized the independence of Slovenia, Croatia, and Bosnia and Herzegovina from Yugoslavia, the legal status of their residents and their rights as citizens also came into question, requiring legal redefinition. The US Committee for Refugees, in its Refugees World Survey for 1998, made the following claim:

> About 550,000 refugees from former Yugoslavia were in the Federal Republic of Yugoslavia (Serbia and Montenegro). About 293,000 came from Croatia, almost all ethnic Serbs. The estimated 241,000 Bosnian refugees in Yugoslavia were also overwhelmingly ethnic Serb. ... Late in the year, a new influx of Serbs began arriving from eastern Slavonia, on Serbia's western border, which was scheduled to be transferred to Croatian government control on January 15, 1998. Many of the departing Croatian Serbs had previously been displaced from the Krajina into eastern Slavonia, and were fleeing for the second or third time. By year's end, at least 20,000 Croatian Serb refugees had newly arrived in Yugoslavia.
>
> The wars in Croatia and Bosnia have left Serbia and Montenegro with more refugees than the other four republics of the former Socialist Federal Republic of Yugoslavia combined. The effects of previous international sanctions imposed against Yugoslavia because of its role in the wars, the machinations of Yugoslav politicians, and a relative lack of international sympathy and support for ethnic Serb refugees have contributed to the precarious economic situation of refugees in Yugoslavia. Without a federal refugee structure, host families, municipalities, and republic governments have shouldered much of the burden of assisting refugees in Yugoslavia's two republics (U.S. Committee for Refugees and Immigrants, 1998).

Such institutional deterioration and international neglect made the lives of most post-Yugoslav refugees and many locals unsustainable in Serbia. In the absence of other immediate solutions, many Bosnian and Croatian refugees found themselves staying in the newly recognized states of post-Yugoslavia for several months or even several years. As a result, the spontaneous emergence of the post-Yugoslav refugees' community in Serbia confirms the first proposition about community ties, as noted by Barabasi (2014), suggesting that these ties can be somewhat random. However, the vulnerabilities and traumatic experiences that these refugees accidentally shared also suggest the validity of the complementing proposition, as equally recognized by Barabasi (2014) and Kim (2014), that communities can also form around a specific cause. In this case, the shared experience of displacement and the search for safety and belonging brought them together to form a unique and resilient community amidst challenging circumstances.

Especially in Serbia, such a concentration of refugees brought together their shared pain and traumas, which were further exacerbated by a set of institutional voids resulting from the collapse of the former Yugoslavia. Collectively, these factors generated a lack of representation and, consequently, further exclusion of post-Yugoslav refugees from the local society in Serbia. Apart from already mentioned UN economic sanctions introduced as a response to Serbia and Montenegro's intervention in conflicts in Croatia and Bosnia, these institutional voids contributed to increasing activities of the local criminal groups and rapid inflation. One of my conversers, who also became a refugee as a teenager recalls this experience.

> Living as a refugee in Serbia for four years was devastating experience. There were sanctions, poverty, criminals and nationalism everywhere…, and in all that, I felt as …an alien. Neither had I shared with them their feeling of 'Serbness', nor I was at home. I was a refugee, I did not come there willingly, and still I shared a punishment with them. A punishment for the deeds of Serbian politicians towards Bosnia, one of the things that forced me to leave my home. It was absurd, but a reality (personal communication, May 2014).

As a consequence, by 1994, a significant number of refugees from Bosnia and Herzegovina, using Alioua's (2014) concept, had de-re-territorialized to countries with better capacities for accommodating and integrating refugees. The effects of economic sanctions also contributed to displacement and emigration from the Balkans, affecting the populations of Serbia and Montenegro between 1992 and 2000. As a result, these two republics mainly became places of emigration and transit migrations. Due to the UN sanctions, there were no flights operating from either Serbia or Montenegro. However, several privately-owned air transport companies emerged to replace the sanctioned national air company Yugoslav Airlines (known as JAT), offering flights from international airports in neighboring Hungary, Romania, and Bulgaria, along with transfer buses from Belgrade's square, Slavija. Over time, as more people were leaving and more friends and relatives came to see them off, this square became a symbol of emigration and parting, capturing the emotional impact of the mass migrations from the region. The motives to stay or leave were highly personalized and contextually driven, making it challenging to establish any particular rule to distinguish among displaced former Yugoslavs who settled across former Yugoslav republics and those who chose to leave for other destinations. Still, a considerable number of Bosnian and Croatian refugees settled in Serbia, and some smaller number of Bosnian refugees in Croatia. They integrated with the locals, however gradually. As one of my conversers told me,

> For twenty years, Bosnians mostly surrounded me. We could understand each other better as we shared some pre-war backgrounds and problems that we encountered here as refugees.... So all my closest friends and my ex-husband — all are from Bosnia. We continued speaking in Bosnian dialect....The situation in Serbia itself was horrible when we came here, therefore, I cannot blame locals for anything. They provided the best reception that they could. ... Then, after I divorced, I changed the circle of people significantly. Now most of my friends are locals, or from Serbia more broadly, and since I spend the most of time with them I switched to Serbian — *ekavski* – dialect (personal communication, November 2022).

This integration path also influenced not only linguistic transformations, but also sense of loyalty to the surrounding community replicated in the sense of national identity for my converser.

> When I came here, I undoubtedly considered myself a Yugoslav. However, since even the Federal Yugoslavia ceased to exist in the early 2000s, I somehow started to consider myself Serbian. To me it does not matter, whether people around me are ethnically different. To me being Serb and Serbian

means sharing the state, and that means sharing the destiny. Ethnic belonging is rather individual. For example, I learned some time ago that my origins are Greek. I am an ancestor of Greeks, who were traders and travelled the Balkans. I was pleased to learn about it, but these origins do not affect my everyday life. On the contrary, the place, state where I live, and the people who surround do affect my everyday life (personal communication, November 2022).

The striking features that I initially noted by analyzing narratives of Bosnian and Croatian refugees in Serbia were silencing the disadvantages of the refugee status, justifying locals' negative reactions to their arrival, and emphasizing commonalities with the locals as advantages. Though found in a different context—featuring Romanian and Hungarian immigrants in the UK after the EU eastern enlargement—Fox, Morosanu et al. (2014) referred to this phenomenon as migrants' 'denying discrimination', namely silencing legal and cultural disadvantages of migrant status, and emphasizing common 'race' with the locals. This usually unconscious coping mechanism proved to become successful 'soft'—psychological and to a large extent political resilience.

Furthermore, some refugees spend several months in several countries before settling for the long term. The testimony of one of my acquaintances vividly illustrates relatively typical migration path of most refugees from Bosnia and Croatia.

At the time of the outbreak of the war in Bosnia, my older child was ten and my younger one was only two. My husband could not leave, as men were supposed to defend the city and the newly independent Bosnia. Therefore, I took kids, and we went to Belgrade first—Yugoslav army was evacuating women and kids from Bosnia. We stayed in Belgrade with my relatives for several weeks. Other refugees from Bosnia and Croatia overcrowded it. I realized that staying longer in Belgrade is not an option as the social and economic situation there was also close to catastrophe. So we moved further to Italy. My cousin is married to Italian, and they have a large house…, thus, they could accommodate us. …In the meantime, the connections with Bosnia collapsed due to bombing, and I had no idea whether my husband and my parents are alive at all. Luckily, after couple of months, I received a call from Germany—it was my husband. He managed to escape from Bosnia to his cousin, who already lived in Germany. He could not leave Germany, so we moved there to join him. Soon after our arrival, he found a job, and we settled in Germany (personal communication, January 2000).

Likewise, as the war prolonged, a growing number of young refugees and their local peers chose to emigrate further abroad from the remnants of Yugoslavia, with the small exception of Slovenia, which remained relatively calm and socioeconomically stable during the turbulent period. Those, who reached the age of 18, spontaneously formed small groups searching for jobs and accommodations abroad. They were learning about the possibilities and choosing available options to emigrate. In this way, some of my slightly older cousins and peers jointly moved to London, Prague, or Copenhagen just to name few relatively frequent destinations.

Many of the refugees eventually settled in foreign countries long after the war ended, and some chose to make these destinations their permanent homes. Notably, in places like Great Britain and the Czech Republic, many of them expressed that they integrated relatively smoothly into the local communities. In the case of the Czech Republic, according to them, relatively smooth social integration was facilitated by the similarity between their native language and the Czech language. Additionally, the physical resemblance between the refugees and the Czechs played a role in their seamless integration (personal conversation, May 2008). Similar to Bosnian and Croatian refugees in Serbia, my post-Yugoslav conversers, who moved to the Czech Republic usually portrayed commonalities between Czechs and former Yugoslavs as advantages in their integration process. Significantly, these usually were conversers, who moved as adults. Overemphasizing advantages of similarities—again resembling the 'denying discrimination' argument made by Fox, Morosanu et al. (2014)—seemed to be major soft resilience for these post-Yugoslav emigrants. On the contrary, those, who moved as teenagers and young adults usually openly talked about the legal obstacles that they encountered in the Czech Republic (personal communication, 2001; 2010; social media discussion, 2010). For most vulnerable among them this claim of structural discrimination constituted their tangible, in this case legal resilience. Some of them also noted differences in mentality between them and the Czech youngsters, portraying themselves as "less fortunate, but more capable" than their local peers (personal communication, September 2010). At the same time, such 'voicing' against structural discrimination suggests the emergence of certain degree of loyalty of coercion towards the host country.

Similarly, in Great Britain, some of the refugees noted that they integrated well due to their relatively proficient English-speaking abilities prior to immigration. Moreover, they also tend to mention the presence of many other foreigners, particularly among Indian and Pakistani communities, made the refugees feel less like outsiders (personal conversation, June 2001). This implicit note of 'Europeness' and 'whiteness' among my post-Yugoslav conversers coincides with much newer experiences of Romanian and Hungarian immigrants in the Great Britain, in which denying discrimination turns into better integration strategy than claiming it (Fox, Morosanu et al., 2014). Equally, for my former Yugoslav conversers residing in the Great Britain, this often-unconscious strategy turned into the psychological and later political resilience.

Furthermore, in addition to long-term emigration, seasonal work in more prosperous European countries remained a crucial source of socioeconomic resilience for many individuals from the affected regions. The opportunity for seasonal work allowed them to support themselves and their families during challenging times.

> The short-time unplanned migrations for seasonal work across Europe were among major strategies for survival. It was equally important and paralleled with social networks, which helped to find jobs. All social networks were already existing, and most of people were very sympathetic towards us, they were emphatic towards us too. Their empathy helped a lot (online communication, March 2023).

Some of these social networks were established through professional and family links in the newly independent countries of the USSR, primarily in Russia, Ukraine, and Moldova. Many professionals temporarily relocated to these countries by joining former Yugoslav engineering and construction companies, with the intention of sending remittances back to their families and relatives residing in calmer parts of the war-torn homeland. However, as the conflict persisted and the situation became more uncertain, an increasing number of these professionals decided to relocate permanently, especially when major breadwinners made the decision to leave their home country for better opportunities and safety.

> When I realized that the war would last long, I started to search for the place to live with secure income and without bothering relatives. It turned that my husband also succeed to escape from Sarajevo relatively safely. We called it *izaci iz Sarajeva* 'went out from Sarajevo' because it was under siege... For him staying in Serbia was dangerous because they tried to mobilize all male adults, especially refugees, and to send them to Bosnia and Croatia frontlines as soldiers. Luckily, through his colleagues, he found a job in Russia's Black Sea coast, so we moved there as a family. The salary-based job was the direction where to go and how to organize the source of income (online communication, March 2022).

As a result, emigration not only represented individual responses to the challenges posed by the collapse and war but also served as a form of hard resilience and a socioeconomic strategy. The majority chose the 'beaten' but, in terms of social mobility, downward path of refugees in Western Europe and Northern America. Others tried to continue their professional careers by working in other post-socialist countries and sometimes in decolonized third-world countries, where their qualifications continued to provide them with at least the same levels of social status as they had before the collapse.

Emergence of Post-Yugoslav Migrant Communities and Their Resilience Away from Homeland(s)

The majority of initially post-Yugoslav refugees left the former republics of Yugoslavia to go further, mostly to Western Europe — Germany, Austria, and Switzerland — where some members of their families or friends had previously worked as guest workers. Table 4.2 below demonstrates approximate numbers of post-Yugoslav emigrants, and Table 4.3 represents redistribution of refugees from Bosnia and Herzegovina and Croatia in most frequent countries of acceptance.

Table 4.2: Emigrants from former Yugoslavia in the 1996 – 2000

Year	1996	1997	1998	1999	2000
Number of emigrants	1,473,834	1,382,640	1,263,333	1,261, 800	1,051,829

Source: UNHCR 2006 Annual Statistics

Table 4.3: Refugees and asylum seekers from Bosnia and Herzegovina and Croatia 1996-2000 Bosnia-and-Herzegovina/ Number of refugees in host country

Bosnia-and-Herzegovina/ Number of refugees in host country	1996	1997	1998	1999	2000
USA	31,656	53,082	82, 137	97,504	106,410
Germany	332,246	247,348	101,533	51,755	31,638
Netherlands	22,042	23,675	23,833	23,969	24,229
Switzerland	6,413	12,397	7,745	8,800	9,268
France	178	250	294	286	329
Sweden	262	742	1,331	486	4,244
Other	357,033	278,678	232,437	223,876	150,285
Total	749,830	616, 172	449,310	406,676	326,403
Croatia/ Number of refugees in host country					
Germany	408	565	287	107	62
Sweden	1,057	2,114	2,888	2,873	2,949
USA	211	264	298	1,949	4,927
Ireland	1	3	1	2	56
France	15	13	17	33	23
Switzerland	28	27	109	101	31
Other	12,088	14,085	61,696	11,179	12,915
Total	13,808	17,071	65,296	16,244	20,963

Source: UNHCR 2006 Annual Statistics

During the 1990s, due to extensive networks of guest workers and geographical proximity, post-Yugoslav migrants came in large numbers to Austria, mostly to Vienna and Graz. These were predominantly refugees from Croatia and Bosnia and Herzegovina. As the immigration system in Austria at the time was based on the *jus sanguinis* principle — citizenship based on cultural or ethnic origins, thus highly restricted to non-German immigrants (Tepavcevic, 2023), the wave of post-Yugoslav immigrants encountered numerous legal obstacles in integration.

> The largest obstacle that I encountered in the process of integration in Austria was related to the documents. All residence permits were relatively short-term, and I spent all time apart from the work to collect it for me and for the kids. Getting permanent residence was a huge relief (personal communication, April 2023).

On the other hand, as migrant inflows in Austria remained significant and as the programs for integration were gradually developed, kinship-based communities, and culture-based-communities of migrants emerged and through shared immigrant integration interests, experiences and cooperation integrated into parallel multicultural society. Particularly, in largest Austrian cities, Vienna and Graz, this wave of post-Yugoslav migrant communities became very visible through a large number of fast-food restaurants and products shops usually titled either after their owners' hometowns and regions, or after the traditional food that they offer.

Similar to Austria, newly reunified Germany also experienced significant post-Yugoslav chain migration inflows, which led to post-Yugoslav immigrants becoming the second-largest immigrant group after Turks in the country.

> My parents worked in Germany when I was a child, so I grew up with my grandparents and saw my parents once in three months. When the war started, the parents evacuated me and took me with them to Germany. In Germany I went to school, I made friends among other foreigners, less so with Germans. Initially, these were mostly Croatians from Bosnia, but then the circle included all Bosnians and all Croats. … I never became as close with my parents as I was with my grandparents. The fact that my grandparents stayed in Bosnia was very hard for me, I worried for them all the time (personal communication, July 2021).

For those refugees whose origins turned out to be 'multiethnic,' neither integration via dividing and emerging as separate post-Yugoslav migrant communities, nor integration into local German communities was a straightforward option. In this sense, they found themselves in a similar situation as most newcomers and people of foreign origins in Austria. The complexity of their backgrounds and identities presented unique challenges and required a more nuanced approach to integration within the host society.

On the one hand I felt lonely and lost because I did not know anyone. I dis-
liked Germany at first because of the weather that was much colder than in
Yugoslavia. Then, I tried to make friends among fellow Yugoslav, who also
came as refugees and were numerous in Germany. However, they all divided briefly and joined their 'national boxes', even with schools. They divided former Yugoslav schools into Croatian, Bosnian, and Serbian once. I
never related myself to only one of these 'national' groups; I was raised differently, thus, my integration went through the local public school, attended
by many other immigrant students. Most of my friends turned to be immigrants from other post-socialist countries and, less frequently, local Germans (personal communication, July 2000).

Despite the war, many representatives of post-Yugoslav refugees in Germany in the 1990s resembled their Yugo-Schwab predecessors in their perceptions of Germany as temporary destination.

After escaping Bosnia, I found myself in Germany among Bosnian Croats.
We received there the state's support as refugees, and it was enough to survive. I learned German. I could not work, because I was still underage. Mom
worked some part-time, but she also spent time mostly with fellow Croatian
Bosnian women talking about the tragedy that we went through. ... When
the war was finally over, the German government promised 10000 DM to
each Bosnian, who decides to return to Bosnia. I saw it as an opportunity to
get easy initial capital form my small business in Bosnia. Before the war, my
parents held a small retail shop, and I wanted to open a café for the locals in
my town. I took the grant from the German government and went back to
Bosnia (personal communication, July 2017).

As this narrative suggests, despite the war and exclusions in
countries of origin, many post-Yugoslav refuges retained inertial
loyalty to their home places, not lastly because they never felt included in mainstream societies of receiving countries. Following
Austria and Germany, because of the wars of Yugoslavia's dissolution Switzerland encountered significant numbers of post-Yugoslav immigrants, also mostly through family reunion, which also
confirms propositions about chain migrations and also about predetermined emergence of post-Yugoslav migrant communities in
these countries (Barabasi, 2014; Castles, Haas et al., 2019). By 2005,
the number of immigrants from the former Yugoslavia, including
Serbia and Montenegro, Croatia, Bosnia-Herzegovina, Macedonia,
Slovenia, as well as Kosovo, amounted to approximately 370,000
people (Jorio, 2005). Although respected in the past for being hard
workers, their image in Switzerland has worsened because of a

small minority, which had been involved in crime and violence (personal communication, January 2018). As a result, taken as a single group, people from former Yugoslavia represent the largest immigrant group in Switzerland (Jorio, 2005). Most of them have been naturalized and largest communities are concentrated in areas of Zurich and Basel (personal communication, July 2016). Several smaller communities were concentrated in Geneva area, and these are small business owners, staff of the higher education institutions, and staff in hospitality industry (personal communication, July 2003). Personal communication with representatives of the post-Yugoslav communities in Switzerland proved that levels of their integration into the local communities vary from one place to another and heavily depends on the time and pattern of their immigration. While the second generation of migrants has generally experienced better integration, some of my interlocutors mentioned that even they do not completely identify as Swiss and often maintain relatively close connections with people living in their parents' places of origin. Simultaneously, some of these second-generation individuals emphasized that their parents prefer not to return to the former Yugoslavia and instead choose to maintain contact with their places of origin (personal communication, August 1998). Similarly, significant numbers of post-Yugoslavs also migrated to Sweden, Denmark, Great Britain, Spain, Canada, and Australia based on the refugee acceptance quotas system. These countries provided opportunities for resettlement and offered pathways to a new life for many refugees from the former Yugoslavia.

Though relatively small and dispersed across Spain, post-Yugoslav immigrant communities began to emerge as early as 1992. The first of these communities consisted of Yugoslav Jews, mainly descendants of the Spanish Sephardi Jews who were expelled from the town of Lorca by the Spanish Inquisition in the fifteenth century. They found refuge in Bosnia by invitation of the Ottoman Sultan Suleiman the Magnificent. The second type of post-Yugoslav settlers in Spain were mothers with infants and underage children—who arrived in Spain as part of the Kids Embassy program (personal notes, January 1993). The latter were accommodated at the houses of Spanish families.

> First, we were accommodated at small neighboring villages on the Mediter-
> ranean coast. It was so nice, that first month we were very happy. Then we
> started to learn Spanish and to look for some jobs. It turned that in these
> villages it was impossible to find any job. Once we learned Spanish enough
> to be able to work, we moved to the closest larger town (personal commu-
> nication, August 2010).

According to another post-Yugoslav interlocutor who moved to Spain, they learned that the program included an exception from some substantial taxes for those Spanish families who initially accommodated post-Yugoslav refugees (personal communication, January 2018). As the tables above demonstrate, from 1996 to 2000, the overall number of post-Yugoslav emigrants decreased. However, immigration, especially from Bosnia and Herzegovina to certain receiving countries, continued to increase over the same period. In contrast to early post-Yugoslav emigrants who resettled across Europe, the majority of post-Yugoslavs who left for the USA, Canada, and Australia did so either closer to the end of the wars or in their early aftermath. The timing of their emigration coincided with the conclusion of the conflicts or the initial period of recovery and reconstruction in their home countries.

> We understood that there is a real war only by the end of the 1994. We real-
> ized that the city where we lived has changed permanently, that there is no
> way back to the system that we lived in for most of our lives. Thus, we finally
> decided to leave. When we sat to the airplane, I told to myself that I would
> never go back to the Balkans again. And, I did not come by now — it has been
> more than twenty years. … America offered me a new perspective. In Amer-
> ica, I can be godmother to my friend's child even though I come from a Bos-
> nian Muslim family. America has everything that the Balkans will not have
> any time soon, if ever (personal communication, May 2018).

Tragic events in the homelands brought a set of change in loyalty, consequently in identity, and numerous administrative doubts and questions not only to population that resided in remnants of former Yugoslavia at the times of collapse, but also to Yugoslav-era migrants.

> At the time when Yugoslavia collapsed, I studied in the US. The war lasted
> for four years, and my home country disappeared. When the war was over,
> there were several new countries in the place of the previous one, and I had
> to decide the citizen of which of them I should become. Being born and

raised in what became an independent Croatia, I decided that I should become the Croatian citizen (personal communication, February 2018).

Leaving former Yugoslavia for further migrations, many former Yugoslavs did not want only to leave their homeland forever, but also to cut all connections with it. One of my conversers, who like myself was a teenager during the wars of Yugoslavia's dissolution, described her experience of emigration as follows.

> I could not wait to leave the Balkans. I was so sick and tired of nationalism, regional-based, dialect-based, and religion-based discrimination and poor social conditions. I really wanted to quit with my past from the day one when I arrived to Canada. I already spoke fluent English, and I planned to stop speaking Serbo-Croatian once and forever. In such decisive mood, I came the first day to my Canadian school. I sat in the class and looked around. One Asian-looking boy was running while another European-looking one was running after him swearing in Serbo-Croatian: "*dolazi ovamo sunce ti kosooko*" — "Come back you cross-eyed creature". This presence of racist compatriots made me anxious again. My naïve expectations that everything will be simpler in Canada were immediately erased (personal communication, May 2014).

Another converser, a migrant in the US representing post-World-War-II-generation of Yugoslav citizens shared similar disappointment with former compatriots, but more positive perceptions of the receiving country than my peer, who moved to Canada.

> What I feel towards my home country can only be explained as a huge disappointment. It includes both the system and the people. In America, I am a human, a professional, a citizen as anyone else. No ethnic, religious, or any other discrimination. I do my work, I follow the rules and I do not have any problems (personal communication, May 2018).

However, frequent communication with immigrants from former Yugoslavia who relocated to Canada and the USA provided me with insight that most of them, in their receiving countries and localities, formed friendships and communities with fellow post-Yugoslav immigrants. To a large extent, the emergence of these communities echoed the concise description of Bosnian refugees' integration in St. Louis, Missouri, by acclaimed writer and Bosnian immigrant Aleksandar Hemon: "Bosnians, arrived from a country where nothing is like it used to be, build a life like it used to be, in

St. Louis where such life never existed" (Hemon, 2006). This quote aptly captures the unique experience of these refugees in their new homes, as they sought to recreate aspects of their former lives while adapting to entirely new surroundings. While the phenomenon of the community of Bosnians in St. Louis described by Hemon inspired a monograph tellingly subtitled "between the two worlds", other places that received significant numbers of post-Yugoslav migrants simultaneously resemble and differ from St. Louis. Many post-Yugoslav emigrants who relocated as adults knew each other back in pre-war times and translated their habits formed in homelands in new places of residence across the globe (Halilovich, 2013). Their children, who came mostly as young teenagers, initially made new friendships mostly among their other post-Yugoslav peers, and one of my conversers explained:

> Canadians could not imagine, let alone understand what I went through before I came here, and what I miss. How can you explain someone, who saw it only on TV if at all, why you had to leave your home? No way. They all were so nice, so polite, but they had no clue how I felt. The most irritating is when everyone asks you politely "how are you?" It is just a politeness. No one really cares. So many times I want to respond also politely "thank you, I feel miserable", but I always stop myself. Why would I bother them? ... Ours understand me, because they went through similar or even worse troubles. They know what means to be displaced, they know how challenging is to pretend that you are ok, when you are totally down (personal communication, July 1998).

Despite immigrating to Russia, a place vastly different from Canada in terms of formal and informal institutions, my experience of integration closely resonates with the one described by my converser. The experiences of war, escape, being a refugee, and emigration turned into traumatic events for most post-Yugoslav emigrants. As Herman (1997) explains, these experiences represent an unspeakable secret that they try to deflect from, carrying the emotional weight of their past while adapting to their new lives in a foreign land. Similarly, my converser's experience in Canada and my experience in Russia confirm Van Der Kolk's (2015) argument that traumas leave an imprint "on mind, brain, and body," and they fundamentally change not only the way we think and what we think about "but also our very capacity to think" (Van Der Kolk,

2015, p. 33). Therefore, a combination of various factors makes migrants vulnerable, and as a result, most of the early post-Yugoslav emigrants sought meaningful interlocutors and potential friends among their compatriots who shared identical or similar experiences. I discovered similar sentiments among other post-Yugoslav compatriots in Russia as well.

> These Russians think that we came here with a bunch of money because we come from Yugoslavia. They seem to have no clue what is going on in the Balkans, they live in the past, when Yugoslavia was the richest and the most democratic out of socialist countries... I cannot agree with many things that my friends from Serbia and from Croatia think about the war, but otherwise their views and logic are completely clear and close to me, no one else is closer (personal communication, May 2000).

Both of these narratives suggest that most of the first post-Yugoslav emigrants were forced to move, whether due to the war or unbearable socioeconomic conditions in their places of origin. As a result, they emigrated bearing a variety of traumas and feeling vulnerable. Frequently, they felt depressed, which led many of them to keep their distance from the locals, at least during the early stages of immigration. At the same time, these post-Yugoslav migrants differed significantly from their Yugoslav-era compatriots who migrated during Yugoslav times. As noted in Chapter 2, a common feature of Yugoslav-era migrants was the temporality of their migration statuses, as most of them went abroad for several years as either diplomats or, more frequently, as representatives of Yugoslav companies abroad.

> My daughter has never really accepted the US as her permanent home. She waited a summer to go to Yugoslavia; all her close friends were there. She waited for the day to return to Yugoslavia for good. Then the war started, and the return was postponed repeatedly. In turn, she grew up in America, she adapted to it, but she has never liked it. Over the last years, she spends more and more time in the Balkans (personal communication, July 2017).

Similar situations appeared between Yugoslav-era migrants and post-Yugoslav migrants in early post-Soviet Russia. As described in Chapter 2, the former resided in Moscow's special residential buildings for foreigners and were relatively wealthy. Their children attended the same weekend school at the Yugoslav Embassy. However, they viewed Moscow as their temporary residence. "Those who came earlier live in the past; they haven't realized yet that Yugoslavia is not what it used to be. They are arrogant towards the Russians, and their jokes are outdated" (personal notes, March 1995). Thus, traumatic shared experiences constituted in the words of Barabasi (2014), a specific cause for emerging post-Yugoslav migrant communities forming them as an informal hybrid-nation.

Left without jobs and homes due to the state's collapse, most of post-Yugoslavs, who moved elsewhere across post-socialist Europe, such as the Czech Republic, Hungary and Russia did it during the first two years of wars.

> After nights spent in Prague's night trams, which were the only warm places to sleep, we finally collected some money and rented the flat. The flat was small and empty, without any furniture, but it was warm and pleasant to have some kind of a home again, and much better than sleeping in night trams. My friend (name) went out to buy some food. In thirty minutes, she returned with a liter of milk, kilogram of apples, kilogram of bananas, and the blender. She starved for a milk shake (personal communication, January 2000).

This short episode of the life of teenage refugees from Bosnia in the Czech Republic during the war illustrates a striking attempt to 'return to normal' pre-war life in a new space, or an attempt at self-reinclusion into mainstream society. This represents one of two opposite forms of soft resilience—an attempt to revert to the old normal or to embrace change entirely. Apart from Prague, as some of the citations from my personal communication suggest, larger post-Yugoslav communities in the former socialist bloc European countries emerged in Moscow. Smaller communities also emerged in Russia's Black Sea resort city Sochi, the Ukrainian industrial city Dnepropetrovsk, and even in Siberian Tyumen. Many former representatives of the Yugoslav (turning Slovenian, Bosnian, Serbian, Croatian and Macedonian) construction and engineering state-owned companies that had contracts in the Soviet Union and Czechoslovakia privatized or sold the representative offices and their belongings (cars and technical equipment). Further, they used the existing contacts in the host countries to resign contracts as privately owned companies. As many of these former representatives and newly emerged entrepreneurs found themselves in similar circumstances—unable to return to their home country due to wars but having established connections in the host countries, including informal networks and grey market business schemes—they continued their existing cooperation and friendships. As the conflicts in Yugoslavia continued and escalated, these small post-Yugoslav entrepreneurial communities grew by welcoming their former colleagues, who were escaping conflicts in Yugoslavia in increasing numbers. Still, Yugoslav-era migrants played certain roles in the adaptation and integration of post-Yugoslav immigrants.

> There was someone who gave me the contacts of some Yugoslav, who were already there and who spoke Russian too. I contacted him and he helped us to enroll the kids to the school. His kids were already enrolled to that school. I think that he also was the one who helped us to find the Russian language teacher for the kids and for us. Because knowledge of the local language was essential for the school (online communication, March 2023).

Simultaneously, numerous post-Soviet citizens found themselves in relatively similar situations as post-Yugoslav migrants.

> I was offered the job in Moscow. I was told that the job is related to my profession—I am a chemist, engineer. However, the job turned to be trade-related: I was a small Yugoslav company representative in Moscow. It was no salary-based job, but the one based on the percentage of sales. The company traded lemon acid and clothes—everything at the same time. Therefore, the trade of lemon acid was the closest link to my profession as a chemist. … I was lucky to meet the secretary in the company where my husband worked. She was also a refugee like me, but from Baku, from Azerbaijan. She was native in Russian and could speak quite some our language, and she also needed an extra job. As a result, we traded the clothes together and shared the profits. Once we gave to "realization" large amount of clothes to one shop and we signed the contract—everyone was so truthful, so nice, though it was risky job, and they paid as they were selling. I did not speak a word of Russian, but I tried so hard, and once you have no other choice, you learn as you work. It was learning by doing (online communication, March 2023).

This testimony suggests that even people from remote geographies and different cultures, but with similar traumatic experiences and finding themselves in similar situations, naturally became allies. Cooperation with them became one of the building blocks of socioeconomic resilience, leading to a sense of personal loyalty among them.

In the countries remnants of the former Soviet Union, Yugoslav engineers involved in construction and other infrastructural projects gained a positive professional reputation during the Cold War. In the early post-Soviet years, they continued to capitalize on this popularity by developing their own enterprises. These communities consisted of former Yugoslav citizens from all across Yugoslavia, including Kosovo Albanians. With the dissolution of the country, post-Yugoslav republics gradually started to build diplomatic relations with their post-Soviet counterparts. Nevertheless, until approximately 2008, these communities remained post-Yugoslav in essence: they visited the same public spaces, including restaurants, where adults usually were meeting, and nightclubs, where post-Yugoslav youth usually visited and socialized. For example, most of them continued to have Sunday family lunches in former Yugoslav Trade Representative Office restaurant in the *Mąsfil'movskaya* street. The excerption from one of my occasional conversations with fellow post-Yugoslav immigrants in Russia vibrantly depicts the difference in perceptions among Croats who lived in post-Yugoslav Croatia and post-Yugoslav Croats immigrants in Russia.

> The last time I traveled to Zagreb, in the restaurant I ordered *Karadjordjeva* stake, as it was referred in Yugoslavia titled after a Serbian prince. They looked at me as to the public enemy number one—now in Croatia the title is changed to a '*Zagreb* stake' (personal communication, June 2005).

A significant post-Yugoslav contribution to the emerging post-Soviet market in Moscow was evident through the first signs of the entertainment industry. Post-Yugoslavs, mostly Serbs, who had fled from Belgrade under the Milosevic's regime and Western-induced economic sanctions, played a major role as founders and promoters of the first Moscow nightclubs. In the early 1990s, one of these clubs was named "011," after Belgrade's telephone code, and was located on Moscow's internal Garden Ring, with a restaurant of the same title situated in the neighboring quarter. Similarly, the

"Jazz club," established in the early 1998, was located in close vicinity to the Tretyakovskaya Gallery.

By approximately 2013, the group of post-Yugoslavs had become the most important organizers and promoters of Moscow's elite nightclubs, including series named after the four seasons, such as Zima (winter) and Lyeto (summer), and Dyagilyev, all located in top locations in downtown Moscow. My own experience of coming to Moscow as a post-Yugoslav migrant in the beginning was characterized by a weekly routine.

I was preparing for my exams to finish school and get into university. I spent most of my time in the international library. On Sundays, my father and I went to a telecommunication company located on Novy Arbat Street to talk via radio amateurs with my grandparents, who were in besieged Sarajevo. As soon as I entered the university, I started working for an international radio, and my grandparents could listen. When organizing some special issues, I read my poems, which were about Yugoslavia's nature and the ways it was destroyed during the war, and about Sarajevo before and during the war. They listened together with their neighbors, and these listening sessions proved to be a crucial element of their collective soft resilience to the challenges posed by the war and siege. This possibility to inform and entertain my grandparents remotely, at a time when there was no internet, provided me with some comfort and compensation for my inability to rescue them from the siege. As a result, my student job as a radio reporter and presenter became a simultaneous source of tangible and soft resilience: the former in the form of a small but stable income, and the latter through the awareness that my work helped my grandparents and their neighbors feel important and engaged, even while living under suboptimal conditions. Therefore, while wars across the former Yugoslav territory prompted processes of exclusion, division, and discrimination, and generated new identities for smaller nations and states, in Moscow, post-Yugoslav migrants naturally composed the Yugoslav immigrant community by default. This made them different from emerging nation-state communities in the republics-remnants of former Yugoslavia, reinforcing the notion of 'former', keenly noted by Kovacevic-Bielicki (2017). At the same time, many of my acquaintances, who emigrated during the war elsewhere to Austria and Germany, also noticed quite clear divisions between themselves, and Yugoslav-time guest workers, so-called Yugo-Schwabs.

> Those *nashi*—ours still consider that they are temporarily here, and when they go to the Balkans, they say that they go 'home'. We, who came here during the war, from the very beginning realized that there is no a way back, and that this is our only home. We go for a holiday to the Balkans, but we return home to Austria. They do not take much care of their homes here, as they consider them temporary accommodations, though they live here for the most of their lifetime. In contrast, we are the part of the Austrian society (personal communication, October 2021).

Therefore, while in some receiving countries, such as Austria, Germany, and Switzerland, the Yugoslavia-time hybrid-nation, which—in contrast to local hybrid-culture communities found, for example in the Vojvodina and Transylvania (Agardi, 2022; Schwartz, 2018)—was essentially a transmigrant community, was numerous, in other countries, it was much smaller but still visibly different from the wartime post-Yugoslav emigrants. In essence, these two types of migrant communities differed only in their loyalty to the homeland and host country: the Yugo-Schwabs or Yugo-slavia-time hybrid-nation continued to be loyal to their country of origin because they did not experience its collapse directly. Their loyalty, therefore, has been inertial. The later—wartime post-Yugo-slav emigrants, who experienced this collapse directly, have displayed a coercive form of loyalty to their host countries. Therefore, they felt different as a more numerous class, distinct by traumatic experiences and views, from both Yugoslav-era migrants and locals. As a result, if Yugoslav-era migrants formed hybrid-like-nation communities based on their geographical origin, common culture and common citizenship, post-Yugoslav migrant communities formed hybrid-sub-nations based on shared or similar traumatic experiences and close but not entirely shared geographical and cultural origins. However, several expressed their loyalty of commitment to their host countries, most frequently among those who emigrated to the US after the wars of dissolution and because of being included in the mainstream society. These principles were emerging unconsciously during the processes of emigration and integration, constituting the foundation of their soft resilience—both psychological and cultural. These post-Yugoslav communities remained mostly informal networks of people linked by similar experiences, which played a crucial role in their ability to cope with challenges and adapt to new environments.

> Of course, I have many former Yugoslav friends here, but they rarely get along with *nashi* of other 'ethnic' groups. I and my small group of friends are rather an exception, as there are Serbs and Bosniaks and Croats among us. However, in Austria it is very rare (personal communication, October 2021).

Therefore, following Mijic's (2019) argument that post-Yugoslav migrants in Austria form rather 'ethnically' homogenous migrant communities, these post-Yugoslav 'ethnic' groups represent the second type of hybrid-sub-nation. They are based on common origin and shared experiences, making them equally distinct from both Yugoslav-era migrants and their co-ethnics who stayed in the homeland. These groups are usually joined by Yugoslav-time state-corporate migrants and diplomats, and they often become initiators and organizers of the embassies of the emerging post-Yugoslav states (personal notes, November 1996; personal communication, July 2022). In summary, with the exceptions of Germany, Switzerland, and Austria, which were often prompted by the existence of Yugoslav guest-worker communities in these countries, the emergence of post-Yugoslav communities was determined by the need and readiness of the receiving countries to accept a certain number of refugees based on the availability of financial and accommodation resources. Initially, post-Yugoslav migrant communities either appeared as different emigration-motive-based extensions of Yugoslav guest-worker-based communities in continental Europe or as emerging shared-traumatic-experience-based communities elsewhere. Nevertheless, these early post-Yugoslav migrant communities formed as distinct from their Yugoslav-era predecessors in their perception of the receiving country as their new and only home. In some places in Austria, the US, and Australia, by the mid-2010s some of these communities formed some of the diaspora's features such as local and transnational compatriots' organizations. The types of post-Yugoslav migrant communities found and conceptualized throughout the present analysis are demonstrated in Table 4.4 below.

Table 4.4: Situating post-Yugoslav migrant communities in existing theoretical framework

Type	Foundation—Community ties	Characteristics
Benchmark type—Diasporic communities	common origins (either historical, cultural, or geographical) and common place of permanent residence = loyalty to origins and host country	organizational infrastructure, sustained participation in other diasporic networks around the world, the presence of two or more generations in a host country, and permanency in settlement and employment
Ethnic hybrid-sub-nations—Example: Bosnians	common ethnic/cultural origins and war and trauma as common motive for emigration—loyalty to similar migrants and host country = loyalty of coercion and commitment	Emerging and sustained participation in diasporic networks, initiating and organizing embassies
Benchmark type—Migrant communities	foreign origins and common place of temporary residence—loyalty to similar migrants	unstable, transient, and unincorporated
Hybrid-sub-nations—example: post-Yugoslavs	war trauma as motive for emigration and uncertainty in integration—loyalty to similar migrants = inertial loyalty of convenience	transient
Benchmark type—Transmigrants—Hybrid nations—example: Yugo-Schwabs	common country-of-origin, common country of destination—inertial loyalty to 'phantom' country-of-origin	immigrants who live their lives across national borders, participating in the daily life and political processes of two or more nation-states

In all cases, post-Yugoslav migrant communities emerged as a mean of soft resilience in response to emotional vulnerability generated by war and displacement traumas.

On the other hand, these traumas provided a firm foundation of soft resilience in the form of understanding and decisiveness that they would not return to their homelands. As a result, their loyalty to host societies and systems, along with their determination to adapt to and integrate into their new places of residence, became evident.

Emergence of Post-Soviet Migrant Communities and Their Resilience in Emigration

Due to either separate or parallel loss of employment and changes in legal statuses from equal citizens to minorities, as demonstrated in the previous Chapter 3, the collapse of the Soviet Union intensified migrations between former Soviet republics. Along with ethnic emigration flows to Israel, Germany, and the USA that characterized the late Soviet period (Remennick, 2012), post-Soviet migrant communities emerged across the post-Soviet states. These communities represented the continuation of the Soviet-era popular trend of relocation to the capitals of the Soviet republics, most notably to Moscow due to the more accessible higher quality of education, employment, medical services, and overall social security. Thus, in the early post-Soviet period, these ethnic and regional migrant communities grew through chain migration and firmly established themselves in Moscow, with a lesser presence in St. Petersburg and the neighboring regions.

> My mom is Russian-speaking, she grew up in Russia. I went to a Russian school, and the University was also in Russian ... we did not learn much about the Armenian culture. It was the Soviet Union when I studied, and there was a Russian school, Russian language, Russian literature, everything was Russian. We learned about Armenian history, about the history of ancient Armenia, and that was it. ...Thus, I am a Soviet, neither Russian, nor Armenian (personal communication, December 2019).

Simultaneously, an implicit message from this narrative provides an explanation as to why post-Soviet migrants tend to constantly refer to the Soviet era: it is more inclusive than the ethnic aspect of their identities, and thus, it is perceived as more important to them. Additionally, as mentioned in Chapter 3, the majority of Armenia's population continued to perceive Russia as a guarantor of Armenia's security, and this loyalty extends coercively to Russia among most of them. By default, they also perceive Russia as a safe destination for relocation, while Armenian migrant communities remain a major source of communication and social resilience.

> I worked in Moscow for a while, and I have been many times to Los Angeles. In both places, I felt at home because all the time there I spent mostly with Armenians. Armenian diaspora is huge both in Moscow and in Los Angeles. Most of my friends now live either in Los Angeles or in Moscow, fewer stayed in Armenia (personal communication, January 2020).

As the narrative of my converser suggests, Armenian migrant communities display features of both ethnic diasporas and transmigrants. Despite constituting a physical 'exit' from the place of residence, this migration, considering Hirschman's (1970) framework, in practice was a form of 'voice' against the change and loyalty to the previous system. Therefore, this migration represented a simultaneous expression of 'voice' and 'exit' in the search for socioeconomic resilience. For some of my other interlocutors, a clear 'exit' was prompted by a combination of negative factors in their home country and intervening personal factors, as Lee (1966) put it in his emigration analytical framework. At the same time, many post-Soviet citizens continued to relocate across post-Soviet republics in an equally desperate and unsuccessful search for a new home.

> Coming from Uzbekistan to Russia, we could not get the citizenship and sustainable employment there, so we moved to Ukraine, where I originally come from and where I had an extended family. ... The situation in Ukraine proved even more complex than in Russia... I started to knock on the doors of many European embassies in Kiev asking for an asylum ... After being rejected by several of them, I sat on the bench in a park and started to cry. A young man approached me and asked have I been rejected the visa, and maybe he can help me, and he offered his help in applying for the asylum in Hungary. That is how in the summer 2005 we emigrated and received a refugee status in Hungary (online communication, April 2020).

As this narrative suggests, after the collapse of the USSR, many of my interlocutors initially envisioned settling in one of the former Soviet republics. However, emigration from the former USSR — Hirschman's (1970) initial 'exit' option — appeared as the only solution, though not an easily accessible form of survival and resilience. Concurrently, due to their socialist bloc ties and geographical proximity, the countries neighboring the former Soviet republics to the West became popular initial destinations for the emigrants from post-Soviet republics.

> I married a Hungarian woman... she was in Baku once. My initial idea was to live in Baku with her, I had there a job, and I had friends. There was sun, sea, what else one needs in the life? However, when the war started, the mass emigration started from Baku, and my friends all told me that since my wife is a foreigner, it is better for me to live. I thought for quite some time, and I realized that they were right. I ... left to Budapest (personal communication, January 2020).

In addition to the existing socioeconomic hardship that stemmed from the Soviet system and emerging post-Soviet institutional voids, individual motives were also driving emigrations from the former Soviet states. "In 1996... my mom got married for the second time. My dad allowed her to take me with her, and we moved ... Mom's new husband was from Hungary, and we moved there" (personal communication, January 2019). For my interlocutor, who was only eleven when she emigrated, the differences between life-style and customs of home and receiving country appeared as revealing and positive.

> In Hungary, the life is focused on a family and it is organized around the family. The family always has a lunch together, for example. They are very close to each other. That impressed me, that surprised me. ...We are the kids of the Soviet Union, we did not have families at all! That is roughly speaking. We raised ourselves independently, while the parents worked. In Hungary, parents took care of kids, family members were taking care of each other. At the age of my parents, Hungarians were all quite successful. Their kids all had bicycles. To me it looked wow! Every family member had a bicycle! That was really cool. They went on touring! They had many various family-focused programs. That was impressive! (personal communication, January 2019).

In addition to post-Soviet emigrating adults and children, many young people in former Soviet republics perceived the demise of the USSR and politico-economic transformations merely as an unexpected opportunity for their own personal and professional development.

> I was preparing to study in Austria and that was my dream. I had to study for another year in the Russian university to get to the level of German that I needed for studying in Austria. I was studying at the part-time program, and I spent three months of that year in Germany, in Munich (personal communication, February 2020).

As a result, most post-Soviet emigrants, who in the time of collapse were teenagers and in their early twenties perceived their emigration experience as an adventure rather than a mean of survival. Their experiences corroborated Byford and Bronnikova (2018) 'normalization' or 'de-politization' of post-Soviet emigration.

> The most challenging was to organize my life independently. By that moment, my parents were organizing my life, … I learned how to cook and what food to buy to be able to cook. Of course, I did not have money to go to restaurants to eat, so I had to learn to prepare the food for myself. Therefore, I was preoccupied with such kind of my sweet little problems (personal communication, February 2020).

Therefore, post-Soviet citizens' emigration motives ranged from political discrimination and socioeconomic hardship to individual motives such as marriage and opportunities for travel and education abroad.

> I came here, because Austria is a country of music and higher education was free from charge.… I knew only my cousin, who invited me.… In the beginning, I was earning money as a street musician. … I met a wonderful Austrian family, who practically adapted me. I was extremely lucky because they took me to their home and because I could live there peacefully and I did not have to pay flat rents. As a result, I had a possibility to study quietly and to save some money. Therefore, my integration went quite smooth (Tepavcevic, 2021 a, p. 147).

Therefore, during the 1990s, Austria experienced the first large inflow of migrants from the newly independent post-Soviet countries, prompted mostly by socioeconomic instability, exclusion, and increasing institutional voids. The emergence of post-Soviet Russian-speaking migrant communities in Austria was evident through restaurants offering Russian and Caucasian food, magazines published in the Russian language in Vienna, and an increasing number of art schools teaching in Russian. These communities consisted of Chechen refugees, Russian, Ukrainian, and Kazakh students (Tepavcevic, 2020a). When discussing the adaptation and integration, most of my conversers noted that their first points of contact were Soviet citizens, who moved to the same receiving countries earlier.

> There were friends of the friends of the friends of my father. Therefore, my dad agreed with them, that since they had a half-empty house, they accepted me to stay there for the beginning. …They were Jews from the former Soviet Union. They rented the house to the Representative Office of the USSR ….They took me from the airport, they showed me the flat and gave me the keys. …They were adult people like my parents. In the beginning, they were calling me once a week to ask is everything ok, then once a month … Apart from that, I did not have friends as I was very shy. Back then, I saw the possibility to make friends only in the university …My first friend was a girl from Austria… on my own initiative, then that contact somehow disappeared. The second friend of mine was a Russian girl, her dad worked for one of international organizations… she spent here all of her life. We were friends for a very long time, and we had a good friendship, but later our paths divided (personal communication, February 2020).

In this way, early post-Soviet migrations in Austria were individual and spontaneous, suggesting the correctness of the proposition postulating the randomness of migration flows. In contrast to Austria, early post-Soviet immigration to Germany appeared in three major forms. The first form represented a continuation of programs for the immigration of ethnic Germans and Jews from the former Soviet Union as explained by Remennick (2012). Second, and much less known, was the group of post-Soviet, Russian-speaking scientists and innovators. I met a group of these post-Soviet scientists during my dissertation-related fieldwork. All of them owned small and medium enterprises (SMEs) in the science and technology sector in northern Germany, and they were concentrated in several smaller towns in Westphalia and in Hamburg. These technical scientists immigrated to Germany between the mid-1990s and mid-2000s in search of better technical conditions and finances to develop their innovations. By the late 2000s, they had founded the Union of Russian-speaking Entrepreneurs in Germany — ARGUS, and worked under the umbrella of this organization. Some of their projects were successful.

> In 1996, the Russian scientist and entrepreneur Alexandr Filimonov developed a new generation of small airplane models, 'Bella', and unsuccessfully sought Russian financing. As a result, with the help of ARGUS, he expanded his search abroad to Germany, and with Kronstadt GmbH marketing support, obtained 700,000 euro from the European Commission for testing and developing his innovation (Tepavcevic, 2013).

As the example of Bella, a small airplane, suggests, with the marketing support of their fellow post-Soviet Russian-speaking entrepreneurs from small consulting agencies, these innovative companies received financial support from European funds for the development of their innovations and for cooperation between European and post-Soviet scientists. Therefore, particularly this post-Soviet immigrant community in Germany built its socioeconomic and cultural resilience through the commonalities of its members: shared socioeconomic difficulties faced in their newly independent countries of origin, shared native-level use of the Russian language, and shared interest in developing their innovations. At the same time, the lack of support from the Russian state and the subsequent need to emigrate abroad in order to develop innovations turned many owners of small Russian science-based companies into opponents of the Russian authorities, while their loyalty towards Germany and the EU in general grew stronger. Their cooperation and its institutionalization into an official organization is a striking confirmation of the proposition that community ties emerge around a specific cause. Additionally, the example of ARGUS fully embodied Kontos (2003), who pointed out that social capital is linked to a sense of community, also based on examples of immigrant entrepreneurship in Germany in the early 2000s. At the same time, the example of ARGUS confirms an argument made by Aldrich and Zimmer (1986) that strong communication within the immigrant community enhances social capital and creates a pool of resources that can foster business and increase the likelihood of success. At the same time, this simultaneously profession- and common-culture-based migrant community embodies two — connector and corporant — out of eight types of migrant entrepreneurship[3] based on their role in integration of immigrants (Tepavcevic, 2023).

The third group of post-Soviet immigrants emerged between the mid-1990s and mid-2005 in Germany and simultaneously in Switzerland, driven mostly by Russian capital that often came through offshore registered companies based in the Netherlands, Cyprus, and British offshore zones. Particularly in Switzerland, these companies fostered a relatively small post-Soviet community, whose second generation is only beginning to emerge. Until recently, this community has represented business elites and representatives of Russian transnational corporations. Initially coming to Switzerland as employees and representatives of Russian energy corporations to establish joint ventures with EU, mostly German energy companies, these post-Soviet immigrants were bringing their families with them. Their kids attended Swiss schools and universities and integrated into the global cosmopolitan elites that Vailati and Rial (2016) characterized as 'rich migrants'. Coming in small groups of professionals serving particular companies and their partners, these migrants initially came on temporarily contracts. Most of time, they spent working, while their families and spouses connected and organized other activities usually together and in immigrant groups. Usually, main offices of these joint ventures are located in smaller towns. As a result, contrary to mainstream theories of integration postulating that the larger the immigrant community, the less it integrates into the host society, these professionals and their families formed a small immigrant community, mostly focused internally, and with limited contacts with other local inhabitants. One of my random interlocutors described the life and connections of Russian-speaking immigrants in Switzerland as follows.

---

[3]   In my recent study, I found eight types of post-Soviet migrant entrepreneurship based on its role in migrants' integration across three EU countries representing different models of market economies.

Switzerland is a small and very expensive country. For shopping, we always travel either to Germany or to France. Kids cannot move or stay at home alone—without adult's following—until they turn 12, so women usually cannot undertake full-time jobs for a long time, which is the obstacle for women's careers and burden for men as the only bread-winners in a family with kids, That is my situation, and it would be unimaginable if we stayed in Russia.... Apart from us, there are several more post-Soviet Russian-speaking families in this and neighboring towns. We usually socialize with them meeting at someone's home for dinners and gatherings, because restaurants are terribly expensive and they usually offer horrible food... My German is still poor, because at work, I usually use either Russian or English, and the local dialect is very different from the German that we learned at the school. Only kids speak fluent Swiss German (personal communication, January 2018).

Therefore, the identities of these post-Soviet citizens seemed to have three significant components: a corporate component overlapping with their place of origin or nationality, and their place of destination—the local community. Taken together, these three commonalities constituted the ties of the post-Soviet migrant community in Switzerland. They worked either in the same company or in another post-Soviet-founded company and maintained friendships outside of work. In its internal dynamics, this type of immigrant community seems closest to the Yugoslav-era migrant communities in Western Europe and Northern America, which were initially planned as temporary but turned into long-term, if not permanent, due to the breakup of Yugoslavia. Given its introverted character, this community can be conditionally labeled as *mono-culti-corpo-nation*. However, under the pressure of further global crises, this type of migrant community may display the most unstable character.

One of the significant crises that hit post-Soviet countries soon after the collapse of the Soviet Union was the Asian financial crash that occurred in 1998. This crash had a profound impact on many multinational corporations that were making investments in the emerging post-Soviet markets and creating employment opportunities for the post-Soviet population. As a result of the crisis, some of these corporations made the decision to relocate their operations to more stable Central European emerging markets.

> In 1998, there was a financial crisis in Russia, and my mom worked for the manufactory, for an international company. Therefore, when the crisis started, the company transferred her here as an important employee. It was planned as temporary transfer, for one or two years. As a result, we live here more than twenty years. … The only person that we knew was mom's director, who worked in Russia, but he was foreigner, and he was also transferred here as the director of the company's branch. Thus, he was the one, who helped us to move here (personal communication, January 2019).

In turn, citizens of post-Soviet countries not only became part of the emerging global class that Meier (2015) referred to as "migrant professionals," but they also gave rise to what Kovacevic-Bielicki (2017) termed as "1.5 generation immigrants." The emergence and existence of these *corpo-nations* — distinct from earlier discussed *monoculti-corpo-nations* in their multinational and transient character — however, does not mean that existing Soviet-times migration communities did not play any role in integration of the early post-Soviet emigrants in receiving environments.

> I felt as if I came to a very different world as I went to an American school, everything was in English…. The school was very convenient, because the first half a year they did not grade me…. I came to the ninth class—I just continued… There were also other five kids from the USSR, four from Russia and one girl from Ukraine. In the beginning, they were helping me…My circle of friends and people that I communicate with is very international, and not many of them are Hungarians (personal communication, January 2019).

Therefore, early post-Soviet emigrants arrived in post-socialist Central East Europe simultaneously with other MNCs-generated migrations from the West. Consequently, their 'exit' was a part of the corporate collective resilience strategy, and they formed a corponation — a truly multinational, usually geographically transient, temporarily local migrant community consisting of migrant professionals and their families. These *corponations* were indeed formed around a specific cause — corporate expansion — often combined with individual professional careers. In a somewhat predetermined or chain migration fashion, these communities share similarities with ethnic diasporas. However, they differ from diasporas in their multinational character and their typically temporary settlements. In this way, their existence confirms two propositions — one related to chain migrations and the other concerning migration prompted by a long-term specific cause. These two characteristics also distinguish *corporations* from transmigrant communities. Although not entirely predetermined, corporation emerges through the global market dynamics—driven by profit-seeking and common professional interests. This community plays a major role in emigration from the place-of-origin and further migrations shaped by business rationality, but—as some cases analyzed in the concluding chapter demonstrate—also by elementary human security. In sum, based on their role in resilience to the crisis of the Soviet dissolution and its aftermath, three additional types of post-Soviet migrant communities emerged, in addition to the previously recognized diaspora, transmigrant, and migrant communities. One is the institutionalized profession-and-common-culture based community embodied in the post-Soviet scientists-founded ARGUS organization based in Germany. Another is the post-Soviet monoculti-corporation found among representatives of post-Soviet firms in Switzerland. The third, and largest one, is conditionally titled corporations.

Table 4.5 below summarizes the types of post-Soviet migrant communities, making bold the types that were found among post-Soviet migrant communities and positioning them among the previously recognized types of migrant communities.

Table 4.5: Types of post-Soviet migrant communities

Type	Foundation	Characteristics
Benchmark type – Diasporic communities – example among post-Soviet: Armenians	common origins (either historical, cultural, or geographical) and common place of permanent residence – loyalty to historical homeland and co-ethnics – loyalty of commitment	organizational infrastructure, sustained participation in other diasporic networks around the world, the presence of two or more generations in a host country, and permanency in settlement and employment
Ethnic hybrid-sub-nations – Example: (post-) Soviet Jews, (post) Soviet Germans	common ethnic/cultural origins and discrimination as common motive for emigration – loyalty to compatriots and to host country-of-origin = loyalty of coercion and commitment	sustained participation in other diasporic networks, permanency in settlement
Benchmark type – Migrant communities	foreign origins and common place of temporary residence	unstable, transient, unincorporated
Monoculti-corponations	Post-Soviet origins and culture, corporate-interest-driven, and common place of (temporary) residence – loyalty to compatriots in the host country = loyalty of coercion and convenience	Small in size, geographically relatively stable, and unincorporated, potentially highly volatile
Corponations	Professional, corporate interests – loyalty to the employing organization = loyalty of convenience and commitment	Multinational/global, temporally local, constant
Benchmark type – Transmigrants		immigrants who live their lives across national borders, participating in the daily life and political processes of two or more nation-states

Conclusions: Post-Yugoslav and Post-Soviet Migrant Communities and Their Resilience in Emigration Compared

This chapter has shed light on the significance of identity boundaries in the formation of migrant communities, as previously proposed by Kovacevic-Bielicki (2017). The contribution of this chapter is twofold. Firstly, it highlights that identity boundaries in post-Soviet migrant communities are not solely based on 'ethnic', cultural, and geographical factors, but are significantly shaped by shared experiences related to the motives and timing of emigration. These shared experiences play a crucial role in strengthening these identity boundaries even more than the traditional factors. Drawing on the works of Spenser and Darwin, Brooks, Hoberg et al. (2019), the chapter emphasizes that adaptation is the key to survival, and there are two ways to adapt: either returning to the previous pattern or striving to survive and thrive in new circumstances. The chapter shows that post-Soviet migrants, depending on the context in the receiving society, adapt various identity boundaries and form migrant communities to attain soft — psychological, and later tangible — socioeconomic resilience. The loyalty of individuals to these communities arises as a result of the resilience and support that these communities provide during the challenges of emigration and adaptation.

Emigrants from both former Yugoslavia and the former Soviet Union, who migrated during and soon after the dissolution of these two socialist federations appeared different from both their compatriots who left during the Cold War and those of them who continued to reside in the places of origin, or in other post-Soviet republics. The timing and conditions of migrations led to relatively similar experiences for these post-Soviet migrants, creating a shared bond and a common search for sources and ways of resilience. Consequently, these communities evolved into hybrid nations, distinguishing themselves from older socialist-time emigrants, especially in their perception of the homeland as a place they would not return to, and viewing their current place of residence as either a new permanent home or a temporary stopover on the way to another receiving country or destination, distinct from their place of origin.

Post-Yugoslav migrant communities emerged as a transferred form of the previous society into different geographies, depending on the specific receiving localities and host countries. In the countries of Western Europe, they mostly appeared as a geographical extension of the societies in their home countries, experiencing separation and segregation. Thus, they formed separate 'ethnic' communities, dividing the leftovers of Yugoslav or organizing new separate embassies, trade offices and schools. In receiving localities where national diasporas—long-existing national communities—already existed, these post-Yugoslav migrants—forced out of their homes in social, economic, or political way—were initially supported and integrated into these existing diasporas, which reinforced divisions from home. Others, who escaped not only from the physical danger but also trying to avoid these divisions created their small anti-division 'bubbles', and 'circles of friends' mostly among other groups of immigrants, with locals, or the combination of both.

The stronger the community ties, whether socioeconomic, such as working for the same or similar corporations, or through the foundation of joint ventures and migrant entrepreneurship, the greater the socioeconomic resilience experienced by the members of these communities. Soft resilience has been achieved through shared traumatic experiences among post-Yugoslav migrants and through common-culture-based communication and communities among post-Soviet migrants. The remaining chapters of this book will discuss the ways in which the experiences discussed in this and preceding chapters have influenced these communities and their members in the face of further global crises.

PART III

Chapter 5
From Digitalization to Great Recession: Effects on Post-Yugoslav and Post-Soviet Migrations and Resilience

"We lost our country, but we conquered the world. Yugoslavs are now every-where. Well, except in our homeland" (personal communication, January 2007).

"Meanwhile, many of us became the jet-setting, English-language-proficient, smart-phone-wielding, globally nomadic citizens of the twenty-first century" (Budjeryn, 2022, p. 3).

Great Recession and Migrations

Explaining the sources of global financial crisis (GFC) or The Great Recession, economist Ivan Berend (2012) traced it to

the age of globalization, characterized by exceptional increase of three-and-a-half times in trade...Deregulations changed "the rules of the game" and the characteristics of the capitalist market economy. The morals of solid banking, together with trust in institutions, were lost. Gambling replaced a solid business attitude and increased both gains and risks. The boom culminated the first years of the twenty-first century... that make old sectors obsolete and declining, while new sectors, based on new technologies, gradually emerge" (Berend, 2012, pp. 1-2).

Addressing the scope of change in the relationship between the global economic crisis of 2008-2009 and the migrations, Roos and Zaun (2018) found that the crisis had immediate effects on migration patterns in two ways: first, migrants left crisis-stricken countries, and second, they naturalized in non-crisis countries where they had previously settled. They also stopped migrating to formerly attractive countries negatively affected by the crisis. Additionally, whereas before the crisis, the majority of migrants were highly skilled, during the crisis, there was a shift to vulnerable groups such as low-skilled workers and women. Meier (2015) provides a concise description of the impact of the global economic crisis on migrations globally:

> The economic crisis with a heavy rise of unemployment in many countries in southern and eastern Europe led to heavy job losses also for those employed or at least trained as tertiary-educated people and has led to general rise in migration (OECD-UNDESA 2013). Social and economic transformations are spatially unequal and create new spatial settings with new possibilities for the employment of migrant professionals, or in the other case, spatial settings without the former employment possibilities (Meier, 2015, p. 3).

Paralleling these arguments, many studies of migrations suggest that the quantity and quality of migrations depend on the type of crisis. For instance, Castles, Haas et al. (2019) note that when the Great Recession peaked in 2008-2009, scholars of migrations expected large return of migrants from developed to developing countries. However, this expected return did not happen. Instead, immigration to most developed countries only decreased during the peak of these two crises but gradually increased afterwards. However, scholars who focused on particular countries and regions provided a more nuanced picture. For example, discussing effects of GFC on Spain, Prieto-Rosas, Recaño et al. (2018, p. 1885) pointed out that "[R]eturn migration and emigration to an unknown destination increased significantly with respect to interregional mobility at early and late stages of the crisis. In contrast, interregional migration was more likely than international emigration before the first stage". Similarly, exploring migration flows in Poland, Brzozowski and Pedziwiatr (2016, p. 1) noted that

> after 2008, we can observe a decline in the dynamic of departure from the country, symptoms of re-immigration, and a rising number of foreigners deciding on a long-term stay in Poland. For this reason, migration researchers suggest that our country may in the near future experience a "migration reversal".

In addition to these arguments, Joseph Daher (2022) underlined the influence of intervening factors on migration flows during and in the aftermath of the Great Recession focusing on the Middle East and North Africa (MENA) region.

> In the MENA region, states have cut public services, removed subsidies to basic necessities such as food, and privatized state industries, often selling them to businessmen connected to the centers of political power. As a result, all the region's countries are characterized by extreme class inequality, high

rates of poverty, high informality (which strips labor of their protection rights, even if those were limited) and high unemployment, especially among youth. Those with education and valued skills leave for opportunities elsewhere. And, in the case of the Gulf monarchies, the local economy relies on temporary migrant workers who make up the majority of the laboring population and are deprived of political, labor, and civil rights.

The outbreak of popular uprisings in the MENA region in 2011 was, therefore, not simply the result of the 2008 global economic crisis. Certainly, the Great Recession helped trigger them, but the region had deep structural problems compared to the rest of the world. These shortcomings have deepened since then, as the MENA region was declared the most unequal in the world in the World Inequality Report 2022, which stated that the top 10 percent of income share there is equal to 58 percent, compared to 36 percent in Europe (Daher, 2022).

Taking these arguments as macro-level-based propositions about the influence of global financial crisis on global migrations, the present chapter aims to answer the following questions: To what extent and in what ways did global financial crisis affected post-Yugoslav and post-Soviet citizens and migrant communities? To what extent and in what ways did their experiences from previous global crises influence their resilience to global financial crisis? What other challenges did they experience along with the global financial crisis?

Building upon the findings from preceding parts of the present book, the present chapter explores the effects of the Great Depression and the related socioeconomic changes on post-Yugoslav and post-Soviet migrants and citizens. The chapter demonstrates that underpinned by the Great Recession, socioeconomic, environmental, and sociopolitical challenges in former Yugoslav and former Soviet republics combined with the emergence of social media influenced both dynamics of post-Yugoslav and post-Soviet migrant communities and further emigration, rather than the global crisis alone.

The remainder of the chapter proceeds as follows. The next section discusses the emergence of social media and their influence on emigration and resilience of the post-Yugoslav and post-Soviet migrants. Section 3 analyzes the influence of the great recession and the related factors on citizens of post-Yugoslav states and their approach to the resilience through it based on experience with previous global crises. Similarly, Section 4 analyzes influence of the great recession and the related factors on citizens of post-Soviet states and their approaches to resilience considering their experience with the collapse of the USSR. The last section compares resilience in the light of Great Recession and migration paths of post-Yugoslav and post-Soviet citizens.

Emergence of Digital Transnational and Migrant Communities

The development of post-Yugoslav and post-Soviet migrant communities was paralleled with the increasing digitalization of political, business, and social processes. As Palankai (2013, pp. 120-125) correctly noted, "The new information society brings dramatic qualitative changes in terms of social identities... Information technologies give birth to a new society, while challenging all the traditional values of identity, in national, social, or religious terms". While for existing migrant communities, their long-established contacts were a major source of information about possibilities for work abroad, and therefore, socioeconomic resilience in the face of various local, regional, and global challenges, younger generations of post-Yugoslavs and post-Soviets, as well as those who became first-time migrants since the mid-2000s, increasingly relied on new technologies. As a result, the period slightly prior to the Great Recession was marked by the rise of social media and their broad use. They gave a great push not only in connecting global communities. Particularly for post-Yugoslav and post-Soviet migrants, social media has played a crucial role in reestablishing connections lost during the collapses and collapse-prompted migrations. Personally, social media represented the first successful attempt to find and reconnect with many of my school-time friends. All previous attempts to find them, whether via other common friends or in the places of their previous residence, were unsuccessful, demonstrating the devastating effects of the wars on migrations within and from former Yugoslavia. Most importantly, social media created rebonds between, as Kovacevic-Bielicki (2019) put it, "those who stayed, and those who left" and blurred the dividing lines between them.

This is especially visible among citizens of post-Soviet countries, where an entirely different set of social media is used more than the ones usually used in the 'Western' hemisphere. As one of my conversers, an immigrant from Ukraine in Austria, told me, even post-Soviet migrants in Austria use completely different social media than what is typically used among the population of post-Soviet countries.

> When I came here, I had no idea about Facebook, I was mostly in "VKontakte" social network.[4] It surprised me when I realized that here nobody is interested in "VKontakte". I see now that Instagram is also very popular. I was not even registered in any of them (personal communication, February 2020).

One of key outcomes of emergence and widespread use of social media has been that emigration, adaptation, and integration became much easier and faster than they were before.

> I had to register on the Facebook and to learn how it functions. I was looking for a job, and I found the pages, where people publish their job offers. There I also found the people, who discuss topics of their particular interests: some of them were discussing cats, others were discussion dogs; others discussed sightseeing in Vienna, and through them, I got to the people, whose professions are creative. Schools are publishing various information (personal communication, February 2020).

Apart from quick access to contacts, the emergence of social media has provided a possibility for migrant compatriots residing in the same or neighboring countries and cities to easily connect and cooperate in many ways: to organize compatriots' associations, groups of support in integration, and increasingly to find jobs and founding businesses.

Post-Yugoslav Countries in the Dawn of the Great Recession: Returns and Further Migrations

The period between 2000 and 2008, prior to the Great Recession, saw most of the post-Yugoslav republics only starting to recover

---

[4]   the most popular social network in post-Soviet countries, an analogue of Facebook

from the collapse crisis, and their governments were trying to build state institutions, a process known as the transition crisis that other post-socialist European countries experienced throughout the 1990s. As Keil and Stahl (2023) noted,

> the evolving state- and nation-building processes after the violent break-up of Yugoslavia significantly deviated in the post-Yugoslav states, with some countries focusing strongly on portraying themselves as Continental European states (Slovenia and Croatia), while others struggled with the establishment of new statehood (Bosnia and Herzegovina, Kosovo, Serbia, North-Macedonia).

The end of the war, the process of slow recovery and the hope for full recovery and prosperity influenced decision of many post-Yugoslav emigrants to return to their homes.

> People were returning after the war. Especially intellectuals, who left during the Milosevic rule. Djindjic was a positive factor. In 2006, people were returning to re-build the country. And there was enthusiasm. That was very important factor of the country's and my stability (online communication, February 2023).

Apart from positively perceived political changes, for some post-Yugoslav migrants, who left their homes as teenage refugees, personal and professional factors led them back to their home countries. For one of my conversers from Serbia, the return from Russia proved prosperous both socioeconomically and in terms of career.

> I was stable, forceful, the best age, without any fears. I had many interesting jobs, I could use my education to get any job I wanted. In Serbia back then the situation was completely different than now. In these years, three governments changed in Serbia, but it did not affect me in any way. I worked for UN, and I did not feel political instability. I got great job offers and I had great salary (online communication, February 2023).

In the same way, many post-Yugoslav migrants who emigrated when they were children decided to return to the country's remnants of the former Yugoslavia and found their families there, hoping that major crises and wars became a thing of the past. Similarly, tired of being refugees, many Bosnians, mostly Serbs and Croats, who left for neighboring former Yugoslav republics during the war, were returning to Bosnia with similar enthusiasm. One of my acquaintances perceived his return as a certain relief.

> Look, the country is destroyed, obviously, and the people are down, but being back home and being no refugee anymore is such a good feeling. Many of old gang is back together, so we continued where we stopped in 1992 (personal communication, July 1999).

Another converser, who during the war escaped from Bosnia to Croatia, decided to return due to lack of prospects of legal integration in Croatia.

> We spent eight years in Croatia, where we came during the war as refugees. I counted on help of my relatives, who lived in Croatia permanently, but they had enough of their own problems to help me much. My husband and I settled in one of peaceful and relatively cheap areas in Croatia's north. We were taking all available jobs. When our child was born, I tried to get Croatian citizenship, and I was even baptized, but even that was not enough to be granted a citizenship. We became sick and tired of hypocrisy and we went back home to Bosnia (personal communication. January 2008).

Others vividly illustrated that discrimination, which emerged during the war persisted and underpinned with the Constitution, even firmed in post-war Bosnia.

> When I returned from Germany, I immediately went to study. As a result, I received legal higher education in the post-war Bosnia. I also kept small retail shop and a cafe in my town. I was satisfied with my income and I was happy to be back home. I like Bosnia. The only thing that bothered me was continuous divisions on Croats and Bosnians. As a Croat, I appeared as a minority in my town. It was inconvenient, to put it softly, because many war criminals, who by some Bosniaks were perceived as heroes moved to my town and were trying to put forward their criminal rules (personal communication, July 2016).

In the context of such hampered social and political recovery, the Great Recession initially was not much noticed. The effects of it became visible only a couple of years after the peak of the crisis.

> The people started to leave the country around 2010 again. By then they already understood that nothing will be better. With their experience of the collapse, they realized that better system somewhere else is more attractive than home country. Especially intellectuals. People who worked in UN — because they wanted to re-build the institutions. They left because of the wars in the 1990s. There is no stability — there is no system, there is wide-

spread corruption, it is impossible to build the institutions. And people—the intellectuals—simply did not want to be the part of it (online communication, February 2023).

Like Serbia, in Bosnia and Croatia, the effects of the global financial crisis started to feel much after the peak of the crisis.

Since I have children, I realized that we as a family need another source of income. During summers, my wife and I went to Croatia and rented apartments there. Over the winter, I took additional job at the airport customs. As a result, we earned enough (personal communication, August 2018).

In all countries of former Yugoslavia with the exception of Slovenia, and to a smaller extent in Croatia, conflict-related divisions continued to humper the development of formal state institutions based on the rule of law. Combined with the lack of financial resources for reconstruction, the continual institutional voids prompted further emigrations from the region, though in slower pace than during and immediately after the collapse.

I like to be at home, I love Bosnian mountains, I like the city, but it is quite unsafe ever since the war started and ended. Jobs are fewer, short-term and poorly paid. My goal is to defend my MA thesis here and to learn German enough to be able to work in Germany. I joined the program for guest workers in Germany. I will go myself first, and then I will try to bring over the family (personal communication, December 2012).

While the new wave of emigration from the Balkans grew, the period of the Great Recession also sought the most massive return of former Yugoslav migrant communities from the countries of the former Soviet bloc. This return migration wave included migrants representing generations of 1945 – 1965, and 1970 – 1985.

Some projects were postponed because of increasing difficulties with financing them. Payments for some of finished projects were frozen, so the work stalled. As the work slowed down, I felt that I am tired and that I have already worked enough. The kids grew up and became independent, the elderly back in the Balkans needed our support. Thus, I had no more motivation to stay abroad (personal communication, summer 2008).

Depending on the age, financial crisis prompted many post-Yugoslavs on further migration. Older generations to large extent made the decision to return to the Balkans, though not always to their previous places of residence.

> I came to Belgrade in 2007, because it was already hard to find a job in Moscow. That was quite frequent that firms do not pay salaries. One firm was a Croatian one, where my husband worked – it did not pay a salary at all. …Another was a Russian-Serbian firm, where my husband also had a contract, but because of the looming crisis, there was no more work. Therefore, they paid the last salary, and my husband quit. …I already had some pension in Serbia, which I earned long ago as a refugee. When I turned 65, I got also my pension from Bosnia, and we had savings. …As former Yugoslavs, we could receive the citizenship in Serbia, and we could receive the pension, so it was the easiest solution for us to the crisis. … I have continued to work at least one multilevel marketing side jobs, and I still work in this way. I trade the cosmetics, pharmaceutical cosmetics, vitamins, and cleaning equipment (online communication, March 2023).

Therefore, the Great Recession urged post-Yugoslav migrant communities to 'exit' from Russia and pursue further migration to places that were more inclusive to them, generating a certain loyalty of convenience towards these communities and individuals. Many re-migrated to the old member states of the EU, while the majority returned to the Balkans. As a result, these re-migrations, to some extent, quantitatively compensated for a new wave of emigration from the countries remnants of the former Yugoslavia. Still, this new wave of emigration mostly comprised middle-aged and young citizens in the years following the peak of the Great Recession. Most significantly, 2014 sought two important events in the region. First, overall influence of Great Recession combined with post-conflict political and economic inertia left socialist time created and later privatized factories in most post-Yugoslav republics bankrupt, especially in Bosnia and Herzegovina. Five of these factories were located in the northeastern Bosnian town of Tuzla, resulting in the loss of jobs and incomes for their former workers. As most of them had worked in these factories for most of their adult life, they rallied and voiced their demands for compensation and repayments of healthcare and pension payments from the cantonal government (Jukic, 2014). However, officials rejected the protesters' demands and instead blamed them for allowing the collapse of these companies. This led to the organization of the police against the protesters, triggering clashes between the police and protesters in Tuzla, and sparking protests in all regional centers in Bosnia, including the capital Sarajevo. These were the first post-conflict mass protests in Bosnia and Herzegovina, which despite all 'ethnic' divisions, were generally anti-establishment and violent, fueled by frustration with poverty and a dysfunctional state. In mid-February 2014, protests were held in support of the protesters in Bosnia and Herzegovina in most capitals of the former Yugoslav republics and in Kosovo (Avaz, 2014; Vision, 2014). The protests ended after the resignations of four regional officials with no other protesters' demands fulfilled, while several protesters were arrested and sentenced for causing damage to buildings (tportal.hr, 2014). One of my post-Yugoslav migrant acquaintances, who visited Bosnia at the time of the protests, told me that during the protests, the focus of media and observers was on material damage: "In Bosnia, society is focused on outcomes; no one really talks about the cause of protests. Everyone commented on the fact that important buildings are burning, not thinking of why they are burning" (personal communication, May 2014).

Second, soon after the protests ended, in May 2014, the region bordering Croatia, Bosnia, and Serbia was hard hit by floods, resulting in the largest humanitarian disaster since the end of the war. The floods were a direct result of climate change. According to the Organization for Security and Cooperation in Europe (OSCE) report, "[o]ver 90,000 people lost their homes, and a large number of schools, health centers, and other buildings were damaged or destroyed. The floods also caused landslides which dislocated previously marked minefields" (OSCE, 2015). Following regional solidarity with protesters in Bosnia, the floods also hit neighboring Croatia and Serbia. The population of the affected neighboring countries displayed solidarity and helped each other escape and find accommodation. This was the first post-conflict post-Yugoslav collective resilience in its tangible form. Overall, about 1.5 million people in Bosnia, 38,000 people in Croatia, and 1.6 million people in Serbia were affected by the floods (Reliefweb, 2014). As a result, floods prompted a new wave of migration outflow from the remnants of former Yugoslavia. As Euronews reported, the floods generated the largest exodus from Bosnia after the wars of the 1990s. For example, many Croatians and Bosnians owning Croatian passports—thus, as citizens of the EU did not need visas for moving further to the EU—joined their family members, who worked in Germany.

> A friend of mine was picked up on the first day of the floods by her husband, who came for her from Germany. She just got in the car and left, her house wasn't even flooded. For her it was the trigger. She left and never came back (Montalto Monella & Carleone, 2022).

Therefore, the floods generated the first large post-conflict emigration wave from the post-Yugoslav countries, turning them into climate migrants (Montalto Monella & Carleone, 2022). Disappointed, desperate, and tired of unsuccessful attempts to organize life at home as it was before the war, many representatives of the generations that were teenagers at the time of the war tended to blame the generation of their parents for the dissolution of Yugoslavia. Consequently, they blamed older generations for being forced to emigrate to survive, both for socioeconomic and political reasons.

> My older son is about to start the school, and the only relatively reasonable school in our vicinity was the Catholic one. They asked to baptize my son. My wife, his mother, is a Muslim (meaning Bosniak—the author), and I do not want to make her son a Catholic. Therefore, the divisions persist, and I have them. I realized that there is no future for my kids in Bosnia (personal communication, August 2017).

Through informal communication, the absence of Yugoslavia again appeared as the essential motive for emigration.

> If there still was Yugoslavia, I would never leave from here. I told to my parents that it was wrong that they voted for Bosnia's independence. Now, they will have to live far away from their grandchildren, and from me. I have to go to Germany and to work as *Gastarbeiter* if I want my kids to live peacefully and to have any future (personal communication, August 2017).

This absence of Yugoslavia has constantly appeared in the narratives of my friends, family, and other conversers. Most of them expressed their continuous loyalty of convenience to the system that the former country displayed as convenient and inclusive.

> It was so convenient back in Yugoslavia. Not that I am nostalgic about Yugoslavia itself. I was a child when it collapsed and I live in Austria for most of my life. But that system that Yugoslavia had — the work between 8 and 15, the time for a rest every day, secured employment, secured salaries, secured summer vacation, slow pace of life — that is what I still miss (personal communication, September 2021).

Thus, in many cases, emigration after the Great Recession was an expression of voice through exit, driven by a set of sociopolitical factors in the home country. Most frequently, for post-Yugoslav citizens, this emigration was not their first experience, and it stemmed from their previous experiences during the collapse of Yugoslavia, which taught them that emigration and exit are more effective responses than voicing their concerns in their home country. These emigrations from the region were followed, and to a large extent overshadowed, by mass migrations from the MENA region and Afghanistan through the Balkan route towards the core EU countries (Krasteva, 2021), which generated a migration crisis in Europe even larger than the one prompted by the wars of Yugoslavia's dissolution.

Dynamics of Post-Yugoslav Migrant Communities in Times of Great Recession

Those who lived in the countries remnants of Yugoslavia left abroad. Germany remained the top receiving country, followed by Austria. Scandinavian countries, most notably Norway and Sweden, also remained at the top of the list of receiving countries for post-Yugoslav emigrants. The population of former Yugoslavia was also attracted to emigrate to post-socialist countries of Central and Eastern Europe, most notably Czech Republic, though to a lesser extent. Spain and Italy remained top host countries of post-Yugoslav immigration in the Mediterranean. As EU migration statistics dating from 2019 demonstrated, a large majority of emigrants from former Yugoslavia reside in the EU 27 countries. More than half of emigrants from Bosnia and Herzegovina and Serbia reside in the EU 27 countries, while slightly over half of emigrants from Montenegro and about 20 percent of Bosnian citizens are settled in Serbia. Similarly, around 20 percent of citizens of North Macedonia reside in Turkey. About 10 percent and smaller number of emigrants from these countries reside in the USA, Switzerland, Australia and Great Britain (Bildung, 2022).

Table 5.1: Emigration from countries remnants of former Yugoslavia as of 2019

Country	Total number of emigrants	Emigrants share of total population	Projected population decline in 2020-50
Bosnia and Herzegovina	1,653,056	50.1%	-18.2%
Croatia	990,012	24.0%	-18.0%
Montenegro	153,009	24.4%	- 6.2%
North Macedonia	658, 264	31.6%	- 10.9%
Serbia (with Kosovo)	950,485	10.08%	- 18.9%
Slovenia	147,593	7.1%	- 6.7%

Source: Kondan (2020)

For example, post-Yugoslavs who had integrated into Spain by the time of the global financial crisis experienced mass job losses. One individual mentioned, "It was hard to find a long-term job, therefore, despite having prestigious higher education and being highly qualified, I took the first available job as a waiter at the railways" (personal communication, January 2015). Discussing the effects of the Great Recession on migration flows in and from Spain, González-Ferrer and Moreno-Fuentes (2017, p. 447) pointed out that "[T]he complex and multidimensional economic crisis experienced by Spain since 2008 significantly altered migration patterns in this country. Large-scale unemployment contributed to slowing down migrant inflows and accelerated out-migration flows from Spain." Losing their jobs, some Spain-based post-Yugoslavs sought their resilience in the face of the crisis as seasonal workers in Great Britain. "I went to Britain as a baby-sitter to one British family. In this way, I also improved my English and earned some savings. So, I returned to Spain better qualified with a higher level of English knowledge that gave me better chances to find a new job" (personal communication, December 2014). Some post-Soviet citizens, who emigrated to Spain in the 1990s shared similar comments regarding the effects of the global financial crisis. "In Spain you can live great only if you come with a lot of money, or if you are based in Spain, but work remotely or freelance for an organization in another country" (online discussion, July 2022). The Great Recession affected young and middle age immigrants in Spain, while senior generations of them appeared rather as observers of the situation in Spain.

> Losing jobs, many Spaniards lost their income and, consequentially, their ability to cover loans taken to purchase homes. Then the police was knocking to the doors with order to move them from the flats. Therefore, Spaniards were massively jumping from the windows to avoid the police! It was a big 'circus'.... We were lucky to own the flat before the crisis and savings from the sale of real estate back in Yugoslavia (online communication, December 2022).

Like Spain, during the global financial crisis and its' early aftermath, both Germany and Austria experienced only larger inflows of post-Yugoslav migrants.

> Overall social, economic, and political situation in Bosnia and Croatia pushed me back to Germany after almost twenty years of trying to settle in the Balkans. Now, being middle age highly educated, I work as a blue-collar in one factory in Germany, nevertheless, I am grateful and satisfied to get this opportunity for my kids to live in more stable and better organized country than our unfortunate Balkans. ... I kept in touch with my friends who moved to Germany as refugees, and stayed there after the war ended. They helped me to find a job and move this time back to Germany. They also helped me to bring my family along, as it is not always easy to find a flat for rent and to bring your family having one and not very high salary. Now we live several families from the same town in Bosnia in the same town in Germany, and apart from work, we spend most of the time together (personal communication, July 2020).

Simultaneously, in Bosnia as well as in Croatia some programs reopened for foreign workers with particular skillsets that were in high demand in Germany and in Austria. Most frequently, these were medical personnel, elderly care and childcare professionals. Though small in scale, these programs provided German courses.

> After almost a year of working on temporary visa, I got a long-term contract and could bring my family. I cannot explain how much I missed them here. We had enough to pay the rent for a studio, where three of us lived, but we

were happy to be together again. My husband and daughter learned German, and I worked (online communication, July 2015).

Digital connections with migrant compatriots living elsewhere in Europe turned to be helpful in finding more job opportunities and new friends.

> Coming to Germany, my husband started to look for a job, but there was no immediate opportunity among the local Croatian community, where he asked first. Unexpectedly, my school-time friend, who during the war immigrated to Austria, wrote me that her Bosnian friends, immigrants in Germany owners of a small business look for someone with the EU citizenship to work for them. My husband owns the Croatian passport, so we connected to learn about the job. It turned out, that these friends live in the same town as we do. Moreover, my husband's skills matched their demand. He has been working with them several years for now, and we gradually became friends (personal communication, September 2017).

This example demonstrates the interplay of several influential factors that helped post-Yugoslav migrants to overcome the negative effects of global financial crisis combined with other regional crises. Elements of tangible resilience included emigration, ownership of an EU country passport, and connections with the local Croatian community. Digital media and transnational networks of post-Yugoslav migrants provided the missing link for the socioeconomic integration of the new wave of immigrants, namely the job and income.

> Huge number of people from Serbia and Croatia moved to Austria. Some of my friends, who worked for international companies were offered positions in Vienna within the same company. Their families followed, and spouses usually found jobs in other multinational companies, mostly as sales persons in retail. Others, who previously did their undergrad studies in Austria returned to work there. There are also those, who applied for postgraduate studies and used it to relocate to Austria permanently (online communication, May 2021).

As a (rather unanticipated) result of these migration flows, post-Yugoslavs represent the second largest (after Turks) immigrant group in Austria, while post-Soviets are a much smaller immigrant group in Austria. Among former Yugoslavs, citizens of Serbia, Bosnia, and Croatia are the most numerous, followed by (Northern) Macedonians. Since 2013, when Croatia joined the EU,

Croatian citizens who migrated to Austria have been included in Austrian migration statistics as EU citizens. However, Austria, as an older EU member, has kept certain restrictions on labor migration, along with Romanian and Bulgarian citizens. Meanwhile, citizens of Serbia, Bosnia and Herzegovina, and Northern Macedonia retained the status of third country nationals, although since 2012, they do not need a visa to enter Schengen-member states for short-term stays (under 90 days). This allowed them to provide seasonal services as transmigrants and temporary workers, becoming a tangible resilience strategy for many of them. For some, it was a way out of the Great Depression, functioning as chain and seasonal migrant workers from Croatia, Bosnia, and high-qualified representatives of *corponations* from Serbia. Some Serbian citizens received Hungarian passports and moved to Austria as Hungarian citizens (personal communication, September 2021).

Commenting on one of her frequent experiences with other post-Yugoslavs in Vienna, one of my acquaintances from Croatia recalled:

> I went to a café with my friend from Serbia. We were talking in our language, when a bar tender approached us asking also in our language "Ladies, where do you come from?" I said that I am from Croatia, my friend said that she is from Serbia, and the bar tender excitingly said "And I am from Bosnia!" It turned out that she was the owner of the café. We spent the rest of the evening together talking (personal communication, February 2020).

In Hungary, migrants from former Yugoslavia represent a small and linguistically diverse group, consisting mostly of the cultural Hungarians from Serbia and Croatia, some refugees from the eastern parts of Croatia—Slavonia and Baranya—Croats, Serbs, and Hungarians, respectively. Together they count only about 6000. They have resided for more than a decade in Hungary and have fully integrated into the Hungarian society.

> In the very beginning, when we escaped Croatia, there were several families in the neighboring to Croatia Hungarian towns, and we continued to live as we did back in Yugoslav-era Croatia. As the situation was changing, some of us left to calmer parts of Croatia, others, like us, moved to Budapest. My

kids went to the Croatian school. Still, with several post-Yugoslav exceptions, their friends were mostly Hungarians (personal communication, September 2017).

Most of them have also obtained Hungarian citizenship since
2011. Serbian citizens also increasingly moved to Hungary, especially those from the northern parts of Serbia, where Hungarian is
one of official languages and is taught at schools. Therefore, the formation of the post-Yugoslav immigrant community in Hungary
was prompted by the Great Recession. In contrast to most other receiving countries, these post-Yugoslav migrant communities
merged with official national minorities in Hungary, which appeared as separated Croatian and Serbian ones after the breakup of
Yugoslavia. Due to their small numbers, the post-Yugoslav immigrants integrated with the existing national minority communities
in Hungary.

> During the Cold war, we had a status of one Serbo-Croatian minority. After
> the breakup of Yugoslavia, Hungary became the EU candidate and started
> to receive pre-accession EU funds. Then we realized that we can receive
> more as separate minorities. As a result, we made separate Serbian and Cro-
> atian minorities (personal communication, December 2012).

Post-Yugoslav immigration to the South African Republic
(SAR) increased during the 1990s and has continued over the last
thirty years. The first wave of post-Yugoslav immigrants in SAR
occurred in the 1990s, primarily consisting of middle-class Serbians
and Bosnians seeking to escape violent conflicts, economic sanctions, and the general anarchy generated by the collapse of the socialist federal system in their home countries. These immigrants
were drawn to SAR due to its easy visa regime, relatively low cost
of living, and favorable climate. These post-Yugoslav communities
integrated through existing immigrant institutions that were concentrated in major cities such as Johannesburg, Cape Town, and
Pretoria. The largest post-Yugoslav immigrant community on the
African continent can be found in SAR, with an estimated 20,000
immigrants from former Yugoslavia residing there, predominantly

of Serb and Serbian origin. The largest concentration of this community is in Johannesburg, where Serbian language teaching is offered at a local school (Gucijan, 2014).

> When I announced that I move to SAR for some time, my senior colleagues alerted me to be careful with Serbian immigrants there, because they are mostly 1990s law fugitives. ... First time when I went to grocery shop in Joesburgh[5], hearing a different accent, a shop lady asked me where do I come from. I answered that I am from Serbia, and she pointed towards the shop's owner saying that he is also from Serbia. I made a small talk with both of them and there was nothing inconvenient or negative about them. Nevertheless, following the alert of my colleagues, I did not go to that shop again to avoid potential troubles (online communication, December 2021).

My inquiry included several personal testimonies by post-Yugoslav immigrants in South Africa. It is interesting to note that some of these post-Yugoslav immigrants in SAR were previously immigrants in Russia before coming to SAR. The majority of respondents were employees of multinational corporations (MNCs), and their stay in SAR was primarily temporary. As a result, their communities were mostly international, aligning with the concept of "corponations" defined in the previous chapter. For these migrants, the corporations they worked for provided comprehensive support in adapting to the local customs, which were quite different from those in most of Europe and even the countries of the former Soviet Union, owing to the legacy of Apartheid. This support ranged from assisting in finding long-term accommodation and offering guided local tours to providing mandatory bodyguards during the initial months after their arrival, due to the high risk of street attacks and lingering racial inequalities in social statuses and educational levels. Furthermore, integration into the local society often involved taking left-side driving lessons, especially for professionals with no prior experience of driving on the left side of the road (online communication, September 2021). According to Barabasi (2014), individuals are part of social networks that create small social worlds. In the case of corponations in SAR, as well as in other places, representatives often used country-of-origin or ethnic ties to

---

[5]   Shortened and locally widely used title for Johannesburg

connect with immigrants, who were predominantly marriage migrants. Among the most numerous and long-standing post-Yugoslav immigrant communities in SAR are Serbian war criminal groups, which left the Balkans in the early 2000s following the violent collapse of Yugoslavia (Jutarnji.hr, 2018). However, Serbians are not the only gangster immigrant community in SAR. According to Mandy Wiener (2018), a renowned investigative journalist in SAR, there is an entire network of Eastern European criminal gangs. These fugitives, with fake documents and identities, undertook long journeys, often passing through countries in the Global South (for example, via Ecuador), before settling in SAR with their families. Upon arrival, they connected with local gangsters and integrated into existing Serbian immigrant communities under false identities. In many cases, these fugitives organized businesses in international trade, such as grocery shops, which primarily served as a front for their main criminal activities, including drug trade and security services jobs.

Influence of the Great Recession on Post-Soviet Citizens and Migrant Communities

Discussing the emigrations from Commonwealth of Independent States CIS after 2000, Denisenko (2020) pointed out that

> the geography of emigration from the CIS expanded and become in line with global mobility trends. As a result, new migrant communities emerged in many countries. Permanent residents from post-Soviet countries are especially numerous in Germany, Israel, the USA and Italy (Denisenko, 2020, p. 55).

As discussed in Chapter 4, Asian financial crisis of 1998 had disastrous effects on the emerging market economies of the newly independent post-Soviet republics, especially on Russia, and it prompted emigration from them.

> I wanted to study MBA abroad. That would allow me to move upward in my career anywhere in the post-Soviet countries. Once reaching European Union, the financial crisis resulted in cheap relatively to post-Soviet space opportunities to start my own business, so I stayed abroad and organized

> my small business, that would be much harder to do back in Ukraine or in Russia (personal communication, summer 2015).

Libman and Vinokurov (2011) pointed out that large wave of emigration from the former Soviet states in 2010s

> represents one of the most surprising changes of the last decade. For the last two decades, five CIS countries—Armenia, Kazakhstan, Moldova, the Kyrgyz Republic and Tajikistan—have been among the nations with the highest emigration rates in the world. Tajikistan, the Kyrgyz Republic and Moldova are also among the top 10 countries in the world in terms of their ratio of migrant remittances to GDP. The migration corridors between Russia and Ukraine, and Russia and Kazakhstan, are among the world's top 10 migration corridors, with Russia being the second destination (after the United States) and third origin country in the world.

In the summer of 2007, Russia had achieved a full economic recovery from the collapse of the USSR and the economic default of 1998, which was influenced by the Asian financial crisis. This economic revival was supported by the booming oil and gas prices, contributing to the emergence of a middle class in Russia that was becoming increasingly integrated into global economic, educational, and political networks. Furthermore, liberal economic reforms had led to Russia having the lowest income tax rate in Europe, at only thirteen percent. The Russian market was also experiencing significant growth, offering a wide range of products from all over the world at lower prices than in many other countries. These favorable economic conditions attracted both foreign investors and immigrants to Russia, seeking opportunities in its thriving economy and promising market.

> During the global financial crisis, I went to Hungary to study. Then I returned to Moscow to work. The only impact it had on the currency, because it was volatile, but all my savings were in rubbles, I received the salary in rubbles (personal communication, February 2023).

At the same time, continuous economic dependence on oil and gas exports and incomplete and inconsistence reforms (without stabilization and institutionalization, but going straight to liberalization and privatization), led to increasing social inequalities, and simultaneously, into political power disbalance, resulting in increasing autocracy.

> I did not have the reason to emigrate because I had all I needed: a good job, good salary, friends, a car. Nevertheless, I felt slightly bored and my friend and I wanted to change the scenery a bit. I agreed with my boss to keep the position for me for a year, while I study abroad. The plan was to go abroad for a year, to do the Master studies, and to return. I planned to apply to Harvard. … I had already submitted all the documents for an exam. However, just a month before the departure, I had a car accident and got to the hospital for a month. I had broken bones of my spine. That is how I missed the exam, and the next possibility to get it was only a year after (personal communication, December 2019).

Although indirectly, the narratives of my interlocutors revealed that emigration from the former Soviet republics, particularly Russia as the most populated and the largest of them, was the long-term effect of the Great Recession as Aleshkovski, Grebenyuk et al. (2018) described as follows:

> The second half of the 2000s was characterized by another economic crisis (2008–2009). Rising unemployment and a shrinking domestic market made the Russian business people look for business opportunities abroad. According to experts, they made up the largest proportion of emigrants at that time. Other forms of emigration such as migration for study or migration of graduates in search of jobs were still widely spread… It is even more difficult to estimate the quantitative scale of emigration during the period than in previous periods. The official statistics record only approximately 30 per cent of total emigration. According to Rosstat, about 227 thousand citizens left the country during the fourth wave (2006–2011). However, the USA, German, Spanish and Israeli official statistics show that about 237,000 immigrants from Russia entered those countries. Therefore, taking into account all countries that attracted Russian emigrants, whose numbers had increased significantly by that time, the total number of those who left the country may be as large as 400 thousand.

It is noteworthy that the peak of the global financial crisis coincided with Russia's invasion of Georgia on the significant date of 08.08.2008. The invasion was led by Russia's President at the time, Dmitri Medvedev, who had initially come to power with ambitions to modernize the Russian economy. Despite the invasion and subsequent occupation of a significant portion of Georgian territory, Russia's leadership did not face international sanctions. However,

Russia's economy, which heavily relied on natural resources exports, was impacted by the global financial crisis, leading to a slowdown in the global economy. The true effects of the Great Recession in Russia became apparent in 2010 and 2011, coinciding with Vladimir Putin's third presidential term. This term was met with opposition from a majority of residents in Russia's large cities, leading to the largest protests in post-Soviet Russia, known as the 'Snow Revolution' due to its white bow symbol. These protests lasted from October 2011 to May 2012, during which the incumbents re-inaugurated Putin as President and continued to govern through increased repressions.

These developments led to a new wave of emigrants, mainly consisting of students, young and middle-aged corporate professionals, and entrepreneurs from Russia. As Byford and Bronnikova (2018, p. 20) correctly noted, these events influenced further divisions among Russian and wider post-Soviet migrant communities on those more conservative, who have replicated the notion of "Russkii mir", and those more liberal, who have projected their "global Russianess".

Within this group, there were both individuals who remained apolitical, similar to the majority of citizens from post-Soviet countries with experiences from at least the late Soviet era, and post-Soviet Russian citizens who openly expressed anti-establishment political views. This wave of post-Soviet emigrants clearly demonstrated a dividing line between their country of origin and the political regimes governing post-Soviet states. Their loyalty was characterized by a mixture of commitment, convenience, and cost, and many openly expressed their disloyalty to the political regimes. This was particularly evident among emigrants from post-Soviet Russia. Notably, this wave of emigrants formed the first organized post-Soviet transnational community, united by the goal of providing democratic remittances (Fomina, 2021).

During the 2011-2012 parliamentary and presidential elections in Russia, Russian emigrants utilized social media to connect with official oppositional political structures in Russia and with each other. Their aim was to ensure free and fair election procedures by serving as observers in Russian consulates and embassies around the world (personal communication, April 2012). Apart from election-related migrant community ties, Fomina (2021) found another five thematic areas of mobilization, including human rights and civil freedoms, fighting corruption, environmental protection, anti-war activities, and counteracting Russian propaganda. In addition, these areas of the transnational Russian migrant community mobilization included activities directed to the Russian society, and activities directed to the political elites and societies in receiving countries (Fomina, 2021).

During the period of 2013-2014, as the effects of the global economic crisis slowed down across the former Soviet bloc, Ukraine faced a new political challenge. The EU offered Ukraine an Association Agreement, but then President Viktor Yanukovich rejected the deal, citing opposition from Russia's leadership and concerns about sacrificing trade with Russia (BBC, 2013). Additionally, he was offended by the lack of prospects for full EU membership (Piper, 2013). This rejection led to mass protests throughout Ukraine, known as Euromaidan or the Revolution of Dignity. The protests persisted for several months, with attempts by the special police—Berkut—to quell them. As clashes escalated, the protests turned violent. In mid-February 2014, after deadly clashes with state special police, protesters together with the representatives of the activists, opposition parties, and with the support of some units of the regular police entered the Parliament and suspended Yanukovich from power. As a result, clashes continued between the protesters and Yanukovich's supporters, which further evolved into the violent conflict in Eastern Ukraine. As the conflict escalated, Russia's President Vladimir Putin ordered parts of the Russian army to occupy Crimea Autonomous Republic, a peninsula that had been granted to Ukraine by Russia in 1954, and where the Russian Black Sea Navy remained after the breakup of the USSR. On March 14, 2014, Russian authorities held a referendum on Crimea joining Russia, and only four days later, they claimed Crimea as part of Russia. These events triggered significant waves of migration from the conflict-torn Eastern Ukrainian regions, both towards central Ukraine and to Western Russia, as well as further away from Ukraine to the EU.

The testimony of one of my conversers, who happened to be a emigrant from Donetsk, Ukraine is insightful, especially regarding the relationship among loyalty, voice, and exit following Hirschman's (1970) framework.

> We registered LLC in 2011. ...We were helping people to develop their talents as artists. We made a short feature movie as the study project: people were coming to us for a training, and they were casting in the movies. Then we also organized festivals: we had two seasons, when we presented our movies. It was all offered in various cinemas in Donetsk in the festival format... The project was successful, so ... we applied for a grant, and in 2014, we received that grant. However, in 2014 you understand that the situation radically changed.
>
> ...When the war started, people started to leave Donetsk rapidly. We had many people, our team was more than seventy people. They divided according to their views: some started to support one side, others started to support another side, some stick to pro-Ukrainian views, another defended pro-Russian views. Others became neutral, and some others aggressively neutral. Some became the members of The Right Sector ...
>
> And the conflict started even among the members of our team. It was very sad, of course. My sister and I tried to remain neutral and we did not even touch upon the political themes during our creative events. Unfortunately, we recorded our last short-feature movie in the Hotel Victoria while outside there were explosions and the fights were very close to the city. It was very traumatizing experience. ... I watched through my window how the airplane is flying above our building and I saw the rocket that targets directly to it: at that moment, I realized that it was not a movie, but the reality and it was a horrible feeling! I was so afraid that I sweat. Three days after that, we left Donetsk. There was the state program that supported temporary refugees; therefore, we first went to the suburb.
>
> There were two of my mom, our two cats, and us. We thought that we would return home soon. However, it has not happened: we lived in that tent camp about a week, and then they sent us to another small town (name), where they helped us to rent a cheap flat, so we lived there for about 2-3 months. However, in a very small town, there was nothing much to do, but we found a local club, where we were filming our movies. We made there one movie with the kids: the kids themselves wrote the script for a study movie. ...We even established the cooperation with the local TV channel, there we were synchronizing movies by the way. For them it was exotic that the creative company from Donetsk comes to such a small town (name). For them it was the event, so they were ready to support.
>
> People sympathized with us, because they did not want the same to happen with them. Nevertheless, they got sick and tired of it quite quickly. They realized that the war is ongoing, that nothing is changing, and gradually they stopped to support us. Then they moved us to some dormitory, but after the meeting with the local authorities they told us that we could not stay there anymore, and to move back to the flat, but they did not provide a

money for the rent. They said that the program is over. People, who were also refugees, were shocked, because some of them did not have where to go back. Nevertheless, nobody needs someone else's problems! Therefore, we went to Kiev. We rent the flat. Interestingly, it was very hard to rent the flat, because even when you write the advertisement, people from Kiev did not want to rent a flat to someone from Donetsk or Lugansk. Even in their advertisements, it was written: "We do not rent to people from Donetsk and Lugansk", because they consider us separatists, public enemies, and because they think that we do not have money. … There were precedents that refugees were coming, renting flats, and then they could not pay for a rent and the owners could not move them away. Our problem was even bigger, because we had animals with us (personal communication, February 2020).

This dramatic testimony provides valuable insights directly from a witness of the beginning of the war in Eastern Ukraine. It sheds light on the various sources of exclusion, including ideological, regional, and conflict-driven division lines, which simultaneously created a spectrum of emerging communities with varying degrees of resilience and loyalty. These communities ranged from state-based 'pro-Ukrainian' and 'pro-Russian', to those adopting an 'aggressively neutral' stance and disloyalty to all conflicting sides. The testimony also confirms D'Anieri (2019, p. 2) argument that

> the roots of the conflict are deeper than is commonly understood and therefore will resist a simple change in policy. The violent earthquake that took place in 2014 was the result of deep "tectonic" forces as well as short-term triggers. Conflict between Ukraine and Russia is based on profound normative disagreements and conflicts of interest, and therefore does not depend on mistakes by leaders on whom we can easily pin blame. These disagreements undermined relations even in the 1990s, when post-Cold War mutual trust was at its highest.

Further exclusion that my converser and her family encountered in other parts of Ukraine, as refugees from Eastern Ukraine after being forced to leave their home, also implies a feeling of double exclusion: not only as being displaced but also as unwanted. While they found short-term resilience in internal migration, their previous strong loyalty to the Ukrainian state, society, and their community shrank to only include their family and work. As a result, this diminished loyalty provided them with a form of soft resilience, allowing them to rely on themselves and to consider moving further abroad without regret.

Dynamics of Post-Soviet Migrant Communities in Times of the Great Recession

Post-Soviet citizens moving to Spain because of the Great Recession and consequent Euromaidan and violent conflict were lower middle-class Ukrainians, and mostly wealthy Russians. The analysis of investments in the real estate sector in Spain clearly demonstrates that the desire for system-escape or exit, in Hirschman's (1970) terms, has a much more social character than previously portrayed as purely political or economic/business-driven. It is evident that the motive behind purchasing real estate in Spain for many ordinary citizens of post-Soviet countries is to provide their children with better and relatively inexpensive education, obtain resident permits abroad, and find "additional airports" for their families. Concerns over high real estate prices, pollution, and security also contribute to their decisions. During the Great Recession and its early aftermath, post-Soviet communities in Spain grew, with only a few cases of temporary or long-term emigration from the country. Thus, the proposition suggesting that the global financial crisis prompted emigration from countries heavily affected by it cannot be generalized. Instead, the situation is more complex, and individual motivations and circumstances play a significant role in shaping migration patterns.

Immigration from post-Soviet countries in Austria included middle class Ukrainians and wealthy Russians. My converser, a post-Soviet Austria-based lawyer, envisioned the link between various global and regional crises through her work.

> Political and economic crises significantly influence my work. The essence of the work is changing. If, for example, in the beginning of my independent career as a lawyer my clients had significantly more financial resources and they were ready to spend them on anything, they also faced less problems in their home countries, where they really lived, or no problems at all, since 2014 political situation changed and it had a major impact on people. They became poorer to 50%, and on the territory of the former Soviet Union, it became much more complicated to earn money, therefore people started to think more about their spending. Therefore, my work that initially was quite flat and peaceful sphere, after that crisis moved towards more conflictual sphere (personal communication, February 2020).

For most of my conversers originating from Ukraine, Vienna appeared as one more capital city on their list of international relocations.

> After years of working in New York, I was offered to relocate to Vienna. ...In Vienna, I feel closer to Ukraine and I actually am geographically much closer. I am lucky that I work for international organization, so I can afford renting a nice apartment in a good place. Not all of my compatriots are as lucky. Many of them came to Vienna after 2014, because of the political crisis and the conflict in the east of the country. Many of them are highly qualified, but they do not speak German, so they are forced to take low-skilled jobs. For example, the woman, who cleans my apartment worked as a school-teacher in Ukraine, but in Vienna she cannot even dream about getting similar job (personal communication, August 2018).

As demonstrated in previous chapters, and confirming Lee's (1966) theory of migrations, emigration can be influenced by both 'pull' and intervening factors, including individual motives. Despite the backdrop of the global financial crisis, political instability, and the war in Ukraine, she chose to emigrate for seemingly unrelated personal reasons — to unite with her spouse. "We met through one of the matching websites. I was on that website for quite a long time, mainly because I wanted to practice my English" (personal communication, February 2020). While a visa has always been required for any type of travel to Austria for the former Soviet citizens, since 2014 Ukrainians have been allowed on visa free entry up to ninety days. Similar to citizens of Bosnia and Herzegovina, Serbia, and North Macedonia, Ukrainian citizens utilized the visa-free regime between Ukraine and the EU to find temporary employment in EU countries. They also sent remittances to their relatives in Ukraine, serving as both an exit and voice response to the evolving circumstances in their home country, while retaining loyalty primarily to their family. Consequently, despite the differences in legal statuses resulting from various agreements between the EU and sending countries, both post-Yugoslav and post-Soviet immigrant communities in Austria and Germany function as common-culture-based migrant communities, providing a source of tangible and soft resilience during times of crisis, particularly for newcomers. However, it is important to exercise caution when interpreting their actions and impacts on the host societies.

> First, you meet one person, and then that person introduces you to another person, and then that third person to the fourth person, so it is like a snail — the circle is widening. There are many circles. You know, people told me that Vienna is a big village and that there are few Russian-speakers, so the gossips are spreading quickly. If you, for example, talk to one person, soon he will transfer the information to another person, and that someone else will know something about you, and these are not always the facts about you. Therefore, I try to be very cautious and not to tell to people too much about myself (personal communication, February 2020).

Unlike in Austria, post-Soviet immigrants represent the second largest immigrant group in Hungary — second to sum of ethnic Hungarians from Romania, Ukraine, and the former Yugoslavia. Those who migrated to Hungary starting from 2000 have usually been highly skilled labor migrants with families and small-to-midscale businesspersons.

> I met a Hungarian girl … We met in Kyiv, then we strengthen our relationship in Bulgaria… back then it was very unpleasant political situation prompted by ex-president Yanukovich and his gang, so we decided that it is better to be in Hungary… Before I came here, of course, I studied the market — with whom I can work here, I read some articles, I looked for Russian-speaking people here, Ukrainian-speaking people, I monitored job vacancies and currency exchange rates… Back then I was freelancer, I had relatively stable income, so I was not worrying about finding a job in some large company. I worked from home …After sometime, I got bored and felt isolated … Thus, I decided to find a job, and I found an employment in one MNC, technical services provider. There was a small Russian-speaking team working there, people from the former Soviet Union, who, as I remember, were always commenting the Hungarian food, they viewed Hungarians as boring people, they definitely felt some kind of unacceptance of the Hungarians. I never felt anything similar, but I observed such unacceptance from this small group of people that I worked with. You know, it looked like as if you transplanted some part of your body, but it did not take a root (personal communication, January 2020).

Similar to early 1990s, many post-Soviet youth, Russians, Ukrainians and Belarussians alike envisioned the Great Recession as the push to study abroad in the post-socialist countries, new EU member states, most frequently in Czech Republic and Hungary.

I decided to continue my studies abroad when I was on the last year of my undergraduate studies in Odessa. After the graduation, I went to Prague for an MA. Then I wanted to do some internship to try myself in the real work, and I had some friends in Budapest, so I came to Budapest. It was not really well-thought and balanced decision, it was rather irrational. I was young, and it was interesting, I feel convenient here. At the same time, there is no too big difference between Czech Republic and Hungary, they are quite similar, in a way that this is not the US for example, which would be going far away from home. This is all quite close (personal communication, January 2020).

Many of this wave of studies-prompted immigrants have lived in these two countries interchangeably.

Czech Republic is the most Russian-populated, and the most Russia-hating country in the EU! They are such nationalists! In Hungary, if they are nationalists, they openly say and demonstrate that they are nationalists, such as Jobbik (far-right Hungarian party — author). Czechs all pretend that they are liberals, but in fact, they are so arrogant in communication, they consider their country as a very cool one! They also have arrogant comments about Russians and Ukrainians quite frequently. Once some person stopped to talk to me in bar when hearing that I am a Russian. He just turned his spine to me. …Not in my experience. Usually they are ok when I say that I am from Russia. Moreover, Czechs immediately ask, "what do you think about Vladimir Putin? Why are you here?" Therefore, it left some negative impressions from the Czech Republic. It is maybe slightly cleaner (than Hungary), maybe in the aspect of politics, it is slightly more liberal, but these factors do not define the quality of life, and of communication with the people. To me, communication with Czechs was not much pleasant. That is even the point: here in 1956 it was much harsher than in Prague in 1968, and nevertheless, Hungarians are not angry, while the Czechs are. They also think that if you are Russian, you must be stupid. Moreover, they extensively ask and explain what was happening in 1968! I always say "yes". Moreover, they think that in Russia people still do not know what happened in Prague in 1968. In Hungary they may ask something after sometime, but in Czech Republic they immediately put you on test — whether you are good or bad Russian! If you like Putin, you are bad, and if you dislike, you are ok! Even if I liked Putin, which I do not, I know that they expect me to say that I dislike him, and I would anyway say that I dislike him. Why on Earth then you ask such question?! (personal communication, November 2019).

This wave of post-Soviet immigrants in Hungary mainly consisted of highly-skilled labor force, many of whom arrived as employees of multinational corporations (MNCs), eventually establishing their own local corporations.

> When, as the part of market diversification, the international company where I am employed offered to relocate to Hungary from Russia as a part of promotion, I agreed almost immediately. I visited Budapest before, and I liked it. I envisioned calmer atmosphere than in Moscow, and opportunities for my kids to get European education. ... The company organized visas, the local colleagues cooperated with local real estate companies to arrange the accommodation, so everything went smooth. ... Our colleagues from the local office as well as from other branches of the company are our most frequent contacts. Other important contacts and friends are Russian-speaking immigrants who already lived here when we arrived (personal communication, April 2018).

Many post-Soviet migrants who moved to Hungary during the wave prompted by the global financial crisis, along with the political crisis in Ukraine, were middle-class Russian and Ukrainian citizens who successfully established themselves as migrant entrepreneurs (Tepavcevic, 2023). "I came to Hungary to study and was integrating through the study. The studies were in English, not in Hungarian, so it was hard to integrate to the local society. It was rather an international 'bubble' (personal communication, November 2019). In 2017, the number of immigrants from the former Soviet Union in Hungary reached approximately 15000. In certain cases, these communities overlap with official Ukrainian and Armenian national minorities in Hungary. Still, as in other countries, these numbers have been highly volatile due to two consecutive global crises — COVID-19 pandemic and Russia's full-fledged invasion in Ukraine.

Conclusions: Effects of the Great Recession on Post-Yugoslav and Post-Soviet Migrant Communities

In sum, the Great Recession had rather long-term effects on existing post-Yugoslav and post-Soviet migrant communities and generated new waves of emigration from the countries remnants of former Yugoslavia and the USSR. Following the global migration trends correctly noted by Meier (2015) and Roos and Zaun (2018), many post-Yugoslav emigrants returned from the countries of the former Soviet Union to some extent balancing increasing outflow of new emigrants from the Balkans. Similarly, new waves of post-

Soviet emigration continued the trend of massive outflows from these countries during the Great Recession. However, influential regional factors also contributed to the negative effects of the crisis on emigration.

In the Balkans, the loss of jobs and subsequent mass sociopolitical protests, along with devastating floods in bordering regions of Bosnia, Croatia, and Serbia, played a significant role in emigration from the region. Just a year later, the Balkans became a major route for mass migrations from the MENA region and Afghanistan. In Ukraine, uprisings arose due to disagreements among various political forces regarding the Accession Agreement with the EU, leading to mass protests and escalating into violent conflict in Eastern Ukraine, ultimately resulting in Russia's annexation of Crimea from Ukraine. These events further exacerbated the socioeconomic and political crises in the post-Soviet space, generating additional emigration flows from the countries remnants of the Soviet Union.

Both post-Yugoslav and post-Soviet new emigrants tended to harbor a complex mixture of loyalty driven by coercion and convenience towards the receiving countries. Simultaneously, they openly opposed the regimes in their countries of origin while increasing their loyalty of cost and convenience, towards their migrant communities as sources of hard resilience. For both post-Yugoslav and post-Soviet communities, digital social media became an important tool for reconnection with friends and compatriots, and consequently for achieving resilience in the face of the long-term consequences of the Great Recession. The next two chapters are devoted to the analysis of the influence of these two crises on post-Yugoslav and post-Soviet migrant communities, their experiences during these crises, and their resilience.

Soviet emigration continued the flood of massive outflows from these countries during the Great Recession. However, influential regional factor also contributed to the negative effects of the crisis on emigration.

Chapter 6
Post-Yugoslav and Post-Soviet Migrants' Experiences of COVID-19 Pandemic: Resilience and Lessons from Previous Crises

With COVID pandemic, things only get better for me: I don't waste my time traveling to work and back, and I take my daughter from the school at 15 instead of 18,
so I spend more time with her ... I have a family, and few friends there, I live in my
own bubble... It would probably be different if I was 32 and if I was in the Balkans,
where I have a bunch of friends. In Netherlands, I live a different life
(online communication, October 2021).

We are friends with Russian wives of my husband's friends, but they like to stay at
home, they are homemakers, none of them works. I need communication with active people, there are very few of them here. ... I made friends via Internet. I had a
good friend in Budapest, but during the pandemic their work stopped and they left
back to Russia (personal communication, January 2022).

COVID and Migrations

The global spread of the COVID-19 virus has been one of the most
hazardous results of high human mobility that marked the first two
decades of the twenty-first century. Contrary to most previous
global crises, due to almost simultaneous lockdowns in nearly all
parts of the world, the COVID-19 pandemic heavily limited "the
number of people crossing borders, especially on permanent or a
long-term basis" (Gamlen, 2020, p. 10). Migrant populations in the
world became considered the worst victims of COVID-19, and simultaneously the worst spreaders (Ullah, Nawaz et al., 2021). Though
scholarly literature has rarely related the effects of the pandemic to
the migrations in the broader context of global crises, analyses of
the COVID-19 pandemic and its' impacts generated a certain body
of literature on migration discussing its short-term and long-term
effects on migrants across the world.

On one hand, media and scholarly literature have equally focused on the immediate negative effects of the pandemic on migrants. For example, in January 2021, The Economist published an
article about the return of Eastern European labor migrants from

Western Europe, stating that "waiters and cleaners, many of whom are migrants, cannot work remotely" (Economist, 2021). Similarly, research exploring the impact of the global health crisis on agricultural migrant workers in Southern Italy found that the COVID-19 pandemic interacted with previously existing structural vulnerabilities, resulting in adverse outcomes for these workers and exposing vulnerabilities in the agricultural labor market, migration and asylum, and healthcare systems (Tagliacozzo, Pisacane et al., 2020). Similar situations have been observed in other parts of Europe.

On the other hand, various media outlets have noted the trend of highly skilled East Europeans returning to their countries of origin. Some have portrayed this trend as a positive "brain gain" effect of the COVID-19 pandemic (Economist, 2021). This stands in contrast to the frequently discussed "brain drain," which refers to the trend of well-educated and highly skilled Eastern Europeans emigrating westward and its immediate effects on economies.

> In 2020, Europe saw a great reverse migration, as those who had sought work abroad returned home. ... An estimated 1.3m Romanians went back to Romania... Politicians in eastern Europe had long complained of a "brain drain" as their brightest left in search of higher wages in the west. Now the pandemic, a shifting economy and changing work patterns are bringing many of them back. A "brain gain" has begun... A new grey economy has sprung up across the EU, with white-collar staff living in one country but illicitly working in another (and paying tax in the wrong place, as a result). Often these people are expats in their own country, physically at home, but telecommuting across a border (Economist, 2021).

These observations generated three broad propositions about the impact of the COVID-19 pandemic on migrants and migration flows. First, the most significant mobility patterns during the COVID-19 pandemic were the number of white-collar migrant workers, who — at least temporarily — re-migrated to their countries of origin; some of them continued to work remotely for their host countries, while others used their skills and knowledge obtained in emigration in a home country workplace. The second proposition suggests that this trend has given rise to a new 'grey economy,' where white-collar migrants continue to pay taxes in host countries while living in their countries of origin. The third and most general

proposition is that blue-collar migrant workers were more negatively affected by the pandemic compared to white-collar workers.

In this chapter, I aim to test the three propositions mentioned
earlier by examining the impact of the COVID-19 pandemic on
post-Yugoslav and post-Soviet migrants. I will focus on their strategies of tangible resilience, taking into account exclusion and loyalty, which have proven to be crucial throughout the analyses in
previous chapters. To do so, I continue to rely on an analytical
framework that combines Lee's (1966) theory of migration and
Hirschman's (1970) framework that relates concepts of exit, voice,
and loyalty. Additionally, for the analysis of 'soft' resilience, I also
continue to apply Foulkes' (2021) concept of 'psychological immunization.' The chapter will explore the relationship between tangible
resilience, which involves legal, physical, and socio-economic coping mechanisms, and 'soft' resilience, which involves psychological,
political, and cultural coping mechanisms of both post-Yugoslav
and post-Soviet migrants under the unique condition of globally
limited mobility caused by the pandemic. By examining these aspects, we aim to gain a comprehensive understanding of how these
migrant communities responded to the challenges posed by the
COVID-19 pandemic and how they navigated the uniquely limited
opportunities for mobility during this time.

The chapter aims to address two significant questions. First, it
investigates whether there were any differences in the experiences
and perceptions of the COVID-19 pandemic among post-Yugoslav
and post-Soviet migrants across three broad clusters of receiving
countries. Second, it explores whether and to what extent their past
experiences from previous global crises influenced their reactions
and adaptation strategies during the COVID-19 pandemic. In other
words, the chapter seeks to understand how the combination of
loyalty, voice, and exit as forms of resilience played a role in their
responses to the challenges posed by COVID-19. To achieve these
goals, the next section of the chapter delves into the experiences of
post-Yugoslav migrants in the three clusters of host countries, offering personal insights into the spectrum of challenges they faced
and the coping mechanisms they employed. Through these per-

sonal accounts, the chapter sheds light on the resilience demonstrated by these migrants during the COVID-19 pandemic. Similarly, Section 3 explores experiences of COVID pandemic among post-Soviet migrants and discusses in what ways experiences with previous global crisis influenced their resilience during COVID-19 pandemic. Section 4 reflects on findings by comparing them and provides some conclusions by situating findings in the literature discussing migrations during COVID-19 pandemic.

Post-Yugoslav Migrants' Experiences of COVID-19 Pandemic and Resilience Learned Through Previous Global Crises

Many post-Yugoslav migrants, upon reaching the age of retirement, either established second homes in their home countries or returned from their emigration after reaching the pension age. Meanwhile, the majority of their children, belonging to the middle-age generation, continued to live abroad. As a result, prior to the COVID pandemic, as partially revealed in the previous chapter, post-Yugoslav migrants were accustomed to frequent travel, moving between their different homes seasonally. This transnational lifestyle and the existence of post-Yugoslav communities across multiple countries became even more apparent during the COVID-19 pandemic lockdowns. Some of them felt compelled to relocate back to their country of origin as soon as the lockdowns were announced.

> Our real estate rental business in the US simply stopped as soon as the first lockdown was announced. Understanding that it may last long and that other our income will not be sufficient to cover living costs of the whole family in the US, we took the last flight to Europe and went to Croatia. ... Since the school and the work went online, the kids continued their education online, so did I with my work (personal communication, April 2021).

Several post-Yugoslav immigrants, who until the pandemic lived in the Western Europe made similar move after the first lockdown.

Since there were no vaccines yet, and since we were not allowed to work in the office, we made tests on COVID, and when they displayed negative results, we sat to the car and went to my family house to Croatia. The kids continued their education online, we continued to work online. It was cheaper to be in Croatia than in Austria... because it is warmer climate and less need for heating ... and being close to the nature was much pleasant (personal communication, October 2021).

After work and school, we were making barbeques in the garden, spending time with the family outdoors. ..Soon, it turned out that many of our fellow wartime emigrants also brought their spouses and kids to the homeland during COVID,... so we went on tours to the woods in small groups, or made picnics on the empty beaches. It turned to be one of best periods of lives over the last twenty and more years (personal notes, May 2022).

Therefore, the experiences shared by several of my acquaintances, mainly representing *corpornations* (as conceptualized throughout previous chapters), not only align with the 'brain-gain' trend but also support the proposition that it generated a new 'grey economy'. This was evident as white-collar migrants continued to pay taxes in host countries while relocating to their countries of origin. Similarly, faced with lockdowns in their host countries, they found 'exit' in Hirschman's (1970) original concept—through remigration to their homeland—as the most logical option for them and their families. However, such decisions were by no means a reflection of limited loyalty to host countries, as Hirschman's framework would suggest. Instead, as Ivan Krastev (2022) in his recent book keenly noted,

just as people seek shelter in their country, they also look for shelter in their native language. Psychologists have shown that people often revert to speaking in their mother tongue in moments of great imperilment.... The message urging people to 'stay at home' has encouraged them to define their home not just in pragmatic terms... It took me by surprise that, as it became clear that the coronavirus was a pandemic and we were probably facing a prolonged period of social distancing, my family decided to go back to Bulgaria before the lockdown. In many respects, this was not a rational decision. We have lived and worked in Vienna for a decade and love the city; the Austrian public health system is far more reliable than the system in Bulgaria and we could depend on our friends in the city. Yet what brought us back to Bulgaria was the understanding that we should 'stay at home', and Bulgaria *is* home for us (Krastev, 2022, p. 23).

Thus, during the pandemic, this migration return was the reflection of natural loyalty, not to states, organizations, or groups of people, but to a subjective idea and the perception of what the 'home' is. However, such an 'exit' option was not available to a majority of post-Yugoslav migrants. Most of my interlocutors expressed anxiousness because of the ban on travel and lockdowns. One of them, immigrant from Croatia in Germany, who has been employed as blue-collar worker and, therefore, could not travel back to homeland, found a solution locally in the host country.

> The schools were not working, and most of shops were closed. I was the only one in my family, who continued to work, though with reduced time. … It was too claustrophobic to be in the rented apartment all the time. In Germany, almost everyone has a garden somewhere close to the city. My friends told me that there is a one for sale close to their, the Syrian immigrant was selling it, and I bought it. …We spent all the lockdown there, and that saved us physically and psychologically. As our Bosnian friends own the neighboring garden, we spent the time together outdoor keeping the distance, thus without violating the German laws (personal communication, July 2021).

Therefore, unable to travel 'home,' some post-Yugoslav migrants remade their places of destination and 'warmed' them by spending time with other migrant compatriots. One of my interlocutors, a middle-aged female migrant from Serbia, who had been employed in the event industry and had spent about thirty years in Great Britain by the time of the pandemic, felt particularly vulnerable during the lockdowns.

> This pandemic has negative influence on my life. I feel worse than during the war. Due to lockdowns I lost my job, I cannot see my closest family because they all live elsewhere, and we have ban on travel. It looks as a huge hypocrisy, when the politicians move freely across the country and make parties, and ordinary people have to stay at home and think of how to pay their bills (online communication, September 2020).

Struggling with this feeling of isolation and inability to visit her closest family, she 'voiced' her anxiousness through the arts: writing poetry and making songs, which she then shared via social media with those whom she missed. Combined with frequent and rather long online communication with family members living in her home country and elsewhere abroad, her creativity provided soft resilience not only for her but also for those to whom she devoted her poetry and songs. Similarly, during the pandemic lockdowns, some other post-Yugoslav emigrants reactivated and further developed their YouTube channels and balanced decreased income from their main jobs by capitalizing on them. However, this soft resilience was not sufficient in situations when retired and elderly family members appeared physically far away from their younger and physically more capable children and relatives. Digitalization and the rapid growth of online shopping and delivery services provided substantial relief, especially in the places where volunteer numbers were limited. Constant and long online conversations with fellow post-Yugoslav immigrants living in Germany, it seemed that the perceptions of lockdowns varied from one to another generation of post-Yugoslav migrants.

> My parents live in another German land, and we could not travel to see each other during the first COVID-19 lockdown. My mom told me that she feels as if it was a war again, she was anxious. … I found myself alone in my flat, where I lived for a long time before. However, I did not know many of my neighbors, and now, during the pandemic, I befriended some of them. Many of them have also turned to be immigrants, and — in contrast to myself — many do not speak German at all, so we communicate in English (online communication, May 2020).

These comments suggest that migrants who experienced war as adults perceived the pandemic more negatively than those who were underage kids during the war. From my communication with post-Yugoslav immigrants across most of continental Europe, I learned that the majority of them did not face serious economic problems as they continued to receive pre-pandemic levels of income. The results of online surveys placed in several immigrant groups on Facebook confirmed this impression. Among seventy respondents, over sixty percent wrote that the pandemic did not influence their employment and financial statuses. One of the online survey respondents living in Austria noted, "The pandemic didn't change my financial situation. I find it relatively easy to accept the situation with the pandemic, having experienced the war" (online survey, April 2021). This answer reflects the essence of most of the responses from post-Yugoslav immigrants that I received using mixed methods of inquiry.

These respondents were either middle-level managers of Austrian, German, and Dutch firms or multinational corporations, or they were working in the educational sector. Only six of the seventy respondents reported that they lost their jobs due to the pandemic. As a result, they searched for new jobs through the receiving country's official labor market bureaus and received minimal financial support from states. Those employed as blue-collar workers in factories that had to stop working due to pandemic, reported that they also receive state support, while only one reported the return to the country of origin. This case confirms the assumption raised by The Economist (2021) that blue-collar migrant workers have been the most heavily affected by the pandemic. Moreover, some previous studies have demonstrated that even during the pandemic, particularly Croatians, emigrated to Austria as guest workers (Tepavcevic, 2021 c). Similarly, in social media discussions, several post-Yugoslav immigrants based in the Netherlands actively commented on the situation during the lockdowns. Only one of them, owning a small business in hospitality services, encountered obstacles to continue the work during the pandemic. Still, he used the lockdown to adjust the services and renovate the business venue.

As for the respondents of online surveys, prior to the pandemic, ten of them reported that they were employed in production sites, including agriculture and meat production, cleaning services, and craft, while eight were employed in trade and logistics. The remaining five respondents reported that they continued to work in medical services and an equal number reported that they worked in the education sector. Moreover, the majority of online survey respondents representing blue-collar workers in Germany and Austria noted that their working hours were shortened due to the pandemic. However, as the comment of one middle-aged female Bosnian immigrant living in Austria reveals, the pandemic has made their lives even more complex due to not being able to travel to their countries of permanent residence or visit their families: "I live and work in Denmark, and my parents are in Austria. ... I now have to take a three-week vacation to spend one week with my parents" (online survey, April 2021). At the same time, as online surveys' responses reflected, many post-Yugoslav emigrants during the pandemic perceived themselves as more resilient than their local non-migrant counterparts. "Nothing is in scarcity, I have enough of everything (food, flat, WiFi), all what we did not have during the war"; "Unfortunately, there are situations much worse than the pandemic, and we Bosnians know it very well" (Tepavcevic, 2021 c). The latter comment reinforces the Bosnian identity as a transnational migrant community linked by common traumas of loss and consequent loyalty of commitment to this community. Similarly, some of my post-Yugoslav migrant acquaintances shared anecdotal evidence of higher resilience in comparison to their non-migrant local neighbors during the COVID pandemic, explaining it as an outcome of their experiences with previous global crises.

> In the beginning of the first lockdown, all sanitizers were bought from shops within hours, and for some time in the Netherlands, they were in scarce. I took the first bottle of alcohol that I had at home, it was some vodka, and I put it to the plastic bottle with spray and used it for disinfection. One day a neighbor saw me spraying the door knob, and asked me where did I buy a sanitizer. I told her that I use vodka instead. Her surprise lasted for almost a minute, and I saw that it had just came to her mind that alcoholic drinks may have a multiple application. For me, who went through the collapse, sanctions, and the war the use of vodka as a sanitizer came as a natural solution (personal communication, August 2020).

This small example of tangible, in this case physical, resilience confirms Brooks, Hoberg et al. (2019) thesis that adaptation to sub-optimal conditions is key to survival. Simultaneously, it suggests that migrants' negative experiences from previous global crises contribute to the resilience of the non-migrant population, confirming Foulkes' (2021) thesis about 'psychological immunization'. Following the Bosnian tradition of approaching even the most difficult circumstances with a sense of humor, one of the relatively young male online survey respondents shared his perception of emigration and the pandemic.

> To me the pandemic seems to have lasted throughout my time in Austria, because going-from-home-to-work-repeat is how my life here looks like... but, of course, we live under the pressure of what tomorrow will bring, we live in uncertainty. Above all, I feel sorry for my kids. They always say that

> it is a pity that there is the pandemic, so they cannot go out. I wonder whether this pandemic will destroy my kids' childhood (online survey, March 2021).

At the same time, some of the young female post-Yugoslav online survey respondents residing in Austria noted positive changes happening in their lives during the pandemic. "Quite the contrary to my expectations, I got a job a month before the pandemic, and I still work there" (online survey, May 2021). The experiences of the pandemic seem somewhat different among post-Yugoslav immigrants across post-socialist Europe, most notably in the Czech Republic and Hungary, as a larger number of them through online surveys and online communication revealed their financial vulnerability. Most of them reported decreased incomes, while some noted job losses.

> My Yugoslav friends in Spain all seem terribly stressed with COVID-19 measures. They say that they cannot go out, that they are limited in movements, while they all receive the state's financial support and make barbecue on their terraces. All that we here in Hungary cannot even think of. I listen to them and laugh. We do not receive any state's support and the taxes are the same, while incomes are inexistent (personal communication, June 2020).

Regarding the impact of the pandemic on their lives, they noted reducing their expenditures to essentials. Other respondents pointed out that they "reduced their spending on everything". For example, a middle-aged female post-Yugoslav immigrant, who prior to the pandemic worked in the remnants of the once-flourishing Hungarian textile industry during socialist times, was heavily hit by the pandemic.

> We continued to work remotely for two months, but it is hard to produce individual tailor-made clothes without a face-to-face communication with the client even with a good digital measurement application. As a result, the firm went bankrupt, and I started to look for another job (online communication, May 2020).

Among post-Yugoslav migrants born between 1945 and 1960, the biggest difference was between those who lived alone and those who lived at least with one more family member. For the former, isolation was the most serious challenge. "I was closed at home and could not go out. I felt bad and undermined because I could not go out" (online communication, March 2023). Many of them previously worked in tourism and trade, and during lockdowns, they were left without income.

> Several large tourist groups and their hotel reservations were first postponed, and then cancelled due to the pandemic. Therefore, both my business partners and I lost our incomes. Luckily, our experience as refugees thought me always to keep some conserves and savings aside, so I can survive whatever happens (personal communication, May 2020).

Still, as I learned from my family members representing this age group and were already pensioners when the pandemic began, they organized traditional 'over coffee' meetings, a common practice in the Balkans, via various communication applications and spent hours 'together' talking online. One of them shared, "We turn on cameras, bring some snacks and drinks, and talk and laugh as if we were together somewhere in a café" (online communication, April 2020). Such collective coping mechanisms through digital tools seemed to make my pension-age migrant family members and other fellow migrant interlocutors psychologically resilient throughout the first and consecutive pandemic lockdowns.

Following their example, after finishing my first remotely taught university course, I suggested my students have an online course-graduation party. We all connected at the same time on a late Saturday afternoon, and with drinks and snacks, we chatted, played guitars, and sang for over two hours. Apart from moving teaching activities online, my own soft resilience during the pandemic emerged through following other working routines, attending and participating in online meetings and events, and continuing my research online. I also spent more quality time with my family and engaged in outdoor sports. The time that I used to spend on commuting between home and office before the pandemic, during lockdowns, I utilized for sports and reconnecting online with my friends and family across the world. In that way, the pandemic brought me closer to my old friends and family members living on other continents and in different time zones.

Last, but equally importantly, analyzing reactions to the pandemic via all available channels of communication, I noticed divisions between vaccination supporters, vaccination protesters, and a very small portion of vaccination-neutral reactions among post-Yugoslav migrants. Among my interlocutors, there was no rule based on the host country, level of education, or age determining groups of pro- or anti-vaccination views. However, I noticed that those post-Yugoslav migrants who lived alone both prior to and during the lockdowns were among the most active supporters of both vaccination and a return to the 'old normal,' simply because they felt the most isolated. Some of them coincided with the generations between 18 and 41 that Foulkes (2021) found to be most psychologically vulnerable to pandemic lockdowns, confirming to some extent her findings. Still, the most of them were around higher margin of that age group. In a similar way, there was no pattern enabling for classification of post-Yugoslav migrants inclined to believe in widespread conspiracy theories concerning the pandemic. Some of my interlocutors, spanning from the USA and Western Europe to post-socialist Europe, South Africa, and Australia, displayed deep suspicions of various sorts. Referring to the phenomenon of 'infodemic,' assumptions varied from "an attempt to test new medicines on people" and "making profits from selling the vaccines" to preparation for some big upcoming war. During an online conversation in February 2023, one of my interlocutors expressed suspicions about the origins and motives behind the pandemic. They questioned how a virus could have such a global impact and believed it was not a natural occurrence. They suggested it might be part of a planned and manipulative experiment but admitted to having no idea who could be behind it (online communication, February 2023). Similar impressions of the pandemic were revealed through online surveys, as I discussed in some of my previous works: "If there really were a pandemic, it would not have such a strong impact on my brain. This seems like butchering sheep before killing them" (Tepavcevic, 2022, p. 209).

Allusions to war and "butchering sheep before killing them" perceptions of the pandemic seem to be rooted in previous traumatic experiences of collapse and wars, but it also reveals a deep level of mistrust in the global system. This seems to happens, Bauman (2006) noted, because of the lack of time for social forms and institutions to solidify. Still, as one of my interviewees noted, demonstrating considerable level of psychological resilience, "nothing is end of the world even when there is a global lockdown" (online communication, February 2021). Across many European countries among post-Yugoslav migrant social media migrant groups, I noted some in-person collective resilience during the pandemic.

> In Berlin, we were allowed to go outdoors in small groups, so we went to walks, and, as the weather was relatively warm, we made outdoor parties with loud music, parks were full of people, most were keeping required distance… Overall, for me the first lockdown experience was rather very inspiring, than negative in any way (online communication, June 2020).

Similarly, during the lockdowns in Budapest, where I was located, a group of post-Yugoslav migrants organized several joint jogging meet-ups outdoors. They communicated and coordinated these gatherings through social media groups, using them as a way to both work out and socialize. It is worth noting that, as some previous studies have demonstrated, for migrant mothers with underage children, the pandemic lockdowns provided an opportunity to find a balance between being parents and professionals. One post-Yugoslav immigrant shared her experience,

> In contrast to the war, during the pandemic, we constantly have had water and electricity, we have had constant channels of communication via Internet platforms, so I kept contact with my family and friends… I spend much more time with my kid, and I became much more productive at work, as there was no need to commute to the office and back (personal communication, cited in Tepavcevic (2022)).

In turn, the absence of commuting to work benefited the time spent on childcare (Tepavcevic, 2022).

In summary, the experiences of post-Yugoslav migrants during the COVID pandemic confirmed three general propositions about the impact of the pandemic on migrant flows. First, some post-Yugoslav migrants relocated to their homeland at the beginning of lockdowns, supporting the idea of a temporary "brain gain" and a "new grey economy." Second, blue-collar workers and self-employed entrepreneurs, especially those in post-socialist European countries, experienced a decrease in income or job losses more frequently than those in other regions. This finding adds nuance to the general proposition that blue-collar migrant workers were more negatively affected by the pandemic than white-collar workers. Third, and most importantly, digital communication applications and social media played a major role in post-Yugoslav migrants' resilience during the pandemic. These tools facilitated remote work and allowed for communication with family and peers, serving as a platform for psychological resilience during long-term physical isolations.

The pandemic also generated time for reconnection while digital tools offered the 'space' to do so. Simultaneously, it revealed a place-of-origin and common culture as enduring source of community tie and loyalty of commitment. As a result, pandemic lockdowns resulted in a global re-emergence of Yugoslav-time communities and their replication into the 21st century. Similarly, experiences of previous global crises provided post-Yugoslav migrants certain physical, socioeconomic, and psychological resilience to accept the pandemic relatively calmly. At the same time, their wartime traumas made them vulnerable to various pandemic-related conspiracies. In fact, for senior generations of post-Yugoslav migrants as a truly transnational community, digital communication with their other compatriot friends was a major source of soft resilience. Middle-aged post-Yugoslav migrants displayed tendency to be more oriented to their immediate physical environments.

Post-Soviet Migrants' Experiences of COVID-19 Pandemic

While for post-Yugoslav migrants, COVID-19 lockdowns revoked war memories, for many middle-aged post-Soviet migrants, the pandemic served as a reminder of the scarcity of food and other products that they experienced prior to the breakup of the Soviet Union.

> The COVID-19 lockdown crisis revoked the memories of the late Soviet scarce in products, and expecting 'zombie apocalypses', I bought kilos and kilos of food. For me the lockdown was the signal of something more terrible coming. To keep my sanity, I continued to work, to jog, to meet outdoor with friends (personal communication, February 2023).

Similar to my interviewee, thirty-five respondents to the repeating online surveys placed in the Russian-speaking immigrant groups in spring 2021 and winter 2021-2022 demonstrated that post-Soviet migrants also displayed resilience during the pandemic by maintaining their pre-pandemic routines as much as possible. The respondents mostly held white-collar positions in various economic sectors, ranging from information technologies (IT) and finance to education and manufacturing. They reported that they were able to keep their jobs and maintain their level of salaries during the pandemic. These individuals were mostly representatives of corporations — migrant communities composed of multinational corporate employees as discussed throughout the previous chapters. On the other hand, the pandemic presented significant socioeconomic challenges to many post-Soviet migrants who held blue-collar jobs prior to the pandemic.

> I worked in a Chinese trade company in Hungary as a sales person. The trade was oriented mostly on Chinese tourists, so the company closed simultaneously with the first lockdown in China, much before COVID reached Europe. I was receiving a minimum salary for several months, and, as the company closed, I had to look for another job, but it was challenging to find it as a blue-collar worker during the pandemic anyway (personal communication, May 2020).

Social media groups served simultaneous voice and exit for post-Soviet migrants around the globe. As Molodikova and Tepavcevic (2021) pointed out, the striking example was the post-Soviet women's virtual group "The Frog in Vodka and the Bear in Champagne", which unites women from different countries of the world counting over 43 000 members.

> This is a kind of psychotherapeutic laboratory not only for Russian-speaking wives of foreigners, but also for Russian-speaking women abroad: it is, among other things, a virtual travel agency. Any "frog" can write to members of the group in another country where she is going to travel, and get

not only complete information, but also help in organizing a stay, an excursion program (Molodikova & Tepavcevic, 2021).

In Germany, Austria, Spain, and the Netherlands, post-Soviet migrants, like locals, received state support during the lockdown if they were entrepreneurs or blue-collar workers and unable to continue their work remotely. For instance, the owner of a language and arts school in Vienna described remote teaching and the subsequent decrease in customers as a major challenge for her during the pandemic.

> Teaching … arts and music remotely to kids is not much effective … Parents are afraid of the virus…. There are constant verbal attacks on the Austrian chancellor, but I appreciate his decision to support small businesses during the pandemic… otherwise, we would not be able to survive the pandemic (personal communication, October 2021).

This quotation highlights a high level of convenience loyalty, as described by McGinn (2015), towards the host country's system and its top politician of the time, for being included in the state support when the business was most vulnerable. For those who were also parents, as well as other post-Soviet migrant parents with kindergarten-aged and school-aged children, remote education posed one of the most serious challenges for a variety of reasons. First, it was apparent that both the quality and quantity of online teaching depended not only on the host country or a particular school but even on individual teachers. As one post-Soviet migrant residing in Spain commented,

> Out of two teachers, one was frequently connected and continued to teach remotely. Another was simply sending homework by email, and then parents had to make sure that kids sent the results back, as if parents did not have to do their own work (online communication, June 2020).

In Hungary, similar problems with remote education turned technically difficult for many post-Soviet migrant parents, especially self-employed mothers, who mostly came to Hungary as marriage migrants in the period over the last two decades.

> My kid had just entered the school, and after the first semester, there was a first lockdown. We did not have any gadgets for her, and I and my husband

also had to work remotely. Since the work on smartphone was really inconvenient for the first grade kid, I gave her my computer, and I continued to work from my smartphone as long as her classes lasted. … For me it was important that she attends all classes, because otherwise, unlike the parents of her Hungarian classmates, my knowledge of Hungarian is limited, and I would not be able to help her as much as they can help their kids (personal communication, June 2020).

In this way, many post-Soviet migrant mothers in Hungary during the pandemic experienced "triple vulnerability: being female, a mother, and a migrant" (Tepavcevic, 2022, p. 204). Some corponation parents used their corporate networks with locals to find teachers to help their children with the specifics of the school programs in the host countries' education systems. Others turned to social media's local Russian-speaking groups to find experienced bilingual tutors (Tepavcevic, 2022). Apart from these middle-aged post-Soviet migrant parents, younger generations of post-Soviet migrants, who emigrated either as students or corporate employees, proved strikingly resilient during the pandemic. They displayed a positive mindset and remained active during the lockdowns by engaging in sports, enrolling in online courses, acquiring pets, or simply adopting a proactive approach by focusing on the positive side of the situation. For example, as one of my conversers noted, "Before COVID, we frequently went to restaurants and did a lot of shopping, spending a lot of money. Now, neither restaurants nor shops work, so we are saving money instead" (personal communication, May 2020). Among post-Soviet migrants, there were significantly fewer returners to their homelands during the pandemic compared to former Yugoslav migrants. Nevertheless, some of the wealthier post-Soviet migrants who owned second homes, most frequently in the coastal areas of Spain, France, and Montenegro, or in the mountain areas of Austria and Italy, chose to move there during the lockdowns. This trend of relocation to second-homes during the COVID-19 pandemic was first noted by Krastev (2022, p. 25):

the early stages of the coronavirus crisis were marked not by criticism of foreigners by 'natives', but by the anger of those living in the countryside at the invasion of the 'second-homers'. … city dwellers decamping from the epicenters of the crisis to their second homes, where proximity to the coast or the mountains would lessen the discomfort of confinement – and a decent internet link would permit remote work. Yet their arrival enraged local residents, because of a fear that they would spread the virus to areas with fewer hospitals … The uncomfortable irony is that second homes in Europe are themselves a legacy of plague. After the first few outbreaks of the fourteenth-century Black Death, many inhabitants of cities in Renaissance Italy began to invest in country estates, partly to secure reliable food supplies in times of crisis.

Exactly, as suggested by Krastev, others searched rural estates to rent to be closer to nature and to spend more time outdoors. In Germany, like post-Yugoslav immigrants, they were spending time in their city-based gardens (online communication, June 2020). In Hungary, where city-gardens have not been a common practice as in Germany, my post-Soviet acquaintances from Ukraine used their friendship networks with the locals to rent summerhouses.

The schools and kindergartens were closed, the offices too, and we all were stuck at the flat in the city working online. Being anxious, we used private contacts to rent a house in the woods, faraway from the city. We spent there all the lockdown, and that saved our nerves and improved our health, and also our family relations (personal communication, September 2020).

As the platform economy system became dominant during the pandemic all over the world, self-employed post-Soviet migrants across Europe moved their small businesses online.

When the Hungarian government announced the first lockdown, we quickly installed Zoom and instructed our teachers how to use it online. Though language teaching is much harder in an online format than face-to-face especially for the kids, we continued our language teaching programs and we kept almost all of our clients throughout the pandemic (personal communication, June 2021).

Most chains of stores trading in EU products traditional for the countries of the former Soviet Union began to provide delivery services and offer online selection of goods actively. Many of these stores, which previously used their websites mostly for advertising purposes, changed their formats into interactive platforms. Similar to post-Yugoslav migrants, post-Soviet migrants extended their use of social media to self-organize and help each other. For example, post-Soviet migrants across the EU countries, who were usually self-employed as tourist guides and were among the professions most affected by COVID lockdowns, began to promote walking tours, virtual thematic tours, or nature hikes in small groups on their Facebook pages (Molodikova & Tepavcevic, 2021). Therefore, they overcame the obstacles posed by the pandemic by finding a 'digital exit' from the unprecedented situation. Their socioeconomic resilience was founded on an extended use of digital channels of communication and on transforming their in-person activities into virtual ones. Simultaneously, during the first lockdown, in the early spring of 2020, many Ukrainians, who by the pandemic were frequently travelling for work to the EU, were stuck in Poland, Slovakia and Hungary.

As a result, information about trips by minibuses or private cars to Ukraine became one of the most frequent topics in social media groups focused on these three countries. Similar situations were occurring along the borders of the three Baltic states and Russia (Ryazantsev, Molodikova et al., 2020). Moreover, announcements in various social media groups revealed that during the COVID lockdowns, Ukrainians with dual Ukrainian-EU citizenship or residents of the border zones of EU and non-EU countries were allowed to travel across the border. Similarly, websites for recruitment of migrant labor, intended mostly for Ukrainians and Moldovans, offered jobs in large enterprises, construction, and agriculture in Hungary, Austria, and Italy. Taking these jobs during the pandemic was also a response to other blue-collar job losses. Some of my Hungary-based post-Soviet acquaintances found the pandemic as a moment to change their careers, place of work, or even start a business in areas related to their previous hobbies.

> Being employed in tourism, I went to courses for the cosmetician and I had a plan to practice it as a hobby to bring some additional income. The pandemic made corrections to my plans. First, cosmetology became my major source of income, as during the pandemic I received only a minimal salary. Then, the more clients I had, the more time I worked as a cosmetician. As a result, I quit my old job, and now I work in my own beauty salon (online communication, November 2021).

For one of my youngest interlocutors, a twenty-two old Ukrainian immigrant in Hungary, the pandemic created the conditions for his first job.

> My dad's company needed Hungarian-Russian and English-Russian interpreters, and it was during the spring and summer breaks that I applied for that job, and worked on two construction sites as an interpreter. This was my first serious job and salary (personal communication, September 2020).

Similarly, a respondent of the online survey residing in Austria reported that during the pandemic, she switched to work for another company and to a better position: from a pre-pandemic medium-level professional in tourism to a top manager in marketing (online survey, April 2021). Moreover, similar to their counterparts from former Yugoslavia, most of my post-Soviet migrant conversers noted that during the pandemic, the biggest challenge for them was the ban on travel. Some other respondents found the travel ban difficult because it did not allow for "a change in the environment and scenery." During the COVID lockdown, my interlocutor, an emigrant from the Eastern regions of Ukraine, encountered triple vulnerability through exclusion. First, being employed in the tourism and hospitality sector in Lower Austria, she lost her job due to COVID. Second, because of the ongoing war and subsequent sanctions, the banks in the war-torn Eastern Ukrainian regions have not been able to make international transfers since 2014. Therefore, before the COVID pandemic, she used to send remittances to her parents through friends living in the Ukrainian army-controlled territories. Her friends would then hand over the money to her parents, meeting with them at block posts or checkpoints on the borders of Ukrainian army-controlled and breakout territories. However, with the outbreak of COVID, lockdowns were introduced all across Ukraine, and these meetings at checkpoints became forbidden, making bank transfers to the breakout territories of Ukraine equally impossible.

Along with post-Soviet Russians, Ukrainians, and Belarussians, I also frequently conversed with Armenians and Azerbaijanis, who were post-Soviet migrants. Prior to the second lockdown in late September 2020, for most of them, the pandemic turned into a secondary problem compared to the new outbreak of a thirty-year frozen conflict in Nagorno-Karabakh. The attempts of the Azerbaijani army to regain control over the territory of the self-proclaimed Armenian enclave prompted the Armenian population of Nagorno-Karabakh to evacuate to neighboring Armenia. At the same time, the attempts of the Armenian government to defend Armenians and their property in Nagorno-Karabakh led to mass mobilization across Armenia. Post-Soviet emigrants originating from both Armenia and Azerbaijan, particularly those from the Nagorno-Karabakh region, found themselves under double pressure. On one hand, many of them made individual attempts to bring their relatives from the conflict zone to their host countries to save them from the conflict and mobilization. These examples shed light on the limited loyalty to the state and the system among Armenians, which was compensated by loyalty of commitment to family and fellow nationals.

In these attempts, the COVID pandemic appeared as an additional obstacle to their compatriots' already limited mobility, because embassies and visa centers remained closed. In turn, in host countries, where Armenian diaspora associations already existed, including the US, Hungary, and Russia, these associations along with individual immigrants organized charity activities and meetings for fund-rising and collecting humanitarian aid, and supply chains for delivering aid to Armenia (personal communication, October 2021). The conflict in Karabakh also appeared as a trigger for some long-term post-Soviet emigrants to relocate back to post-Soviet countries, as they believed that being geographically closer to Armenia would enable them to provide more and better support to their historical homelands.

> My friends lived in Hungary for a long time, they had good jobs, good salaries. However, when the war in Karabakh started again, they felt that they could not stay aside and continue their business as usual... They felt that their skills and experience would be better applied to help Armenia from Russia, where the largest Armenian diaspora resides. ... I had a similar urge to go either to Russia or to Armenia to be among the Armenians to support them, because nobody can understand us better in such situation than we can understand and support each other. Unfortunately, here... I neither

could find affordable flights to travel to homeland, nor I had a social network enough trusted and large to support my family in my absence except
from a couple of other Armenians, who also wanted to travel to Armenia
and help there (personal communication, January 2021).

It is significant that my Azerbaijani migrant acquaintances
noted that due to the pandemic restrictions, their relatives who escaped from territories close to Karabakh also mostly found shelter
in Russia, where the largest Azerbaijani diaspora lives (personal
communication, April 2022). Therefore, for post-Soviet migrants
with ties to Armenia and Azerbaijan, the COVID pandemic appeared as a secondary rather than the primary challenge posed by
the global crisis, preventing them from finding individual solutions. As a result, their tangible and soft resilience appeared as collective 'voice' in Hirschman's words, or some form of sociopolitical
participation in events of the home country and the kin-state, as
noted by Hoffmann (2010). In this way, they displayed transmigrants' loyalty of commitment to their homeland and to their less
fortunate compatriots there. At the same time, this collective sociopolitical activism provided Armenian migrants with soft resilience,
in this case a comfort that balanced their inability to be physically
present in Armenia during the peak of the worst local crisis in decades.

I also noted one significant trend: while most of my post-Soviet migrant conversers were not eager to embrace conspiracy theories concerning the pandemic, I observed that those of them who
had previously experienced war or problems with food supply
tended to be more suspicious towards vaccination, though not
openly anti-vaccination as many post-Yugoslav migrants were.
Quite the contrary, most of my post-Soviet migrant interlocutors
were among the first in line waiting for vaccines as soon as they
became available. Interestingly, most of them were male. When I
asked them about their motives for waiting hours in queues for vaccination, one of them told me that he cannot wait to go to an upcoming football match and, for that, he needs confirmation of vaccination. Similarly, another said that he wants to attend a concert of
his favorite musician and, thus, he needs proof that he is vaccinated
against COVID. These explanations, when compared to the fears

from vaccination among my post-Yugoslav migrant peers, suggest the relevance of Foulkes' (2021) concepts of high and mild levels of stress, and their influence on the presence or absence of 'psychological immunization'. They also reveal different levels of trust in international and national medical authorities, highlighting what McGinn (2015) referred to as 'loyalty of coercion' among post-Soviet migrants or the lack thereof among post-Yugoslav migrants.

Though most post-Soviet immigrants perceived the pandemic as an unprecedented experience, they seem to have reacted with resilience throughout the obstacles posed by the crisis. On the one hand, this kind of resilience may be interpreted as personal with generational characteristics. On the other hand, the pandemic can be seen as a learning experience that generates psychological immunity. In summary, during the COVID pandemic, post-Soviet corponation migrants were preoccupied with their well-being and continued to follow their routines. Those who have kids also focused on finding the best solutions for continuing their education under quarantine conditions.

Conclusions: Self-Organization as 'Voice' or Tangible Resilience and Digital Exit as Soft Resilience

The COVID-19 pandemic has acted as a catalyst for almost all aspects and levels of post-Yugoslav and post-Soviet immigrants' lives, affecting their health, finances, society, and family dynamics. The analysis in this chapter highlights that for most post-Yugoslav emigrants and many relatively recent post-Soviet immigrants, frequent travels to their countries of origin were a crucial source of soft resilience. However, the pandemic's lockdowns disrupted the work and income of numerous migrants who relied on small logistics-related businesses and tourism. Despite these challenges, the overall impression from my communication with both former Yugoslav and post-Soviet immigrants of various genders and age groups is that, for the majority, their incomes and socio-economic situations have not been significantly impacted by the pandemic. However, it is important to note that the psychological effects of the pandemic vary among individuals and are only partially influenced by the overall situation.

The findings, therefore, lead to several important conclusions on both theoretical and practical levels. On the theoretical level, probably the most obvious conclusion is that the COVID-19 pandemic represented a transformation in both Polanyi's meanings: while in the beginning it prompted people to change their daily routines and jobs, in the long-term, the pandemic prompted changes in life styles, habits, and even in worldviews. Still, these changes are varied depending on four factors: first the immigrants' socio-economic circumstances prior to and during the pandemic; second, the extent of their psychological immunity developed during previous global crises; third, the time of their emigration and the length of their stay in a receiving country, and fourth, their own personalities.

As pointed out by Foulkes (2021), mild stress can generate psychological immunity, while high stress may lead to psychological vulnerability. This pattern seemed to be observed among immigrants working as blue-collar workers who lost their jobs during the pandemic. Similarly, the level of loyalty to medical authorities, whether international or at the host country level, appeared to be influenced by the level of stress and exposure to the pandemic. Those who were less severely impacted by the crisis demonstrated relatively high levels of resilience, supporting Foulkes' findings. In conclusion, the analysis in this chapter suggests that socio-economic factors play a significant role, but are not the sole determinants, of the psychological resilience to the crisis among post-Yugoslav and post-Soviet immigrants. The interplay between stress levels, loyalty to medical authorities, and exposure to the pandemic seems to be crucial in understanding the varied responses and coping mechanisms of these migrant communities during this challenging period.

Table 6.1 Comparison of Challenges and Resilience of post-Yugoslav and post-Soviet migrants during COVID-19 pandemic

	Generations 1945-1960	Generations 1970-1985	
Challenges during COVID-19 pandemic	Mobility restrictions, loneliness	Mobility restrictions, loss of jobs	Post-Yugoslav migrants
Forms of Resilience	Reconnection with friends via digital apps and social media and re-creation of place of origin and common culture-based communities in digital 'space'	Connection with compatriots via social media and joined recreation activities; finding access to allowed outdoor spaces and activities with neighbors and compatriots; reform in business management; the use of social media for earning and comfort via arts	
Challenges during COVID-19 pandemic	Mobility restrictions, loneliness, the lack of physical support in daily activities	War in country of origin and lockdowns as obstacle to evacuate relatives and send remittances; job losses	Post-Soviet migrants
Forms of Resilience	Connection with compatriots via digital apps and social media and common gender and common-culture-based in digital 'space'; use of digital media for delivery and	Further migration or re-migration to closer regions; changing career path, starting own business, or changing the job	

The present chapter has made significant contributions to understanding the impact of the COVID-19 pandemic on post-Yugoslav and post-Soviet immigrants residing across three continents. One important finding is the re-migration of white-collar workers to their countries of origin, as well as the emergence of a 'grey economy', which are specific to individual post-Yugoslav cases. These trends align with the larger early-pandemic trend observed by The Economist (2021) between Western and Eastern European countries. Moreover, the analysis confirms the larger and longer-term pandemic trend of relocating to second homes in rural and coastal areas, as earlier discussed by Krastev (2022), as a repeating historical phenomenon related to plagues. This trend is also applicable to post-Yugoslav and post-Soviet migrants across both EU and non-EU European countries. To gain a more comprehensive understanding of the consequences of the pandemic on migrants, further research should be conducted in other immigrant groups and comparisons. This would provide additional insights and details about the diverse impacts experienced by various migrant communities during the COVID-19 pandemic. Second, the findings of the present chapter provide an interesting contribution to the proposition that migration changes people's identities and consequently loyalties, including the national one.

As the analysis demonstrates, global crises have a significant impact on shaping various types of identities, especially national and ethnic identities, depending on how they affect people in a specific country and period. This is evident from the comment of one of the post-Yugoslav respondents in the online surveys, who expressed the sentiment that "we Bosnians know that the pandemic is not the worst" that can happen, clearly alluding to the traumatic experiences of the collapse and war in the past. This suggests that such historical traumas have left a profound mark on their sense of perspective, emphasizing that they have endured much worse situations than the COVID-19 pandemic.

Moving on to more general implications regarding the role of the state in social protection during such an unprecedented global crisis, striking differences have been observed among post-Yugoslav and post-Soviet immigrants living in Western and older EU member states, compared to those residing in newer EU member states and post-socialist countries. Despite being EU member states for a considerable time before the pandemic, post-socialist countries still have weaker social security mechanisms compared to their Western European counterparts. In this regard, they seemed more similar to countries like Great Britain and the US, which also took considerable time to provide adequate social security during the pandemic. The next and final empirical chapter of this book delves into exploring how the experiences of the COVID-19 pandemic and previous global crises have influenced the reactions of post-Soviet and post-Yugoslav citizens and migrants to another global crisis—Russia's full-scale invasion in Ukraine. This chapter aims to shed light on how the past experiences of these communities shape their responses and resilience in the face of yet another crisis.

Chapter 7
Multiple Exclusions and Self-Organization of Migrant Communities as Resilience to Global Effects of Russia's Government Invasion in Ukraine

Ukrainian migrant: "We are not victims, we are rather heroes, and we will win" (personal communication, December 2022).

Russian migrant: "I could not believe it, because it is non-sense! My friends in Russia are equally shocked; the invasion was a huge surprise for them" (personal communication, September 2022).

Post-Yugoslav migrant: "We were the general repetition for what is going on now in Ukraine and Russia" (personal communications, July 2022).

Introduction: Is It The Beginning of the World War Third?

The dynamics of international relations have rapidly changed since Russia's full-scale invasion of Ukraine in February 2022. A meme shared among post-Yugoslav Balkan groups on social media in the early days of the invasion, displaying Putin's picture and labeling him a "genius" who healed the world from COVID in only two days, suggested that humanity did not even have a proper 'pause' to recover between the pandemic and the war. The war has been raging to destroy the already fragile international institutions established after World War II in an attempt to balance interests on the global stage built on states. Moreover, the war has prompted millions of people from Ukraine and Russia to flee their homes, creating the largest migration crisis in Europe since World War II (UNHCR, 2022). Residents of Ukraine have been escaping from bombs, shelling, poverty caused by destruction, and the threat of war-related epidemics. On the other hand, residents of Russia initially fled due to increased political and ideological persecutions, as well as political and economic uncertainty. Gradually, mobilization, shelling, and drone attacks contributed to the list of motives for their exodus, particularly from regions along the internationally recognized Russian-Ukrainian border.

Migration statistics provided by UNHCR (2022) demonstrate that between February and December 2022, over seven million people left Ukraine, which constitutes about nineteen percent of the total Ukrainian population. Limited statistics about emigration from Russia aggregated from various sources suggests that for the same period between three and five million people emigrated from Russia in two large waves (ERR, 2022). The first wave of emigration peaked between the end of February and April 2022, and the second at the end of September 2022, when the Russian government announced 'partial' mobilization (Fortune, 2022). As of the time of writing, the war continues to escalate along the internationally recognized border between Russia and Ukraine, leading to more refugees fleeing from both countries towards the first available safe destinations. This emergency post-Soviet migration crisis has even surpassed the Balkans, which has been the long-standing 'champion' among European regions in terms of emigration, as described by Krasteva (2021). More broadly, as Mariotti (2022) correctly noted,

> The war in Ukraine goes hand in hand with other manifestations that signal the non-zero probability of a future of severe economic and political instability and of possible large-scale, if not global, conflicts. Economic protectionism and trade wars are escalating. Global and local economic crises are slowing down the world's economy and are opening up prospects for much lower growth rates than those experienced in past decades….
> Obviously, systemic shocks include the exogenous one of the global COVID-19 pandemic and, in accordance with Clausewitz's dictum that war is merely a continuation of politics by other means, the endogenous shock of the Russian–Ukrainian conflict, which is the most recent expression of the current geopolitical imbalances and international competition for political supremacy (Mariotti, 2022, p. 768).

As this book has demonstrated, global crises are complex and often intersect, revealing imbalances in the global order that shape the forms and dynamics of human communities. As the Russia-Ukraine war continues to be an ongoing crisis at the time of writing this book, this chapter delves into the reactions and experiences of post-Soviet and post-Yugoslav immigrants in response to Russia's full-fledged invasion in Ukraine across different receiving countries. It also explores the roles they have taken since February 2022 in light of this unfolding crisis. My recent work reveals general trends of these migration flows noting that

> Ukrainians primarily migrate to the EU, while Russians, facing increasingly restrictive EU visa policies, mostly flee to countries with visa-free regimes such as former Soviet countries, Georgia, Kazakhstan, Armenia, and Uzbekistan, as well as Middle Eastern countries like Turkey and the United Arab Emirates, and Serbia and Montenegro in Europe (Tepavcevic, 2023, p. 88).

Following the overall aim of the present book, this chapter addresses the question whether and to what extent the post-Soviet and post-Yugoslav migrants' experiences from previous global crises affected their adaptation strategies in an awake of the war? As the epicenter of the current global crises lies in Ukraine and Russia, this chapter primarily focuses on post-Soviet migrant communities, offering insights into post-Yugoslav migrant communities' reactions to the crisis as a point of reflection and comparison.

The chapter is structured as follows. In the next section, I delve into the experiences of post-Soviet migrants, particularly Ukrainian long-term emigrants, and those who were forced to become refugees due to the invasion. Through extensive personal and online communication, I analyze their reactions and the wide range of challenges they faced during the crisis. Additionally, I explore the experiences of Russian long-term emigrants and the refugees and relocators from Russia, shedding light on the commonalities and overlapping identities among various post-Soviet nationalities.

Moving on, Section 2 delves into the emerging forms of self-organization and political movements of Russian immigrants in Europe. This section offers insights into how these communities have reacted and mobilized in response to the ongoing conflict in Ukraine. In Section 3, I shift the focus to post-Yugoslav migrants and their reactions to the war in Ukraine. Drawing on their experiences during the wars of Yugoslavia's dissolution, I also examine the responses of the populations in post-Yugoslav republics to the crisis in Ukraine. By examining the experiences and reactions of post-Soviet and post-Yugoslav migrants to the Russia-Ukraine war, this chapter aims to provide a comprehensive understanding of the ways in which global crises shape and influence human communities across different regions and contexts.

February 24, 2022 and First Reactions among Post-Soviet Migrant Communities

Since February 24, 2022, residents of Ukraine encountered numerous unexpected challenges. Some of them were vacationing in Southern European resorts (online communication, February 2022), while others were starting new job positions in Ukraine after several years of studying abroad (personal communication, March 2022). The full-scale invasion, unfolding rapidly and violently, shattered routines and plans for countless individuals. The relentless bombs and attacks from the Russian army posed a grave threat to basic safety and security. Many Ukrainian residents, including a significant number of foreign students in Ukraine, were left with no choice but to flee in order to stay alive. However, even their attempts to escape were marred by the constant threat of bombardments and violence.

> We were living Kyiv at 8 a.m. with my friend's car after waking up at 5 a.m. because of explosions. It was the first airstrike in the city since fascists attacked it in 1941. ... During the first day, I had to explain my children that this is not a nightmare... We are living in this new reality. We cannot tell what will be tomorrow. ... I am grateful to all of you who were asking and suggested help ... I am grateful to all my Russian friends, who made public statements, went to the streets, were arrested and will be put on trial. Our reality is now divided into "before" and "after" (social media discussion, February 2022).

Invasion was equally unexpected for most of post-Soviet migrants, and many of them could not believe the news. The following citation reflects most of reactions.

> When that morning my colleagues told me that Russia attacked Ukraine, I thought that it was some fake news. It really seemed as a complete nonsense. However, when I double-checked several news sources that confirmed that

this nonsense is true, I got stall and numb for several hours trying to understand what was happening. The first clear thought was how I could help Ukrainians escaping the shelling (personal communication, February 2023).

The invasion in Ukraine triggered an immediate and powerful wave of solidarity among post-Soviet migrants and the majority of the population in Europe. They united in support of Ukraine's residents and citizens, who were the first and most visible victims of the conflict. This solidarity also became a new bond among post-Soviet migrants themselves. In the early days of the invasion, post-Soviet migrants were deeply concerned about the safety of their families and friends residing in Ukraine. They made every effort to understand the situation and find ways to evacuate their loved ones. As the conflict persisted, with the Russian army's bombings and the Ukrainian army's defense, and as Ukrainian civilians, including women, children, and the elderly, sought refuge from the violence, post-Soviet immigrants across Europe and around the world came together and self-organized through various communication applications. They provided much-needed relief to the refugees from Ukraine and offered support to one another during this difficult time. The crisis brought them closer, forging a sense of community and shared purpose in the face of adversity.

Geographically close to Ukraine, Poland, Slovakia, and Hungary served as the first border crossings to the EU for many Ukrainians seeking safety. The local population in these countries, along with post-Soviet immigrants living there, were among the first to volunteer and provide various forms of relief to those escaping the aggression of the Russian army. Among the post-Soviet immigrants in Poland, Ukrainian immigrants have been the most numerous over the last two decades. Many Ukrainians had come to Poland as students, migrant workers, and entrepreneurs. As a result, when the invasion began, a significant number of Ukrainian refugees, totaling over a million, sought refuge in Poland, finding comfort and support among their fellow Ukrainians and the local post-Soviet community.

In Hungary, post-Soviet migrants were among the first to step up and provide much-needed relief to the refugees arriving from

Ukraine. They played a crucial role in assisting at the points of mass arrivals, offering help with translation, finding temporary and long-term accommodations, and facilitating transfers from railway stations to their lodgings. In some cases, these volunteers even traveled to the border with Ukraine to pick up Ukrainian refugees and bring them to their homes. I personally participated in the rescue efforts and noticed that a majority of these volunteers were immigrants from Russia. Prior to the invasion, many of them had been critical of Russia's government policies in general, including those concerning Ukraine. Some were apolitical, but regardless of their political views, the invasion was a shocking and intolerable event for all of them. Their compassion and willingness to assist the Ukrainian refugees in need demonstrated a strong sense of solidarity and shared humanity among post-Soviet migrants in Hungary. "I am ashamed for what they are doing," wrote one Russian immigrant in Hungary in social media group.

"What the Russian army is doing is absolutely monstrous!" reacted another.

"I condemn the invasion" — was the most frequent sentence across social media used by Russian-speaking migrants.

In this way, they all disassociated themselves as citizens of Russia from the deeds of the Russian government and the army. All discussions with my acquaintances — despite their prior positions towards the conflict in Ukraine and politics in Russia — revealed their deep shock, disappointment, and disagreement with Russia's government decision to invade Ukraine. Openly expressing their disloyalty and disagreement with Russia's political leadership actions was an immediate reaction and a key mechanism of soft resilience for post-Soviet migrants. By standing against the invasion, they demonstrated their values and principles, refusing to condone or support such aggression. In addition to expressing their disapproval, post-Soviet migrants showed active empathy and solidarity with those directly affected by the conflict. They provided support and relief to family members, friends, colleagues, and even strangers who were escaping Ukraine. This display of compassion and assistance not only showed loyalty to their fellow humans but also served as a form of tangible resilience for themselves during the crisis. By coming together and helping those in need, they reaffirmed their shared humanity and found strength in unity during this difficult time.

Those post-Soviet migrants representing *corponations* as conceptualized in Chapter 4 of this book, as rarely fluent in local languages, were engaged in transfer and organization of accommodation of their colleagues escaping from shelling in Ukraine and from repressions, and later from mobilization in Russia. As one of my acquaintances recalled in the beginning of 2023,

> First, we were evacuating colleagues from Kiev and Odessa with their families. … Among them, there were oncological patients, and people with special needs…. There were pets. … Because of mass inflow of Ukrainians, it was challenging to find appropriate accommodation. After providing immediate relief, we organized them long-term accommodation and settlement in other countries. … Then, in September, we did the same for our colleagues and friends escaping from Russia (personal communication, February 2023).

Among my acquaintances, there are many couples where one partner is Ukrainian, and the other is a Russian citizen. For them, the situation has created a sense of double vulnerability. These Russian-Ukrainian couples, along with those who identify as Ukrainian citizens but also consider themselves Russians or vice versa, demonstrate the transient nature of post-Soviet migrants' national identities. This fluidity is directly linked to their detachment from any sense of loyalty or association with their home states, particularly with the political leadership of those states. Despite this detachment, many post-Soviet migrants share a common cultural background, which often leads to strong relationships, including friendships and marriages. Some of these migrants, who were previously largely apolitical, have started to identify more with Ukraine. The complex web of identities and loyalties among post-Soviet migrants reflects the intricacies of their experiences and the impact of the ongoing crisis in Ukraine.

> I never had any strong national identity; neither do most of people from my hometown, Odessa. However, since Russia blatantly invaded Ukraine, I started to understand that I am Ukrainian in the first place. Today it means

> paying the highest price in fighting the evil (online communication, June 2022).

This comment from one of the numerous online discussions demonstrates an increasing loyalty to Ukraine as a state through Ukrainian national identity. The same factors have also influenced long-term Ukrainian migrants across Western Europe, Canada, and the US to connect and self-organize in order to help the Ukrainian people and army in their defense efforts. One migrant expressed, "Collecting private donations is entirely new for us... Our fund-raising is for purchasing medicines for children's hospitals in Ukraine" (online communication, June 2022). This support had a significant impact on the sociopolitical resilience of the Ukrainian population and army. Another statement from the online discussion highlights

> the strong sense of freedom and independence that has always defined Ukrainians. Now, we are building powerful networks to aid our country in this time of crisis. The connections and solidarity we have formed have proven to be more helpful than just financial assistance. Now we understand what our president means," the statement adds (online communication, May 2022).

This shows that Ukrainian President Volodymyr Zelensky has become a symbol of Ukrainians' resistance to the invasion, and his stance has prompted the loyalty and commitment of Ukrainian migrants both to their home country and personally to the President. Therefore, Russia's full-fledged invasion has brought about a significant trend among many Ukrainian citizens and residents—the emergence of their political loyalty and commitment to the Ukrainian state. Prior to the invasion, such identification with Ukraine as an independent state was more ambiguous and prevalent only among certain regional and political groups (Abdelal, 2005). The invasion has served as a catalyst for a stronger sense of unity and loyalty to Ukraine, especially among those directly affected by the conflict. It has reflected through their strengthening sense of Ukrainian identity, strengthening ties with other Ukrainians, and their joint activity aiming to support people, who reside in Ukraine under the threat of Russia's army invasion. For example, commenting on the notion of 'Nazism', which Russia's government declared as the official motive for the full-fledged invasion in Ukraine, one Ukrainian refugee residing in Poland noted that "Nazis is not the same as nationalists, and we just want to live in our country with our culture. ... We do not take peace and democracy for granted" (online communication, May 2022).

While some Ukrainians perceived themselves as an 'ethnic' nation, and others perceived themselves as a nation by citizenship, the current war put them under similar physical threat, and the reactions to the invasion have been purely negative despite retaining a large diversity of their views on Russia. Still, some of my conversers aligned their traumatic experiences with their struggle to survive.

> I do not understand why Putin is doing this to us. I have never participated in the politics, I was never interested. I only lived my life, taking care of my family, doing my business... My older son, who turned eighteen and my husband stayed in Ukraine, because they are liable for military service. I took the young one, he is five now, he was four when we were escaping (personal communication, February 2023).

In turn, the current war defined Ukrainians as a separate social construct, as a nation in its own as Harari (2022) wrote:

> Gorbachev left Russians and Ukrainians feeling like siblings; Putin has turned them into enemies, and has ensured that the Ukrainian nation will henceforth define itself in opposition to Russia.
> Nations are ultimately built on stories. Each passing day adds more stories that Ukrainians will tell not only in the dark days ahead, but in the decades and generations to come. The president who refused to flee the capital, telling the US that he needs ammunition, not a ride; the soldiers from Snake Island who told a Russian warship to "go fuck yourself"; the civilians who tried to stop Russian tanks by sitting in their path. This is the stuff nations are built from. In the long run, these stories count for more than tanks.
> The Russian despot should know this as well as anyone. As a child, he grew up on a diet of stories about German atrocities and Russian bravery in the siege of Leningrad. He is now producing similar stories, but casting himself in the role of Hitler. ... Unfortunately, this war is likely to be long-lasting. Taking different forms, it may well continue for years. But the most important issue has already been decided. The last few days have proved to the entire world that Ukraine is a very real nation, that Ukrainians are a very real people, and that they definitely don't want to live under a new Russian empire.

Support for Ukrainian citizens who fled the country as refugees and sought refuge in the EU, US, and Canada exposed them to numerous further challenges. On one hand, the official policies of the receiving countries aimed at assisting the Ukrainians fleeing war-torn Ukraine were not immediately evident and appeared as obstacles to some. As higher education-specialized media, University World News reported,

> the Canada-Ukraine Authorization For Emergency Travel (CUAET) program, under which almost 250,000 Ukrainians have been sheltered in Canada, included one-time, non-taxable grant CA$3,000 per adult and CA$1,500 per each child under 17, access to health care and the right apply for study and work permits. It also provided for free access to elementary and secondary education. The program did not, however, categorise Ukrainians as refugees as defined by the United Nations. .... students who are already in university fall into a grey zone because of the way the CUAET program was structured. It gives Ukrainians sheltering in Canada open work permit holder status, meaning they can work freely in Canada (as if they were Canadian citizens), in contrast to refugees whose work status is more restricted (Greenfield, 2023).

This case points towards the validity of the proposition made in the first chapter of this book and reaffirmed throughout subsequent chapters. As Wood (1994) argued, migrants cannot be simply classified as either refugees or economic migrants, but rather should be understood within their specific contexts. On the other hand, Ukrainians received the right to work and to reside legally in receiving countries. For many of my informants residing illegally in the EU, particularly in Spain and Italy, before the full-fledged invasion of Ukraine started, the change in approach towards Ukrainian citizens brought considerable relief: they finally obtained legal status and the right to employment. This shift in policy demonstrated loyalty of commitment by the EU receiving countries. Additionally, along with their existing inert loyalty of coercion, their loyalty to these host countries became an inert loyalty of convenience.

After fleeing the country due to the invasion, Ukrainian refugees were eager and quick to find jobs, often in low-skilled positions. Securing employment was seen as a crucial first step in their socioeconomic integration in the receiving countries. They also made efforts to find suitable long-term accommodations and to learn local languages and customs. In Spain and Italy, where there were already substantial post-Soviet communities, many of which consisted of Ukrainian nationals who were native Russian speakers, these communities became the first providers of relief and also acted as guides for adaptation and integration for the Ukrainian refugees prompted by the full-fledged invasion. Similar to the post-Yugoslav population during the wars of Yugoslavia's dissolution, these post-Soviet migrants self-organized to support Ukrainians fleeing the war.

> A friend called me from Spain. His parents were trying to escape Ukraine by train and to join him and his family. Being people with special needs, his parents needed more support than the others. They arranged to get to the over packed train leaving Kiev region towards the West of the country. A friend told me that they arrive to the border at the evening of March 2, and I went there to meet them. I had never seen them before, but my friend sent me their photos, so I recognized them at the border and drove them to my home in Hungary. They stayed for several days while we were arranging their travel further to Spain. We became friends, and now I always visit them whenever I travel to Spain (personal communication, December 2022).

The presence of these earlier post-Soviet immigrant groups across host countries provided significant relief for the Ukrainians escaping the war. Having someone who waited, understood, and accommodated them made a crucial difference. Existing friendships played a central role in the tangible and soft resilience of Ukrainian refugees, both on an individual and collective level, in the face of the invasion.

Nevertheless, the invasion of Ukraine by Russia has been perceived differently among Soviet-era and post-Soviet immigrant communities. The reactions to the invasion heavily depended on a set of factors influencing personal experiences. These factors include the time and motive of emigration, the place of origin, and the connections retained with the people who remained there, as well as the host country, place of residence, social and legal status in the host country, and last but significantly influential — the media they usually followed. Regarding media, I noticed an interesting tendency among post-Soviet immigrants, particularly those born between 1947 and 1970 and who emigrated by the mid-1990s. Regardless of their place of origin and current residence, they have tended to follow Russian state media by default.

> As an immigrant boy, I did not have possibility to watch television in my native Russian, so I wanted to give such an opportunity to my kids, and I subscribed for Russian satellite channels. As a result, at home we have TV programs in Russian only (personal communication, July 2015).

With such a way of maintaining connections with their places of origin, most post-Soviet emigrants have inevitably been influenced by the propaganda of Putin's regime, which state-controlled Russian media extensively promoted since 2012. Consequently, despite being shocked by the news about Russia's invasion of Ukraine, many of them initially seemed to believe that the Ukrainian army was preparing to attack Russia and that the invasion was a reaction to a threat. During a heated informal discussion, one representative of this group of post-Soviet migrants commented on the invasion in the following way: "I see it as nothing personal, just business" (personal communication, March 2022). Interestingly, this person's close relatives were Ukrainian citizens living in Kiev. Similarly, even when having social media accounts, representatives of this group of post-Soviet migrants tend to passively follow posts rather than actively participate in discussions. This is how one of my conversers described his participation in social media before the full-scale invasion.

> I do not have any profiles, I do not participate in social media at all. I am a very closed person. In fact, none of my friends and the people, whom I am in touch with do not use social media. If some of them participates, then only incognito — not under real names — and they only follow the comments, but they do not put their photos and their own comments. I do not like to expose myself, thus I do not participate in social media (personal communication, January 2020).

Still, the use of Russian state media as the primary source of information was not the only reason for attempts to understand and, to some extent, even try to justify the invasion. For example, some Ukrainians originating from Russia-controlled Eastern

Ukrainian regions and residing in Hungary for more than a decade commented on the situation in the following way:

> We keep in touch as much as possible, because connections are rare. The situation is even more complicated now than it used to be over the last eight years. Back then, there was heating, electricity, and running water at least. Now it is missing along the frontline, especially in private residential houses, residential buildings receive it at least some time during the day. There are no mobile and internet connections because there each connection can reveal the peoples and armies' positions, and make civilians even more vulnerable to attacks. Therefore, because of the war, we are in the worst position again and by far. We belong neither to Ukraine, nor to Russia. Everything is so uncertain, but our people are the most cunning ever. They accepted Russian citizenship, so they receive Russian salaries and pensions, while they continue to receive Ukrainian ones. And they wait and see how and when the war will end. In fact, otherwise they would not survive (personal communication, May 2023).

Still, among my social networks, the post-Soviet immigrants with such reactions to the invasion have been in significant minority. In contrast, most of my conversers have not seen them as the part of the conflict in any way.

> I am far away from that conflict; I was not recruited, so it has no impact on me at all. If I were the part of the conflict, it would have maybe some effects. I am not a representative sample (personal communication, February 2023).

Ukrainian immigrants were particularly active during this time, as many of them had close family members or friends who were escaping from the endangered regions. For some, the challenge was to evacuate underage children who did not have proper travel documents, but this issue was quickly resolved when the EU adopted a resolution for the automatic acceptance of Ukrainian refugees in accordance with international humanitarian law. Some Ukrainian immigrants, who had the means, offered temporary accommodation for refugees, set up meeting points, and organized the collection of humanitarian aid in their own homes. In these efforts, they received active support from Russian immigrants as well.

> In the EU, post-Soviet immigrants have taken initiatives to provide aid to Ukrainian refugees. ...Some post-Soviet-founded schools used their local

administrative networks and organized accommodation for groups of refugees, and even offered free education to the Ukrainian refugee children. Additionally, post-Soviet-founded companies have relocated their employees from both Ukraine and Russia (Tepavcevic, 2023, p. 88).

As I write this book, I have been actively participating in various informal events within the post-Soviet community in Hungary. One observation I have made is that school-age children, whose parents or one parent are immigrants from post-Soviet countries, tend to group together and speak in Russian, away from school activities. They also participate in various extra-school activities, such as sports and language schools, which provide them multiple channels of communication. Through their children's friendships, the parents have also become friends, and they communicate and support each other in various ways. This circle of friends includes citizens from Ukraine, Russia, Belarus, Moldova, Kazakhstan, and Armenia. During discussions among these groups, issues related to the war in Ukraine are openly discussed, alongside other topics. Their views on the situation often overlap, as they see the war as a conflict among politicians and criminal clans, whose interests have nothing to do with them and their own well-being. They all encounter difficulties due to the war and hope for its resolution. They believe that they would only win if the war comes to an end and its atrocities are addressed (personal notes, May 2023). Interestingly, most of them express equal anger towards the authorities of their countries. Russian citizens are criticized for starting the war, while Ukrainian and Belarusian citizens are blamed for continuing it and promoting mobilization into their armies, which they all try to avoid for their relatives and friends. In other words, they continue to remain largely detached from the politics concerning both their home countries and their host countries. This is striking through their narratives, as they speak about escaping Ukraine and hardships of the war neutrally,

> It was hard to bring my parents here, I went to Ukraine to pick them up, and I experienced all the 'charm' of shelling, sirens, and shelters. ... My parents have been here for sometime, and then they returned as it seemed to become safer in some places. They simply cannot adapt to live abroad (personal communication, May 2023).

Looking Further: Russians' Reactions to Russia's Army Invasion in Ukraine and the Struggle for Re-Inclusion

The vulnerabilities encountered by Ukrainian citizens have over-shadowed the challenges faced by Russian citizens, as well as the even greater vulnerability of Ukrainian citizens originating from and living in Russia-controlled territories of Ukraine. Firstly, mass protests in Russia at the beginning of the invasion, along with a subsequent exodus from Russia during 2022 and continuing into 2023, have shown that many Russian citizens do not want to live under the continuously increasing aggression and repressions of Putinism, which Harari (2022) has referred to as a 'new Russian empire'. Similarly, Russian citizens living abroad have written petitions to Russian embassies in their host countries, appealing to the Russian Ministry of Foreign Affairs to immediately stop the invasion (online communication, February 2022). These events demonstrate that the invasion has not only had severe consequences for Ukraine but has also ignited reactions and protests within Russia itself, further complicating the already complex dynamics of the crisis.

Unfortunately, these numerous appeals have never received any responses, erasing the last leftovers of inertial loyalty to any existing Russian state institutions as completely captured by the Putin's regime (personal communication, December 2022). Others, such as famous cartoon-maker from St. Petersburgh, Oleg Kuvaev, long-term post-Soviet immigrant in Israel, made a several anti-war animated series of his popular "Masyanya". Series include "Sankt-Mariuburg", an allegory on the siege of Mariupol and reminder of siege of St. Petersburg during the World War II.[6] In fact, this episode fully represents the reactions to invasion of majority of Ukrainians and Russians.

> I am Russian, but I have my own understanding of what means to be Russian. To me — as in nineteen and twentieth centuries as well as today, it means the culture of resistance, the culture of dissidents, it is Chanson — Galich, Visotsky. Thus, for me the Russian culture is definitely not Stalinism.

---

[6]   These heartbreaking animated episode of typically humorous "Masyanya" are available at YouTube: https://youtu.be/s-GLAIY4DXA

> The Russian culture for me is a very long tradition of resistance. To me it is a huge and most important part of the Russian culture. Pushkin wrote and was prosecuted, Dostoyevsky was prosecuted, Tolstoy, Cvetaeva — take into account any big cultural figure, and you will see that all of them were resisting the regime and prosecuted in one or another way. Therefore, when I say Russian, I associate myself with them, with these traditions of resistance (personal communication, November 2019).

It is still hard to count how many Russian citizens left Russia since the Kremlin started their invasion in Ukraine, not merely because the rapid migrations, but also because the repressions in Russia make it hard if not impossible to collect and analyze statistical data. Talking about Putin, my conversers from Russia have usually been angry and desperate.

> Due to that insane thwart, I made an internal emigration. On February 24, I woke up in a different country though I did not travel anywhere. … The war that they started made me physically sick. I started to adapt to the situation only in the summer of 2022 (personal communication, April 2023).

This insight into the effects of Putin's decision to invade Ukraine on ordinary Russian citizens reflects on the article from Kyiv Post from the summer 2022 concerning invasion-prompted emigration from Russia.

Russian emigrants can be divided into several groups. The first is big businessmen and apolitical stars who would like to wait out the turbulent times abroad. There is every reason to believe that many of them will return, since their source of income is in Russia, where either their assets or fans are.

The second group is "children's" emigration. Parents take their children away in order to enroll them in Western schools, without political indoctrination and patriotic education — and without the prospect of serving in the Russian army.

> The third group is high-tech emigration. Workers at IT companies can quickly find employment in other countries. Such a "brain drain" seriously worries the Russian authorities. This is why they have exempted IT employees from military service, and provided tax benefits to the companies in which they work. Whether this will be enough, considering that IT specialists need not only economic relief, but also a free environment with the ability to travel around the world is a big question. The fourth and main group is political emigration: journalists, politicians and cultural figures. Some of

them used to work in structures declared to be "foreign agents." Others used to work for media, which were closed after Russian's full-scale invasion. Still others participated in opposition protests. Their return in the foreseeable future looks unlikely (Vedyashkin, 2022).

As the war increasingly affects the internationally recognized territory of Russia, more people from Russia envision their future away from their homeland. The mass waves of emigration—exit in Hirschman's framework—do not merely signify disloyalty to the regime but rather reflect a complete detachment from what the Russian government and the Russian state represent. The majority of post-Soviet citizens share a general attitude of desperation and fatigue, as reflected in the following quotation from social media discussions:

"I can't take this anymore. I am done with this country and its government. It's time to leave and find a better life elsewhere." (social media communication, May 2023). This sentiment indicates a growing disillusionment with the political situation in Russia and a desire to seek refuge and opportunities elsewhere, further contributing to the ongoing migration crisis.

> I am not interested in politics. I don't give a damn about the fact that my country occupied the territory of a foreign country. It's not all that clear, you need to understand ...I just do not give a damn about what happened in the Crimea—I'm a small person, home, family, work. Was I supposed to stop the tanks? What more do I need? ...I do not support Putin, he is a thief. So what? Everyone steals. And, the war ... And what about the war?... God knows what is there and who is fighting with whom. By the way, I'm still that enemy of the regime—I even have a photo from the paddy wagon, two times they were arrested me. After the last time, however, I no longer go to rallies—they said that they would be fired from work. And I have a family, a mortgage (social media discussion, September 2022).

Others observed that while escaping the same source of threat, Ukrainian and Russian citizens have been treated unequally.

> Ukrainians are under threat and it is completely clear, and they receive adequate support and shelter in Europe. Russians, while being at the same threat in the EU are treated rather as criminals. It is much harder for them to escape, than to Ukrainians, they have much less rights in the EU, than Ukrainians. Therefore, while absolutely sympathizing with Ukrainians, I try to help Russians as much as I can, because they are more vulnerable (personal communication, December 2022).

As the war continues, the people adapt to it. Like Bosnians during the war in 1990s, many of post-Soviet migrants, who have Russian-Ukrainian identity, make fun of themselves. The meme in Russian that one of my acquaintances shared via social media illustrates their perceptions of the situation:

> If your parents owe you, it means that you are a kid. If the state owes you, it means that you are a pensioner. If the whole world owes you, it means that you are Ukrainian. But if you are guilty for everything—you are Russian (online mem, April 2023).

Recognizing that the source of the threat is the same as that faced by Ukrainians—the people in the Kremlin and their politics—many Russians sought to support the Ukrainian army as one of the avenues of their own resilience. For example, in an interview to Russian famous journalist—interviewer, Yuriy Dud', a famous Russian poet and author, Vera Polozkova stated: "I support the Ukrainian Army because they fight for my interests. I want to make them capable to defend me and deliberate my country from Putin" (Dud, 2023).

In emigration, Russian citizens faced numerous challenges, including obtaining visas for travel to many countries, facing negative reactions due to being Russian citizens, and encountering obstacles when trying to transfer their savings and money from their accounts in Russia due to the sanctions. Besides these invasion-related obstacles, they also encountered challenges common to almost all forced emigrants: finding affordable accommodations, learning the language of the receiving country, organizing a source of income, and finding schools and kindergartens for their children. In response to these challenges, several social entrepreneurial projects emerged, organized by Russian refugees themselves. These initiatives aimed to provide support and solutions to their fellow emigrants, creating a sense of solidarity and resilience among the community. Additionally, existing organizations of Russian political emigrants, mainly located in London, UK, expanded their activism to assist new emigrants, offering guidance, resources, and advocacy. Despite the difficulties they faced, Russian citizens who chose to leave their homeland demonstrated their determination to seek a better life and resilience in the face of adversity. Their experiences shed light on the multifaceted impact of the invasion and the collective efforts that emerged in response to the crisis.

Similarly, several Russian mass media outlets, which were forced to close and leave their Russia-based headquarters in the early days of Russia's full-fledged invasion in Ukraine, found ways to continue operating online. Channels like *Dozhd'* (TVRain) and Radio Ekho, whose journalists had to flee Russia, resumed their programs through online platforms. For example, TVRain restarted its program after several months from Riga, Latvia, where the channel lost its broadcasting license due to one of its journalists advising Russian citizens on how to avoid mobilization into the Russian Army, referring to them as "our people." Subsequently, the channel obtained a broadcasting license in Amsterdam, the Netherlands. Similarly, representatives of the Russian non-systemic political opposition and large businesses, who had left Russia either much earlier or at the beginning of the invasion in Ukraine, organized some semi-official meetings. These gatherings took place in Riga, Latvia, in the summer of 2022, and in Berlin in April 2023. The focus of these meetings was on humanitarian and human rights issues concerning the support of Ukrainian and Russian refugees. These gatherings aimed to provide a platform for discussion and action to address the challenges faced by those displaced by the conflict.

One of the informal leaders of this expanding Russian diaspora's activism is Mikhail Khodorkovsky, a renowned former Russian oil magnate and political prisoner. After being released from jail in 2013, he moved to the UK and founded the *Russkiy Komitet Deistviya* (Russian Committee of Action), an organization dedicated to providing legal support to Russian political prisoners and political dissidents. According to Khodorkovsky, in cooperation with other humanitarian organizations founded by the Russian forced emigrants, such as *Kovcheg* (The Ark), since the beginning of Russia's army full-fledged invasion in Ukraine, his organization expanded its activity to humanitarian once (TVRain, 2023). In his interview to TVRain's journalist, Mikhail Fishman, in May 2023, Khodorkovsky commented on this Russian migrants' activism highlighting its' democratic character and his own commitment to democratic values.

> There are different groups with different interests, and these interests should remain different. Otherwise, it will be dictatorship, and we aspire for democracy in Russia of the future. The part of these diverse interests are common, and these are the interests that we work on (TVRain, 2023).

These common interests appeared, as many media reported, in the official Declaration resulted from the conference of Russian activists held in April 2023 in Berlin. The document reflects the activists' desired vision of Russia's internal political order, however, without mentioning the specifics of who should be responsible for realizing that vision:

> The Russian troops must be removed from all occupied territories. ... Putin's regime is illegitimate and criminal. Therefore, it must be liquidated. ... Political prisoners and prisoners of war must be freed; forcibly deported persons must get an opportunity to return; abducted Ukrainian children should be returned to Ukraine. ... The declaration's signatories commit to abstaining from conflict amidst themselves until their "joint strategic goals are achieved (Meduza, 2023).

In the spring of 2023, the Russian opposition movement in Europe became increasingly politically active. Soon after the informal conference held in Berlin in early June 2023, the European Parliament organized a conference with the symbolic title "The Day After," inviting Russian opposition politicians, social scientists, and activists residing in Europe to discuss potential relations between the EU and Russia after the Russia-Ukraine war. The last significant event organized by recent Russian migrants and war-related relocators, who prefer not to call themselves 'refugees,' included journalists, academics, and political and social activists. This event took place on the Day of Russia, June 12. Over the last thirty years, this day has been celebrated as a national holiday in Russia to mark the country's declaration of independence from the former Soviet Union on June 12, 1991. They organized a Russian independent media marathon of solidarity called "*Ty ne odin,*" which translates to "You are not alone," aimed at fundraising to support the families and lawyers of political prisoners in Russia. The cooperation among the participants seems to continue, as Russia's renowned political scientist and commentator, Ekaterina Schulman, commented on June 13, 2023, during her program "Status" on Ekho Radio in exile.

> It is hard for us to unite because of symbolism ... it is important to note openly that we are not eager in creation of the political structures, however, we seem good in ... creating human rights-defending structures, not necessarily jurisdictional. Second, we create media structures. These two are our national talents. ... In our nation-building, if we ever get to it, we should rely on these strong points (Status, June 13, 2023, transcript, Ekaterina Schulman Telegram channel).

Therefore, concerning politically active emigrants from Russia, their hard resilience to the repressive regime in Russia and the war in Ukraine is in human-rights-support activities and media-structures community-building. The more inclusive these structures become, the more loyalty of commitment by other Russian and post-Soviet migrants they could receive, and the more chances for building some sort of democratic state in Russia in any near or more distant future.

Post-Yugoslavs' Migrants' Reactions on Russia's Invasion in Ukraine

The meme depicting Putin as a genius who miraculously healed the world from COVID in two days was one of the initial reactions observed among post-Yugoslav migrants. This joke highlighted the fact that the COVID pandemic had been the dominant topic of discussion between January 2020 and February 2022, but Russia's full-scale invasion in Ukraine suddenly shifted everyone's attention away from it. The war in Ukraine was particularly distressing for people in the Balkans, where many still had vivid memories of local wars. Social media groups became more active than usual, as the conflict triggered traumatic memories and deep empathy for Ukrainians. Especially empathetic were the emigrants from Bosnia, who found the scenes of the war in Ukraine to be painful reminders of the sieges of Sarajevo, Bihac, and the fights over Mostar.

> War memories from Sarajevo in the 1990s have been awaken with the
> breakout of the war in Ukraine as flashbacks. ... Once we got three eggs from
> my husband's relative: he had two hens, who slept in the house with him.
> During the day, he would let them walk outside a bit, but he was guarding
> them with a gun. .. My daughter patented her invention: she took the brick,
> put it on the stove, wrap it with dishtowel, and took it to the school, where
> there was not heating. She was sitting on it and kept herself warm. She
> boasted of letting other kids to warm up by sitting on her invention.... We
> found an accumulator, and we spread wires with tiny lamps around the
> flat—it looked lavishly! (online communication, March 2022).
> They call it 'special operation' as the Serbs called 'special operation' their
> attack on Slavonia and Baranya, and then Croats similarly characterized
> 'Storm' and 'Flesh' in 1995. It is horrifying to see that the same tragedy is
> happening with someone else (personal conversation, March 2022).

Diverse experiences of wars across the Balkans have also
translated into a variety of reactions and empathy with various vulnerable groups. One wartime Bosnian immigrant in Serbia explained her position towards the war in Ukraine.

> I see Russia as a preferable ally among several 'evils', including Russia, US,
> the EU, and China just because of language, religious and ethnic similarity.
> It does not mean that it is good, or that I support what they do in Ukraine
> and elsewhere (personal communication, November 2022).

Generally, the reactions to Russia's invasion in former Yugoslav republics were as diverse as the divisions witnessed during the
wars of Yugoslavia's dissolution. For instance, far-right nationalists
in Serbia reacted by supporting Russia's invasion, seeing it as a response to the violent coercion of Russian-speaking Ukrainian citizens from Donetsk and Luhansk regions to remain part of Ukraine,
drawing parallels between them and the Serb self-proclaimed independent regions in Croatia during the 1990s. However, it is important to note that they represented a significant minority (online
communication, April 2022). Similarly, in Croatia, the support of
far-right groups has aligned with the Ukrainian nationalist center-
right actively since Russia annexed Crimea from Ukraine in 2014,
and they also perceived it as analogue of Serb self-proclaimed territories of Croatia during 1990s. They also were in minority in Croatia (online communication, April 2022). At the same time, across
all former Yugoslav republics, as elsewhere, majority have supported Ukrainian refugees and blamed the full-fledged invasion for

peoples' suffering. Like pro-vaccination and anti-vaccination reactions to COVID, among my frequent post-Yugoslav migrant conversers there have been many persons, who perceived the Russia-Ukraine war as a continuation of the war in Yugoslavia. One of my conversers was former Croatian refugees-returners from Germany, and his experience translated into solidarity towards Ukrainian refugees in Croatia.

> Having experienced the war thirty years ago, I understood how these people feel. Close by, there is an old hotel, where the Ukrainian refugees are accommodated. One of them, a middle-aged woman, whom we frequently meet and befriended in some way, once told us that she cannot sleep well in their accommodation as she has some illness. As we rent apartments and we had one, we accommodated her for free, of course. But then the police came and checked whether we rented her. We provided them all proofs, and the problem was solved. But it was still very inconvenient. And we only wanted to help a person, who was in a similar situation as we did long time ago.
> … The war is non-sense anyway. What we got from four years war here? Destruction, death, long-term economic and humanitarian problems. So what we have in the end? Our Serb neighbors returned, and we live again as we lived before. We go to celebrate Orthodox Easter today with them (personal communication, April 2022).

The last significant group have been equally sympathetic with escaping Ukrainians and escaping Russians. "When I heard about the Russia's invasion in Ukraine, I got ill for several days with fewer, numb, and anxiousness" (personal communication, April 2023). Most post-Yugoslav migrants shared these emotions. "We were merely the training ground for what is happening now," told me a Croatian wartime emigrant of the generation between 1945 and 1960, now living in Spain. "Russians and Ukrainians are pushed against one another, while someone else makes profits on their misfortune" (online communication, December 2022). Similar impressions shared another emigrant from Bosnia residing in the United Arab Emirates of a generation between 1970 and 1985.

> Those who stayed they had different story from those who left. They hated those, who left, they called them traitors. And look now to Russia: some of them say that they like Ukrainians and they are ashamed for their country to bomb Ukraine. Others hate those, who defend Ukrainians. Those who left hate those who stayed and vice versa. Everything is the same matrix. Only

the place and the time is different. In my view, it is nothing but being ma-
nipulated, mostly by media and by politicians. Thus, I try to keep away from
media (online communication, March 2023).

Nevertheless, the war traumas and fears of new conflicts was
shared by all groups equally as discussions in post-Yugoslav
groups across a variety of social media demonstrated through most
frequently shared meme declaring the following:

> I hope that we are not on the edge of the Third World War, but if it turns
> that we are, everyone from the Balkans is requested to pretend that we are
> dead. Do not even think of engaging... we already had enough (online com-
> munication, February 2022).

This meme strikingly demonstrates not only the absence of
loyalty to formal institutions in general but also highlights that detachment is the only possible resilience in this global crisis. In my
numerous personal conversations with fellow post-Yugoslav migrants, I also observed a tendency to blame the media and the interest groups behind them for the escalation of the war in Ukraine,
and conflicts in general.

> I do not watch TV and I do not allow to be manipulated by all these horrors.
> ... If the person is not much bombed by media and news, anyone just goes
> on and does not see many changes. ...Almost no one now speaks about
> Ukraine, while people still die as they were dying in the beginning—and
> that is horrible. That means that the human life is not as important as the
> story to cover some other important things— to blame Russia for everything,
> and to weaken them. They are freaks of their own kind, but they cannot be
> guilty for everything under the sun (online communication, February 2023).

Reactions of post-Yugoslav migrant returners from Russia
have been more specific and, in most situations displayed better
understanding of the situation.

> The collapse was between 1990 and 1993, if you ask me, but it all was
> planned earlier. The process of collapse started during Tito's rule. It was all
> preparation for what happened later. I was always in the center of happen-
> ing—the first time in Bosnia, and later in Moscow (online communication,
> February 2023).
> I could never believe that the Russian army would attack Ukraine, for me it
> was huge extremely negative surprise. Russians as I know them are the most
> pacifist nation, and the attack on Ukraine simply does not fit into this picture
> (online communication, April 2022).

Instead of Conclusions

Occasionally, I met a woman from Ukraine in one of the language schools in Budapest, which happened to be owned by a Russian citizen. As we both waited for our kids to finish their language and art classes, I overheard her talking on the phone in Ukrainian, presumably with her family members who remained in Ukraine. After finishing the call, she had tears in her eyes and apologized for speaking loudly. "It's always hard to talk to those who stayed behind," she said. I reassured her that there was no need to apologize, as I understood the situation. I shared with her that I had also experienced escaping from Sarajevo as a child thirty years ago, and she opened up about her own experience of escaping from Ukraine.

> We were escaping from Irpen' to Kiyv, literally running from the bombs. We went by the neighbor's car, three adults and three kids....We followed the information from the radio, but the situation was changing so rapidly that the information seemed outdated. We heard that the closest bridge over Dnepr is safe, but when we approached it, the bomb destroyed it just in from of our eyes. We were in about fifty meters from there, so we rapidly went back and got to the another road towards another bridge. Once we got across the Dnepr, we went out of gasoline. My son is still afraid of the sound of planes (personal communication, February 2023).

During our heartfelt conversation, I honestly shared with her that I still feel uneasy when I hear the sound of planes. Needless to say, our emotions ran high during this coincidental encounter, and both of us shed tears. When our kids finished their classes, we hugged each other tightly and said our goodbyes. It was only then that she remembered to ask for my name, and I introduced myself as well—at that moment, such details seemed inconsequential compared to the bond we had formed through our shared experiences. It was only one of my numerous painful experiences of talking to Ukrainians, who escaped the war. I learned about similar examples of post-Soviet and post-Yugoslav migrants becoming friends through sharing traumatic experiences in Canada, Germany, Austria, and the Great Britain. It remains to be seen whether they will form the new global communities of resilience. As the war in Ukraine continues and escalates to Russia, occasionally to Moldova and Belarus, I meet more people, whose attitude seems to reflect detachment. It reminds me to the major lesson from the war that former Bosnian emigrant in Germany, now famous Bosnian actor and writer, Fedja Stukan wrote in the end of his book titled "Blank" about the war in Bosnia in 1990s as the message to his daughter:

> When the war starts, run away. Life is a zero priority, nothing is more important than that. Do not listen to anyone who says otherwise. There is only one life. The state and the nation are a construct of a very territorial species of monkeys, and are nothing more than a synonym for a larger pack led by a small group of monkeys, ready to do literally anything for money. The flag is a piece of cloth, anthems are a set of tones and words, do not attach any deeper meaning to them. Behind everything, there are the rich who exploit the poor. Patriotism is for the mentally limited persons. The whole world is yours, you have a right to it, explore it. There is no better use of time than traveling. Surround yourself with people who value life. Religion is a cult of death, the most morbid thing man has invented, and it exists only for money. Those who lead it know nothing about life, let alone death. Death is nothing, death does not hurt. Enjoy life. That is the point.

This dramatic message confirms Benedict Anderson (1991) thirty year old theory of nations as imagined communities. Simultaneously, it suggests that individual resilience in global crisis lies in a lack of loyalty to the state, religion, and other imagined communities and their symbols, which enable manipulation of masses; collective resilience is still possible in finding people with similar experiences and mutual understanding and allying with them.

Chapter 8
Conclusions:
(Imagined) Global Crises and
(Imagined) Migrant Communities —
Lessons from the Shortest Century

"We must learn to live with the crisis, just as we are resigned to living with so
much endemic adversity imposed on us by the evolution of the times: pollution,
noise, corruption and, above all, fear"(Bauman & Bordoni, 2014, p. 7).

This short chapter composed situates the findings of the book into
the broad literature on global crises, migrations, strands on post-
Yugoslav and post-Soviet migrants and migrant communities, and
the relationship between sources of resilience and loyalty to various
types of migrant communities. It also offers practical implications
of the findings concerning the approach to global crises.

Post-Yugoslav and Post-Soviet Resilience in
Global Crises: Comparative Summary from Collapse
to Russia's Invasion in Ukraine

The analysis of experiences of citizens from former Yugoslavia and
the former Soviet Union during several global crises that marked
the early 21st century provides important theoretical implications
for the study of temporality and migration nexus. First, the analysis
of early post-World War II emigrations from Yugoslavia and the
Soviet Union during the Cold War reveals that exclusions are integral to authoritarian regimes, leading to divisions within communities and motivating many of the most marginalized individuals
to seek escape through emigration. This finding suggests that emigration from countries with authoritarian regimes is inherently
forced in one way or another, expanding upon Wood's (1994) initial
proposition regarding motives for emigration and their relevance
within the context of authoritarian regimes, as demonstrated

through the example of Soviet citizens' emigrations and post-conflict societies, as illustrated by the early post-World War II emigration from Yugoslavia. In the broader context of migration studies, these findings contribute to the understanding of motives for emigration in general (Baycan & Nijkamp, 2007; Samers & Collyer, 2016) by shedding light on opportunity-driven labor migration to Third World countries as a significant motive and geographic direction of migration. Specifically, it adds to the scholarship on motives for emigration of Soviet citizens (Remennick, 2012; Ryazantsev, Pismennaya et al., 2018; Tepavcevic, 2017) and motives for emigration of Yugoslav citizens (Bakovic, 2015; Bubalo Zivkovic, Ivkov et al., 2010) during the Cold War period.

Second, as demonstrated throughout the analysis of collapses of former Yugoslavia through series of violent conflicts and conflicts preceding and constituting the collapse of the Soviet Union, such crises foster divisions of existing 'imagined' communities, retaining some members of formerly existing communities, and excluding others. These divisions usually happen across the lines of crisis-generated assumed and experienced threats and possible allies in surviving these threats replicating to certain extent some theories of international relations (Hobsbawm, 1994; Waltz, 1979) to individuals.

Thirdly, as highlighted throughout this book, the perception or anticipation of exclusion becomes a significant threat, leading individuals to develop loyalty to a community that offers a sense of safety during times of crisis. Exclusion acts as a stressor, influencing the form and extent of resilience. This can be viewed as a form of 'voice' reaction, as described by Hirschman (1970), in response to the threats posed by the crisis. However, in Hirschman's framework, the decision to 'voice' or 'exit' lies with dissatisfied citizens or employees who seek change or alternative environments that better meet their needs and foster loyalty.

In contrast, the analyses provided in Chapter 3 and Chapter 5 demonstrated that in the context of a global crisis and the collapse of a system, citizens and employees are often forcibly excluded from the communities they once belonged to. This leads to a crucial theoretical implication, suggesting that exclusion tends to reshape an individual's sense of belonging and modify their loyalty and identification with a community or collective identity. This argument aligns with the negative or 'push' factors discussed in Lee's (1966) theory of migration. For many post-Yugoslav and post-Soviet migrants, the lack of loyalty to their communities in their home countries became a catalyst for both soft resilience, leading to the decision to emigrate, and tangible resilience through the act of emigration itself.

Fourth, at the same time, as demonstrated in Chapter 2, apart from recognized in business studies coercive form of loyalty, which is characteristic of authoritarian regimes in politics and monopolies in economics, the present book offers one conceptually new form of loyalty, namely, loyalty of ignorance. This concept differs from the other four—already mentioned loyalty of coercion, commitment, convenience, and contended—in a way that it can be further classified as strong, but not as positive or negative, because it is produced as unconscious persuasion by the regime. For this reason, in the summarizing Table below, it is positioned in the left lower corner.

Table 8.1: Forms of loyalty extended

	Strong	Weak
Positive	Commitment	Convenience and Low Cost (adequate value for money)
Negative	Coercion or Captive loyalty	Contended or High Cost
Neutral	Ignorance	

Fifth, unlike disloyalty or indifference, which often led to 'exit' or emigration in most analyzed situations, loyalty of ignorance typically did not prompt any change in the status quo for individuals who were dissatisfied but remained unaware of their discontent. As a result, this lack of awareness made them resilient under the pressures of an authoritarian regime. This characteristic still exists among many Soviet-era emigrants and post-Soviet citizens. The presence of this form of loyalty, combined with loyalty of coercion and the unavoidable fear it generates, has contributed significantly to the longevity of Putin's regime. This crucial theoretical implication provides further insights into situations where citizens may choose to voice their concerns after emigration, as previously discussed by Hoffmann (2010) and Burgess (2012), as well as democratic remittances, which Fomina (2021) explored in the context of post-Soviet Russian emigrants in Europe. It sheds light on the complexities of loyalty, resilience, and responses to authoritarian regimes, highlighting how unawareness of dissatisfaction can play a significant role in maintaining the status quo.

Sixth, as exemplified in Chapter 3, the interplay between the extent of exclusion over time, available coping mechanisms, and forms of loyalty significantly shapes an individual's reaction to their crisis-related situation. In cases where the existing community proved to be a reliable source of tangible resilience, often materialized through the provision of basic needs, individuals tended to maintain a certain form of loyalty and continued their basic participation in that community. On the other hand, those who experienced higher levels of threat, whether tangible or perceived, tended to escape from it, often resulting in changing their place of residence through displacement, emigration, or relocation. This change of place of residence, as thoroughly discussed in Chapters 2 and 4, represented distant experience aiming generally in re-inclusion into the communities in the places of destination. The change requires multiple adaptive mechanisms because, as Caporale-Bizini, Galhardo Couto et al. (2009) "[M]igration and geographical and inner/psychological displacement are incompatible with a fixed identity: they have to do with the emergence of a non-territorial body".

As discussed in Chapters 4 and 5, migrant communities play a significant role as a form of tangible resilience and as sources of both soft and tangible resilience. In addition to the three general types of migrant communities widely recognized in migration scholarship — diaspora, migrant community, and transmigrants — additional types were identified and conceptualized based on two criteria: a form of loyalty and form of providing or generating resilience. Two types were identified among post-Yugoslav migrants, and three among post-Soviet migrant communities, with one overlapping between the two groups, as represented in Table 8.2 below.

Table 8.2.: Newly conceptualized migrant communities found among post-Yugoslav and post-Soviet migrants

Type	Form	Present among
Ethnic hybrid-sub-nations	Formal	Bosnians; (post-)Soviet Jews, (post) Soviet Germans
Monoculti-corponations	Informal	Post-Soviet migrants
Corponations	Formal	Post-Soviet and post-Yugoslav migrants
Hybrid-sub-nations	Informal	post-Yugoslavs

In addition, one interesting counterintuitive finding of the analysis of this book is that the Cold War times Yugoslav emigrants in Western Europe and the US, and Soviet emigrants in Eastern Europe tend to hold more loyalty of convenience and commitment to former Yugoslavia and the former Soviet Union, than their post-Cold-war emigrating compatriots.

The findings of this book confirm arguments proposed by previous works, suggesting that migrations, especially long-term migrations, reshape the identities of individuals and migrant groups (Kovacevic-Bielicki, 2017, 2019). This reshaping of identities can be seen as a form of soft resilience, with an important contribution of this book being the recognition that these modifications of identity also lead to changes in objects and forms of loyalty. As channels of resilience, these migrant communities become the objects of new loyalties, complementing the previous ones. Consequently, despite spending a long time in host countries and, in some cases, being born there, the majority of post-Yugoslav and post-Soviet immigrants still perceive themselves as 'others' in relation to the mainstream societies in their host countries (Kovacevic-Bielicki, 2017; Tepavcevic, 2022). This implies that they either experience certain forms of exclusion or perceive themselves as different. Therefore, they tend to maintain connections with their former compatriots in host countries and use these networks to adapt when new major crises occur.

The eighth and most significant finding and theoretical implication proposed by this book is that surviving global crises, despite being traumatic experiences, also serve as valuable learning opportunities. Lessons learned from these crises are applied when new crises occur, giving rise to various forms of resilience. The strongest aspect of identity is closely related to the major source of resilience and safety. In essence, the primary source of resilience becomes the strongest community tie and, as a result, it transforms into a form of loyalty. In turn, loyalty is reflected through self-identification with a particular community, be it national, local, professional, or cultural. These different forms of loyalty often overlap, much like the overlapping identities. As individuals are excluded from previous systems, structures, and communities, both emigrants and those who remain create new communities to re-include themselves. The level of re-inclusion, which represents a balanced combination of soft and hard resilience, determines the strength of loyalty and commitment the members have towards their community and its cause. This finding, reconfirms Kontos' (2003) argument made regarding migrant communities, but it also extends beyond just migrant communities and migrant entrepreneurship. Post-Yugoslav migrant communities continue to identify themselves as "post" or "former" due to the lack of stable states and institutions in the place of the previous Yugoslav ones. This argument also applies to most post-Soviet citizens, with the exception of those from Baltic states, for similar reasons. However, for most Ukrainian citizens, this situation has changed since Russia's full-scaled invasion. The tragedy and danger they have experienced have strengthened their sense of nationhood and become a source of both hard and soft resilience. This has generated a loyalty of commitment to Ukraine that previously existed more as inertial loyalty, loyalty of convenience, and even loyalty of cost.

Finally, one of the most important tools of resilience in the most recent and present global crises has been the emergence and widespread use of social media networks, which fostered the re-embeddedness of migrant communities in their countries-of-origin and other migrant communities across various immigration destinations. This phenomenon takes on a new form—digital—and nature—translocal (Halilovich, 2013; Tepavcevic, 2021 c). This finding also aligns with Zygmunt Bauman's (2006) notion of liquid times, where even human communities take virtual forms. These virtual or digital migrant communities add a new dimension to Anderson's

(1991) concept of 'imagined' communities, showcasing their dynamic and changeable nature.

Real World Implications: Preventing global crises through global coordination

A major theoretical argument that this book offers is that global crises have the ability to both split existing communities and generate new ones. Throughout this process, individuals who find themselves included in communities within their settlement tend to stay, while those who face exclusion from mainstream society under the pressures of the crisis tend to migrate. Thus, migration essentially becomes a search for re-inclusion. In the case of post-Yugoslav and post-Soviet communities, including their migrant communities, the division lines appear to be closely related to the system or regime from which they were excluded. As the analysis proposed in this book demonstrates, identity reveals the intensity of loyalty among these communities. Post-Yugoslav and post-Soviet migrant communities that emerged in the aftermath of the socialist federations' demises, as demonstrated in Chapter 4, contributed to Wimmer's (2004, p. 4) plea for more research on "the everyday praxis of group formation' and 'its variability and context dependency".

In turn, the terms of exclusion influence the form of loyalty individuals hold for one community or another. This loyalty is reflected through the expression of their identity. In the case of post-Yugoslav migrant communities, the works of Halilovich and Kovecevic-Bielicki play a crucial role as they explicitly demonstrate the ways migrants' identities are linked to both their home and host countries. In Halilovich's (2013) work, examples of Bosnian migrants in Sweden and their expression of 'our' in relation to Swedish achievements reveal a loyalty of convenience to the host country, whereas 'our' referring to former Yugoslavia demonstrates, as noted by Rowley (2005), an inertial loyalty to the home country.

Similarly, Kovecevic-Bielicki's (2017) interviewees emphasize the notion of 'former' and feeling 'neither in the sky, nor on Earth' as crucial features of their identity, which reflects limited loyalty to the host society — closer to loyalty of 'no choice' or coercion — and inertial loyalty towards the country of origin and the society they are settled in. These limited loyalties and the related transient 'national' identities are present among all hybrid-nations studied throughout the analysis of this book.

As I write up this book, there is another looming global financial crisis, which, according to the world-famous economist and former Greek Finance Minister, Yanis Varoufakis (2023), demonstrates the dysfunctionality of capitalism as a system. As reflections of exclusion and inequalities, most vividly throughout 2022 and 2023, we witness the creation of two broad opposing blocs of states. This is happening primarily because the interests of governments and citizens of the non-Western bloc of countries have either been excluded or neglected by the bloc of economically richest countries. Among other aspects, immigration of citizens from 'the rest' has been heavily limited in the countries of the West.

Venues for further research

As demonstrated throughout this book, it is essential to distinguish between people and states, especially in non-democratic regimes, as they are very different units and actors. Therefore, a major practical implication provided by this book is the need for a horizontal approach to international relations, not only to address the present crisis but also to foster global resilience in the future.

This approach is particularly crucial when dealing with people from countries with a recent history of collapses and dissolutions, including post-Yugoslav and post-Soviet countries, as well as other geographical regions. It is important to consider not only legal aspects but also political and cultural aspects of their identities. In other words, the traditional in-box approaches based on nationality, ethnicity, or citizenship have proven to be dysfunctional and even dangerous. Concerning immediate implications, this means adopting a more nuanced approach towards Russian and Belarusian emigrants and refugees. It is crucial to prevent the extension of human rights violations that are currently widespread under the self-proclaimed Russian and Belarusian authorities.

Bibliography

Abdelal, R. (2005). *National Purpose in the World Economy*: Cornell University Press.

Adams, T., Ellis, C., & S., H.-J. (2017). Autoethnography. In *The International Encyclopedia of Communication Research Methods*: John Wiley & Sons, Inc.

Agardi, I. (2022). *On the Verge of History. Life Stories of Rural Women from Serbia, Romania, and Hungary, 1920–2020*: Ibidem Verlag, Columbia University Press.

Aldrich, H., & Zimmer, C. (1986). Entrepreneurship through Social Networks. In *The Art and Science of Entrepreneurship* (pp. 3-23). Cambridge, MA: Ballinger Publishing Company.

Aleshkovski, I., Grebenyuk, A., & Vorobyeva, O. (2018). The Evalution of Russian Emigration in the Post-Soviet Period. *Social Evolution and History, 17*(2), 140-156. doi:10.30884/seh/2018.02.09

Alioua, M. (2014). Transnational Migration: The Case of Sub-Saharan Transmigrants Stopping Over in Morocco. In F. Düvell, I. Molodikova, & M. Collyer (Eds.), *Transit Migration in Europe*. Amsterdam: Amsterdam University Press.

Anderson, B. (1991). *Imagined communities: reflections on the origin and spread of nationalism*. London: Verso.

Archer, R., Bernard, S., & Papadopoulos, Y. (2023). Introduction: the cold war of labour migrants: opportunities, struggles and adaptations across the iron curtain and beyond. *Labor History*, 1-9. doi:https://doi.org/10.1080/0023656X.2023.2227600

Aron, L. (1991). *Preparing America for the Wave of Russian Immigrants*.

Aslund, A., & McFaul, M. (2006). *Revolution in Orange: The Origins of Ukraine's Democratic Breakthrough*: Carnegie Endowment for International Peace.

Avaz, D. (2014, February, 13, 2014). Skup podrške u Zagrebu građanima BiH: Oni nisu huligani i nasilnici. *Dnevni Avaz*. Retrieved from https://web.archive.org/web/20140214094003/http://www.avaz.ba/globus/region/skup-podrske-u-zagrebu-gradjanima-bih-oni-nisu-huligani-i-nasilnici

Azrael, J., Brukoff, P., & Shkolnikov, V. D. (1992). *Prospective Migration and Emigration from the Former USSR: A Conference Report*.

Baker, C. (2018). *Race and the Yugoslav region: Postsocialist, post-conflict, post-colonial?* Manchester: Manchester University Press.

Bakovic, N. (2015). Song of Brotherhood, Dance of Unity: Cultural-Entertainment Activities for Yugoslav Economic Emigrants in the West in the 1960s and 1970s. *Journal of Contemporary History, 50*(2), 354-375

Barabasi, A. L. (2014). *Linked: How Everything Is Connected to Everything Else and What It Means for Business, Science, and Everyday Life:* Basic Books.

Baruch Wachtel, A. (1998). *Making a Nation, Breaking a Nation: Literature and Cultural Politics in Yugoslavia.* Stanford, CA: Stanford University Press.

Bauman, Z. (2006). *Liquid Times: Living in an Age of Uncertainty* (1 ed.): Polity.

Bauman, Z., & Bordoni, C. (2014). *State of Crisis* Cambridge: Polity Press.

Baycan, T., & Nijkamp, P. (2006). *Migrant female entrepreneurship – Driving forces, motivation and performance* (2006-18).

Baycan, T., & Nijkamp, P. (2007). *Migrant Entrepreneurship In A Diverse Europe: In Search Of Sustainable Development.*

BBC (Producer). (2013, May 20, 2022). Ukraine protests after Yanukovych EU deal rejection. [News report] Retrieved from https://www.bbc.com/news/world-europe-25162563

Beissinger, M. (2009). Nationalism and The Collapse of Soviet Communism. *Contemporary European History, 18*(3), 331–347. doi:10.1017/S0960777309005074

Berend, I. (2012). *Europe in Crisis Bolt from the Blue?* London: Routledge.

Bernard, S. (2019a). *Deutsch Marks in the Head, Shovel in the Hands and Yugoslavia in the Heart: The Gastarbeiter Return to Yugoslavia (1965-1991)* (1 ed.): Harrassowitz Verlag.

Bernard, S. (2019b). Oil shocks, migration and European integration: A (Trans) National perspective on the Yugoslav crises of the 1980s. *National Identities, 21*(5), 463–484. doi: https://doi.org/10.1080/14608944.2018.1498471

Bianchini, S., & Minakov, M. (2018). State-Building Politics after the Yugoslav and Soviet Collapse—The Western Balkans and Ukraine in a Comparative Perspective. *Southeastern Europe, 42*(3), 291-304. doi:10.1163/18763332-04203001

Bieber, F., Galijas, A., & Archer, R. (2014). *Debating the End of Yugoslavia.* Burlington, AT: Ashgate.

Bildung, B. f. p. (2022). Emigration from the Western Balkans. from Bundeszentrale für politische Bildung https://www.bpb.de/the men/migration-integration/laenderprofile/english-version-cou ntry-profiles/505179/emigration-from-the-western-balkans/

Bonifazi, C., & Mamolo, M. (2004). Past and Current Trends of Balkan Migrations. *Espace, Populations, Sociétés*(2004/3), 519-531. doi:10. 4000/eps.356

Braudel, F. (1980). *History and the Social Sciences: The Longue Durée* (S. Matthews, Trans.). Chicago: University of Chicago Press.

Brooks, D., Hoberg, E. P., & Boeger, W. A. (2019). *The Stockholm Paradigm: Climate Change and Emerging Disease* Chicago: University of Chicago Press.

Brown, B. (2017). *Braving the Wilderness The Quest for True Belonging and the Courage to Stand Alone*: Random House.

Brunnbauer, U. (2016). *Globalizing Southeastern Europe: Emigrants, America, and the State since the Late Nineteenth Century*. London: Lexington Books.

Brunnbauer, U. (2019). Yugoslav Gastarbeiter and the ambivalence of socialism: Framing out-migration as a social critique. *Journal of Migration History, 5*(3), 413–437. doi:https://doi.org/10.1163/235 19924-00503001

Brzozowski, J., & Pedziwiatr, K. (2016). *Pushed to the Mainstream Market: The Case of Immigrant Entrepreneurs in Lesser Poland*. Paper presented at the Cross-Border Migration and its Implications for the Central European Area, Bratislava.

Bubalo Zivkovic, M., Ivkov, A., & Kovacevic, T. (2010). Migration in the Former Yugoslav Republics. In *Migrations from and to Southeastern Europe. – (Europe and the Balkans international network; 31)* (pp. 1-10). Ravenna: Longo.

Budjeryn, M. (2022). *Inheriting the Bomb: The Collapse of the USSR and the Nuclear Disarmament of Ukraine.*: Johns Hopkins University Press.

Burgess, K. (2012). Migrants, Remittances, and Politics: Loyalty and Voice after Exit'. *World Affairs, 36*(1), 43-55.

Byford, A., & Bronnikova, O. (2018). INTRODUCTION. TRANSNATIONAL EXOPOLITIES Politics in post-Soviet migration. *Revue d'études comparatives Est-Ouest, 4*(4), 5-25.

Calori, A., Hartmetz, A.-K., Kocsev, B., Mark, J., & Zofka, J. (2019). Between East and South: Spaces of interaction in the globalizing economy of the cold war. . In A. Calori, A.-K. Hartmetz, B. Kocsev, J. Mark, & J. Zofka (Eds.), *Between East and South Spaces of Interaction in the Globalizing Economy of the Cold War* (Vol. 3, pp. 1-31): De Gruyter.

Caporale-Bizini, S., Galhardo Couto, G., Kasic, B., Lund, L., Richeter Malabotta, M., & Skarbak, E. (2009). Introduction. In S. Caporale bizini & M. Richeter Malabotta (Eds.), *Teaching Subjectivity: Travelling Selves for Feminist Pedagogy* (pp. 7-8). Utrecht: Zuidam Uithof Drukkerijen.

Castles, S., Haas, H., & Miller, M. (2019). *The Age of Migration International Population Movements in the Modern World* (6th ed.): Bloomsbury Publishing.

Cavoski, J. (2019). From Alignment to Non-Alignment: Yugoslavia Discovers the Third World, [Press release]. Retrieved from https://www.wil soncenter.org/event/alignment-to-non-alignment-yugoslavia-dis covers-the-third-world

Chamberlain-Creanga, R. (2006). The "Transnistrian People": Citizenship and Imaginings of "the State" in an Unrecognized Country. *Ab Imperio, 4*, 371-399. doi::10.1353/imp.2006.0096.

Connerton, P. (1989). *How Societies Remember*. Cambridge, UK: Cambridge University Press.

Crawley, H. (2006). Forced migration and the politics of asylum: The missing pieces of the international migration puzzle?. *International Migration, 44*(1), 21-26. doi:/10.1111/j.1468-2435.2006.00352.x

Csaba, L. (2007). *The New Political Economy of Emerging Europe*. Budapest, Hungary: Akademiai Kiado.

D'Anieri, P. (2019). *Ukraine and Russia: From Civilized Divorce to Uncivil War*. Cambridge: Cambridge University Press.

Daher, J. (2022). Consequences of the Russian Invasion of Ukraine as an Indicator of MENA Dysfunctional and Unequal Economic and Food System Production *Europe Now*.

De Fina, A. (2003). *Identity in Narrative A study of immigrant discourse*: John Benjamins Publishing Company.

Denisenko, M. (2020). Emigration from the CIS Countries: Old Intentions — New Regularities. In M. Denisenko, S. Strozza, & M. Light (Eds.), *Migration from the Newly Independent States: 25 years after the collapse of the USSR*: Springer.

Diamond, J. (1999). *Guns, Germs, and Steel*. New York London: W.W. Norton & Company

Diamond, J. (2005). *Collapse: How Societies Choose to Fail or Succeed*: Viking Press.

Dictionary, C. E. (2022). Resilience. https://dictionary.cambridge.org/dict ionary/english/

Dragovic, R. (2016, April 16, 2016). Podele i na jugu Afrike: Tri Srbina, dve crkve, Report. *Novosti*. Retrieved from https://www.novosti.rs/vesti/naslovna/drustvo/aktuelno.290.html:600870-Podele-i-na-jugu-Afrike-Tri-Srbina-dve-crkve

(2023). *Poetry and war* [Retrieved from https://www.youtube.com/watch?v=bAzEjV_WXxU

Duranovic, A. (2020). Identity Transformation of Migrants from Bosnia and Herzegovina in post-1960s Germany. *Journal of the Faculty of Philosophy in Sarajevo (History, History of Art, Archeology), 7*(2), 249-264. doi:10.46352/23036974.2020.2.249

Economist, T. (2021, January 28, 2021). How the pandemic reversed old migration patterns in Europe. *The Economist*.

Edwards, L. (2009). Bikini Girl who made a Splash. *The Sidney Morning Herald* Retrieved from https://www.smh.com.au/national/bikini-girl-who-made-a-splash-20091231-ll1h.html

ERR, e. (2022, August 25). S nachala voiny rossijane vhezzhayut v evrosojuz v osnovom cherez finljaniju i estoniju.

Falzon, M. A. (2009). *Multi-sited Ethnography: Theory, Praxis and Locality in Contemporary Research*. Surrey, England and Burlington, USA: Ashgate.

Farrar, J. H. M., D.G. (2013). *Globalisation, the global financial crisis and the state*. Cheltenham, UK: Edward Elgar Publishing.

Fibbi, R., Wanner, p., Topgül, c., & Ugrina, D. (2015). *The New Second Generation in Switzerland: Youth of Turkish and Former Yugoslav Descent in Zurich and Basel*. Amsterdam: IMSCOE Research, Amsterdam University Press.

Fomina, J. (2021). Voice, exit and voice again: democratic remittances by recent Russian emigrants to the EU. *Journal of Ethnic and Migration Studies,, 47*(11), 2439-2458. doi:10.1080/1369183X.2019.1690437

Fortune. (2022, October 18). Russia's population is in a historic decline as emigration, war and a plunging birth rate form a 'perfect storm'. Retrieved from https://fortune.com/2022/10/18/russia-population-historic-decline-emigration-war-plunging-birth-rate-form-perfect-storm/

Fotiadis, R., Ivanovic, V., & Vucetic, R. (2019). *Brotherhood and Unity at the Kitchen Table: Food in Socialist Yugoslavia*. Zagreb: Srednja Europa Zagreb

Foulkes, L. (2021). *Losing Our Minds: The Challenge of Defining Mental Illness*: St. Martin's Press.

Fox, J. E., Morosanu, L., & Szilassy, E. (2014). Denying Discrimination: Status, 'Race', and the Whitening of Britain's New Europeans. *Journal of Ethnic and Migration Studies, 41*(5), 729-748. doi:10.1080/ 1369183X.2014.962491

Fraser, N. (2021). Climates of capital: For a trans-environmental eco-socialism. *New Left Review, 127*(Jan-Feb), 94-127.

Friedman, T. (2000). The Golden Straitjacket. In *The Lexus and the Olive Tree* (pp. 101-111). New York: Anchor Books.

Gagnon, V. (2004). *The Myth of Ethnic War: Serbia and Croatia in the 1990s* (1 ed.): Cornell University Press.

Gallo, E. (2009). In the Right Place at the Right Time? Reflections on Multi-sited Ethnography in the Age of Migration. In M. A. Falzon (Ed.), *Multi-Sited Ethnography. Theory, Praxis, and Locality in Contemporary Research.* Surey, England and Burlington, USA: Ashgate.

Gamlen, A. (2020). *Migration and mobility after the 2020 pandemic: The end of an age?*

Gatarić, L. (2003). U Iraku je radilo 100.000 radnika iz SFRJ. *Večernji list*

Gessen, M. (2012). *The Man without a Face: The Unlikely Rise of Vladimir Putin*: Riverhead Books.

Glick Schiller, N. (1997). The Situation of Transnational Studies. *Identities Global Studies in Culture and Power, 4*(2), 155-166. doi:https://doi.org/10.10 80/1070289X.1997.9962587

Gomberg, L. (2018). *Time-Memory 1990-2010. Israel: articles about people, books, theatre* St. Petersburg: Aleteya.

González-Ferrer, A., & Moreno-Fuentes, F. J. (2017). Back to the Suitcase? Emigration during the Great Recession in Spain. *South European Society and Politics, 22*(4), 447-471.

Greenfield, N. M. (2023, June 1, 2023). Ukrainians sheltering in Canada hit hard by tuition fees. *University World News.* Retrieved from https://www.universityworldnews.com/post.php?story=20230 601205017370&utm_source=newsletter&utm_medium=email&u tm_campaign=GLNL0742

Greitens, E. (2016). *Resilience: Hard-Won Wisdom for Living a Better Life*: Harvest.

Gucijan, S. (Producer). (2014, November 10, 2022). Srpska skola u Juznoj Africi. [Report] Retrieved from https://www.politika.rs/scc/cla nak/291249/Srpska-skola-u-Juznoj-Africi

Halilovich, H. (2013). *Places of Pain: Forced Displacement, Popular Memory and Trans-local Identities in Bosnian War-Torn Communities.* New York: Berghahn Books.

Harari, Y. N. (2018). *21 Lessons for 21st Century*. US: Spiegel and Grau.

Harari, Y. N. (2022). Why Vladimir Putin has already lost this war (Opinion). Retrieved March 5, 2022 https://www.theguardian.co m/commentisfree/2022/feb/28/vladimir-putin-war-russia-ukr aine

Heleniak, T. (2017). Post-Soviet Russian-speaking migration to the UK: the discourses of visibility and accountability. In *Post-soviet migration and diasporas: from global perspectives to everyday practices*: Palgrave Pivot.

Hemon, A. (2006, February 10, 2010). Na Kapiji Zapada. *Dani*. Retrieved from http://www.infobiro.ba/article/172653

Herman, J. (1997). *Trauma and Recovery: The Aftermath of Violence – from Domestic Abuse to Political Terror* Basic Books.

Hinchman, L. P., & Hinchman, S. K. (Eds.). (1997). *Memory, identity, community: The idea of narrative in the human sciences*. New York: State University of New York Press.

Hirschman, A. (1970). *Exit, voice, and loyalty : responses to decline in firms, organizations, and states*. Cambridge, Massachusetts: Harvard University Press.

Hirschman, A. (1993). Exit, Voice, and the Fate of the German Democratic Republic: An Essay in Conceptual History. *World Politics, 45*(2), 173-202.

Hobsbawm, E. (1994). *The Age of Extremes: The Short Twentieth Century, 1914–1991*. USA: Vintage Books.

Hoffmann, B. (2010). Bringing Hirschman Back In: "Exit", "Voice", and "Loyalty" in the Politics of Transnational Migration. *The Latin Americanist, 54*(2010, 2), 57-73.

Holmes, S., & Krastev, I. (2012). Putinism Under Siege: An Autopsy of Managed Democracy. *Journal of Democracy, 23*(3), 33-45.

Hough, J. (1997). *Democratization and Revolution in the USSR, 1985–1991* Washington, DC: Brookings Institution.

Hurley, K. (2022, July 14, 2022). What Is Resilience? Your Guide to Facing Life's Challenges, Adversities, and Crises.

Ioneasco, D., & Chazalnoel, T. (2015). *Climate Change and Migrations*.

Ivanovic, V. (2019). INTEGRAION ON A PLATE: RESAURANTS AND REPRESENTATIONS OF YUGOSLAV CUISINE IN WEST GERMANY. In V. Ivanovic, Fotiadis, R., Vucetic, R. (Ed.), *rotherhood and Unity at the Kitchen Table: Food in Socialist Yugoslavia* (pp. 135-156). Zagreb: Srednja Europa.

Jackson, T. (2009). *Prosperity Without Growth: Economics for a Finite Planet*. London, UK: Earthscan

Jorio, L. (2005). Balkan migrants struggle to integrate. Retrieved from https://www.swissinfo.ch/eng/balkan-migrants-struggle-to-int egrate/4810086

Jovanovic, D., & Stojmenovic, D. (2023). The export of know-how at the (semi-)peripheries: the case of Yugoslav–Iranian industrial collaboration and labor mobility (1980–1991). *Labor History*, 1-17. doi:10.1080/0023656X.2023.2173728

Jovic, D. (2008). *Yugoslavia: A State That Withered Away*: Purdue University Press.

Judah, T. (2000). *Kosovo: War and Revenge*: Yale University Press.

Jukic, E. M. (2014). Redundant Bosnian Workers Protest in Tuzla. Retrieved from https://balkaninsight.com/2014/02/05/workers-protest-in-tuzla-over-labor-rights/

Jutarnji.hr (Producer). (2018). TKO UBIJA SRBE U JUŽNOJ AFRICI: ČEŠKI BOSS NARUČIO SERIJU LIKVIDACIJA MAFIJAŠA ODGOVORNIH ZA SMRT ARKANA? Niz je nevjerojatan, padaju jedan za drugim Retrieved from https://www.jutarnji.hr/vijesti/s vijet/tko-ubija-srbe-u-juznoj-africi-ceski-boss-narucio-seriju-likvid acija-mafijasa-odgovornih-za-smrt-arkana-niz-je-nevjerojatan-pad aju-jedan-za-drugim-7877163

Karabegovic, D. (Producer). (2018). Crossing Borders: An Introduction to Bosnian Migration to Germany (Part I). *BalkanDiskurs*. Retrieved from https://balkandiskurs.com/en/2018/04/03/crossing-bord ers-part-i/#_ftn6

Kavalski, E. (2007). The Fifth Debate and the Emergence of Complex International Relations Theory: Notes on the Application of Complexity Theory to the Study of International Life. *Cambridge Review of International Affairs, 20*(3), 435-454.

Keil, S., & Stahl, B. (2023). Between the Balkans and Europe: The State/Nation Problem in the Post-Yugoslav States. *Journal of Intervention and Statebuilding, 17*(4), 1-17. doi:10.1080/17502977.20 23.2180723

Khanenko-Friesen, N. (2017). Migrant Self-Reflectivity and New Ukrainian Diaspora in Southern Europe: The Case of Portugal. In *Post-Soviet Migration and Diasporas. From Global Perspectives to Everyday Practices*. (pp. 47-63): Springer International Publishing.

Kim, H. H. (2014). Immigrant Network Structure and Perceived Social Capital: A Study of the Korean Ethnic Enclave in Uzbekistan. *Development and Society, 43*(2), 351-379.

King, C. (2001). The Benefits of Ethnic War: Understanding Eurasia's Unrecognized States. *World Politics, 53*(4), 524-552.

Knezevic, A., & Tufegdzic, V. (1995). *The Crime that Changed Serbia*. Belgrade: Samizdat B92.

Kobrinskaya, I. (2005). *Russia – NIS Relations Beyond the Color Revolutions. Are the Shifts Durable?*

Koenig H.G, & Al Zaben, F. (2021). Moral Injury: An Increasingly Recognized and Widespread Syndrome. . *J Relig Health, 60*(5), 2989-3011. doi:10.1007/s10943-021-01328-0.

Kondan, S. (2020). Southeastern Europe Looks to Engage its Diaspora to Offset the Impact of Depopulation. Retrieved from https://www.migrationpolicy.org/article/southeastern-europe-seeks-offset-depopulation-diaspora-ties

Kontos, M. (2003). Self-employment policies and migrants' entrepreneurship in Germany. *Entrepreneurship and Regional Development, 15*(2), 119-135.

Kovacevic-Bielicki, D. (2017). *Born in Yugoslavia- Raised in Norway: Former Child Refugees and Belonging*. Oslo: Novus Press.

Kovacevic-Bielicki, D. (2019). Those Who Left and Those Who Stayed: Diasporic'Brothers' Seen as the New Others in the Bosnian Context. *Ethnoscripts, 21*(1), 176-195.

Kraler, A. (2011). The Case of Austria. In *Migration Policymaking in Europe. The Dynamics of Actors and Contexts in Past and Present*: Amsterdam University Press, IMSCOE.

Krasnov, V. (1986). *Soviet Defectors: The KGB Wanted List*: Hoover Institution Press, Stanford University.

Krastev, I. (2022). *Is it Tomorrow, Yet? Paradoxes of the Pandemic*: Penguin Press.

Krasteva, A. (2010). Migrations: Challenges and Policies. In A. K. a. D. K. Anna Krasteva (Ed.), *Migrations from and to Southeastern Europe*. Ravenna: Longo.

Krasteva, A. (2021). Balkan Migration Crises and Beyond. *Southeastern Europe, 2021*(45), 173-203. doi:10.30965/18763332-45020001

Labov, W. (1972). *Language in the Inner City: Studies in the Black English Vernacular*. Philadelphia: University of Pennsylvania Press.

Le Normand, B. (2021). *Citizens Without Borders: Yugoslavia and Its Migrant Workers in Western Europe*. Toronto: Toronto University Press.

Lee, E. S. (1966). A Theory of Migration. *Demography, 3*(1), 47-57.

Lenta.ru. (2018). The Last Flight of Simeons – Mother and 10 Kids Hijacked the Plane to Escape from the USSR. Retrieved from https://lenta.ru/articles/2018/03/08/7simeon/

Libman, A., & Vinokurov, E. (2011). Regional Integration and Economic Convergence in the Post-Soviet Space: Experience of the Decade of Growth. *Journal of Common Market Studies, 50*(1), 112-128. doi:/10.1111/j.1468-5965.2011.02209.x

Malešević, S. (2010). Ethnicity in Time and Space: A Conceptual Analysis. *Critical Sociology, 37*(1), 67-82. doi:10.1177/0896920510378763

Marcus, G. E. (1995). Ethnography in/of the world system: The emergence of multi-sited ethnography. *Annual Review of Anthropology, 24*, 95-117.

Mariotti, S. (2022). A warning from the Russian–Ukrainian war: avoiding a future that rhymes with the past. *Journal of Industrial and Business Economics, 49*, 761-782. doi:https://doi.org/10.1007/s40812-022-00219-z

McFadden, R. D. (1996, January 29, 1996). Joseph Brodsky, Exiled Poet Who Won Nobel, Dies at 55. *The New York Times*. Retrieved from https://www.nytimes.com/1996/01/29/arts/joseph-brodsky-exiled-poet-who-won-nobel-dies-at-55.html

McGinn, D. (Producer). (2015, September 9, 2015). 4 Types of Loyalty. [Social media blog] Retrieved from https://www.linkedin.com/pulse/4-types-loyalty-dan-mcginn/

Meduza (Producer). (2023). Russian opposition convenes in Berlin, signs joint declaration of political goals. Navalny's Anti-Corruption Foundation abstains. [News report] Retrieved from https://meduza.io/en/news/2023/05/01/russian-opposition-convenes-in-berlin-signs-joint-declaration-of-political-goals-navalny-s-anti-corruption-foundation-abstains

Meier, L. (2015). *Migrant Professionals in the City. .Local Encounters, Identities and Inequalities*: Routledge.

Merriam-Webster, D. (2022). Resilience. https://www.merriam-webster.com/

Mežnarić, S. (1986). *"Bosanci": A kuda idu Slovenci nedeljom?* . Beograd: Filip Višnjić.

Mijic, A. (2019). Together divided–divided together: Intersections of symbolic boundaries in the context of ex-Yugoslavian immigrant communities in Vienna. *Ethnicities, 20*(3), 1-22. doi:10.1177/1468796819878202

Minster, C. (2021). Why Argentina Accepted Nazi War Criminals After World War II. Retrieved from https://www.thoughtco.com/why-did-argentina-accept-nazi-criminals-2136579

Molnar, C. A. (2014). Imagining Yugoslavs: Migration and the Cold War in Postwar West Germany". *Central European History, 47*(1), 138-169. doi:10.10 1 7/S00089389 1 400065X

Molodikova, I., & Tepavcevic, S. (2021). ОСОБЕННОСТИ ДИГИТАЛЬНЫХ КОММУНИКАЦИЙ И ИНТЕРНЕТ-ПРЕДПРИНИМАТЕЛЬСТВО РУССКОГОВОРЯЩИХ СООБЩЕСТВ В ПЕРИОД КАРАТНИНА COVID-19 НА ПРИМЕРЕ ВЕНГРИИ. *Vestnik (Вестник)*(35), 156-163.

Montalto Monella, M., & Carleone, M. (Producer). (2022). How climate change triggered a second exodus in Bosnia and Herzegovina. Retrieved from https://www.euronews.com/green/2022/01/04/how-climate-change-triggered-a-second-exodus-in-bosnia-and-herzegovina

Munro, G. (2017). *Transnationalism, Diaspora and Migrants from the former Yugoslavia in Britain*. London: Routledge.

Nazareno, J., Zhou, M., and You, T. (2018). Global dynamics of immigrant entrepreneurship. Changing trends, ethnonational variations, and reconceptualizations. *International Journal of Entrepreneurial Behavior & Research*.

News, M. E. (Producer). (2013). Yugoslavia Arms Sales. [Report] Retrieved from http://www.mongabay.com/history/yugoslavia/yugoslavia-arms_sales

Novy, A., , 1-23. DOI: 10.1080/14747731.2020.1850073. (2021). The political trilemma of contemporary social-ecological transformation — lessons from Karl Polanyi's 'The Great Transformation'. *Globalizations, 19*(2), 1-22. doi:10.1080/14747731.2020.1850073

Nygren, B. (2007). *The Rebuilding of Greater Russia Putin's Foreign Policy Towards the CIS Countries*: Routledge.

OSCE. (2015). *Bosnia and Herzegovina 2014 Floods Disaster*.

Palankai, T. (2013). European Integration, National and Ethnic Identities and Central Europe. In J. Jensen & F. Miszlivetz (Eds.), *Global Challenges — European and Local Answers*. Szombathely: Savaria University Press.

Piore, M. J. (1979). *Birds of Passage: Migrant Labor and Industrial Societies*. Cambridge: Cambridge University Press.

Piper, E. (2013). Special Report: Why Ukraine spurned the EU and embraced Russia. Retrieved from https://www.reuters.com/article/us-ukraine-russia-deal-special-report-idUSBRE9BI0DZ20131219

Polian, P. (2003). *Against Their Will. The History and Geography of Forced Migrations in the USSR*. Budapest: CEU Press.

Portes, A. (1997). *Globalization from Below: The Rise of Transnational Communities*. Princeton: Princeton University.

Portes, A., & Wilson, K. L. (1980). Immigrant Enclaves An Analysis of the Labor Market Experiences of Cubans in Miami. *The American Journal of Sociology, 86,* 295-319.

Posen, B. R. (1993). The security dilemma and ethnic conflict. *Survival, 35*(1), 27-47. doi:10.1080/00396339308442672

Prieto-Rosas, V., Recaño, J., & Quintero-Lesmes, D. C. (2018). Migration responses of immigrants in Spain during the Great Recession. *Demographic Research, 38*(61), 1885-1932. doi:10.4054/DemRes.2018.38.61

Ramet, S., & Valenta, M. (2011). *The Bosnian Diaspora: Integration in Transnational Communities*: Routledge.

Rath, J. (2006). *Entrepreneurship among Migrants and Returnees: Creating New Opportunities,* Turin.

Ray, N., & Balasingamchow, Y. (2010). *Vietnam. Travel Guide.*

Rekhviashvili, L. (2017). Why read informality in a substantivist manner? On the embeddedness of the soviet second economy. *The informal economy in global perspective: Varieties of governance,* 15-36.

Reliefweb. (2014). Floods in Serbia, Bosnia and Herzegovina, and Croatia 23 May 2014 (Report). from Reliefweb https://reliefweb.int/report/serbia/floods-serbia-bosnia-and-herzegovina-and-croatia-23-may-2014

Remennick, L. (2012). *Russian Jews on Three Continents. Identity, Integration, and Conflict*: Transaction Publisher

Roos, C., & Zaun, N. (2018). *The Global Economic Crisis and Migration*: Routledge.

Rotella, S., & Wilkinson, T. (1998, APRIL 15, 1998). Suspected WWII Criminal at Large in Argentina. *Los Angeles Times*. Retrieved from https://www.latimes.com/archives/la-xpm-1998-apr-15-mn-39518-story.html

Rowley, J. (2005). The Four Cs of Customer Loyalty. *Marketing Intelligence & Planning, 23*(6), 574-581. doi:10.1108/02634500510624138

Ryazantsev, S., Molodikova, I., & Bragin, A. (2020).). The effect of COVID-19 on labour migration in the CIS. *Baltic Region, 12*(4), 10-38. doi: https://doi.org/10.5922/2079-8555-2020-4-2

Ryazantsev, S., Pismennaya, E., Lukyantsev, A., Sivoplyasova, S., & Khramova, M. (2018). Modern Emigration from Russia and Formation of Russian-Speaking Communities Abroad (In Russian). *World Economy and International Relations, 62*(6), 93-107.

Samers, M., & Collyer, M. (2016). *MIgrations* (2nd ed.): Routledge.

Schwartz, A. (2018). Historical Trauma and Multidirectional Memory in the Vojvodina: László Végel's Neoplanta, avagy az Igéret Földje and Anna Friedrich's Miért? Warum? *Hungarian Studies Review, XLV*(1-2), 61-80.

Serbia, M. o. F. A. (2022). Bilateral Relations—Iraq. Retrieved from https://www.mfa.gov.rs/en/foreign-policy/bilateral-cooperation/iraq

Shvarts, A. (2010). Elite Entrepreneurs from the Former Soviet Union: How They Made Their Millions. PhD Dissertation.

Skaaning, S. (2020). Waves of autocratization and democratization: a critical note on conceptualization and measurement. *Democratization, 27*(8), 1533-1542. doi:10.1080/13510347.2020.1799194

Sokolovic, D. (2006). Intelligentsia and the Destruction of Bosnia: Un finest Hour ofIntellectuals. *Critical Sociology, 32*(4), 699-709.

Solnick, S. (1998). *Stealing the State: Control and Collapse in Soviet Institutions.* Cambridge, MA: Harvard University Press,.

Stipić, I. (2022). Whose Is Herceg Kosača? Populist Memory Politics of Constructing "Historical People" In Bosnia And Herzegovina. In J. Jensen (Ed.), *Memory Politics and Populism in Southeastern Europe*: Routledge.

Subasic, M. (2022). Negotiating the Kin-State Citizenship: The Case of Croats from Herzegovina. *Nationalities Papers, 51*(2), 335-352. doi:https://doi.org/10.1017/nps.2022.14

Subotić, J. (2019). *Yellow Star, Red Star: Holocaust Remembrance After Communism.* Ithaca: Cornell University Press

Tagliacozzo, S., Pisacane, L., Kilkey, M., & . (2020). The interplay between structural and systemic vulnerability during the COVID-19 pandemic: migrant agricultural workers in informal settlements in Southern Italy. *Journal of Ethnic and Migration Studies, 47*(9), 1903-1921.

Tepavcevic, S. (2013). *Russian Foreign Policy and Outward Foreign Direct Investments: Cooperation, Subordination, or Disengagement?* Ph.D. Dissertation.

Tepavcevic, S. (2017). Immigrant Entrepreneurship in the Post-Socialist Countries of the European Union: Motives and Patterns of Entrepreneurship of Post-Soviet Immigrants in Hungary. *Migration and Ethnic Themes, 1*, 65-92.

Tepavcevic, S. (2020a). *Homo Sovieticus or the Agent of Change?*

Tepavcevic, S. (2021 a). Changing Geography, Retaining the Mentality: Social and Economic Integration of Post-Soviet Immigrants in Austria and Hungary. *Review of Economic Theory and Policy, 3*, 137-154.

Tepavcevic, S. (2021 c). *Lessons From Previous Global Crises (Un)Applied During COVID-19 Pandemic: Immigrant Experiences in Austria and Hungary.*

Tepavcevic, S. (2022). (Un)Learned Resilience: Impact of the COVID-19 Pandemic on Post-Yugoslav and Post-Soviet Female Immigrants in Austria and Hungary. In M. Crosby & J. Faludi (Eds.), *Whole Person Promotion, Women, and the Post-Pandemic Era: Impact and Future Outlooks* (pp. 194-217): IGI Global.

Tepavcevic, S. (2023). *Diversity of Migrant Entrepreneurship in Varieties of European Capitalism. Post-Soviet Entrepreneurship in Austria, Spain and Hungary.* London: Palgrave Macmillan.

Tepavcevic, S., Molodikova, I., & Ryazantsev, S. (2020). Post-Soviet Russian-Language Migration, Investment, and Entrepreneurship in Eastern and Central Europe (for Example of Hungary, Austria, and the Czech Republic). *Today and tomorrow of the Russian Economy [In Russian], 99-100,* 5-22.

Toltz, M. (2019). Half-Century Jewish Emigration from the Former Soviet Union. Retrieved from https://daviscenter.fas.harvard.edu/sites/default/files

tportal.hr. (2014). Sedmorica osumnjičena za paljenje Predsjedništva i Arhiva BiH (news report). Retrieved May 9, 2014, from tportal.hr https://www.tportal.hr/vijesti/clanak/sedmorica-osumnjicena-za-paljenje-predsjednistva-i-arhiva-bih-20140309

Tsygankov, A. (2022). *Russian Realism Defending 'Derzhava' in International Relations*: Routledge.

Turaeva, R. (2022). Measuring Humans Through Money: Anthropology of Debt in Post-Soviet Economies. *Social Lives of Debts: Ethnographies from Post-Soviet and Post-socialist Economies, 1*(6).

TVRain (Producer). (2023, May 20, 2023). I tak dalee. *I tak dalee.* [TV analytical program] Retrieved from https://youtu.be/zviobyldl2M

U.S. Committee for Refugees and Immigrants. (1998). *Survey 1998 – Yugoslavia.*

Ullah, A., Nawaz, F., & Chattoraj, D. (2021). Locked up under Lockdown: The COVID-19 pandemic and the migrant population. *Social Sciences & Humanities Open, 3*(1). doi:doi.org/10.1016/j.ssaho.2021.100126

UNHCR. (2022). Ukraine-Fastest Growing Refugee Crisis in Europe Since WWII (Report). Retrieved June 6, 2023 https://www.unhcr.org/hk/en/73141-ukraine-fastest-growing-refugee-crisis-in-europe-since-wwii.html

Vailati, A., & Rial, C. (2016). *Migration of Rich Immigrants: Gender, Ethnicity, and Class*. New York: Palgrave Macmillan.

Van Der Kolk, B. (2015). *The Body Keeps the Score: Brain, Mind, and Body in the Healing of Trauma*.: Penguin.

Vasic, M. (2010, June 10, 2010). Gazda-Jezda i Dafina u raljama Sluzbe. *Vreme*.

Vedyashkin, S. (2022, September 8, 2022). Twice as Many People Left Russia in the First Half of 2022 as in the First Half of 2021, Report. *Kyiv Post*. Retrieved from https://www.kyivpost.com/post/5278

Velickovic, M. (2020). Crisis and Resistance at the Periphery: Bosnian responses to Covid-19. Retrieved from https://criticallegalthinki ng.com/2020/05/06/crisis-and-resistance-at-the-periphery-bosn ian-responses-to-covid-19/

Vezovnik, A. (2018). Review of Social Inequalities and Discontent in Yugoslav Socialism by Roy Archer, Igor Duda and Paul Stubbs. *Slavic Review, 77*(1), 230-232.

Vision. (2014). Solidarity protests for Bosnia reach neighboring Serbia (Online report). Retrieved February 20, 2014 https://web.archive. org/web/20140221133810/http://www.vision.org/visionmedia /visionvideos.aspx?id=80306

Vivod, M. (2009). CRIMINALS AND WARRIORS: THE USE OF CRIMINALS FOR THE PURPOSE OF WAR — THE SERBIAN PARAMILITARY UNITS. In A. Hasselm (Ed.), *Crime: Causes, Types and Victims* Nova Science Publishers, Inc. .

Waltz, K. (1979). *Theory of International Politics*. Long Grove, IL: . Waveland Press.

Wiener, M. (2018). *Ministry of Crime: An Underworld Explored*: Pan Macmillan SA.

Williamson, V., Murphy, D., Phelps, A., Forbes, D., & Greenberg, N. (2021). Moral injury: the effect on mental health and implications for treatment. *The Lancet Psychiatry, 8*(6), 453-455. doi:https://doi. org/10.1016/S2215-0366(21)00113-9

Wilson, E. (2007). *Mstislav Rostropovich: Cellist, Teacher, Legend*: Faber

Wimmer, A. (2004). 'Does ethnicity matter? Everyday group formation in three Swiss immigrant neighbourhoods. *Ethnic and Racial Studies, 27*(1), 136.

Wood, W. B. (1994). Forced Migration: Local Conflicts and International Dilemmas. *Annals of the Association of American Geographers, 84*(4), 607-634.

BALKAN POLITICS AND SOCIETY

Edited by Jelena Dzankic and Soeren Keil